A BIBLIOGRAPHY OF THE WORKS OF

DOROTHY L. SAYERS

(Photo: Howard Coster)

A Bibliography
of the Works of
DOROTHY L.
SAYERS

by

COLLEEN B. GILBERT

First published in the United States of America 1978
First published in the United Kingdom 1979

Published by
THE MACMILLAN PRESS LTD
London and Basingstoke
Associated companies in Delhi
Dublin Hong Kong Johannesburg Lagos
Melbourne New York Singapore Tokyo

Printed in the United States of America

British Library Cataloguing in Publication Data

Gilbert, Colleen B
A bibliography of the works of Dorothy L. Sayers
1. Sayers, Dorothy Leigh – Bibliography
I. Title
016.823'9'12   Z8786.55
ISBN 0–333–26267–0

C_e

CONTENTS

ILLUSTRATIONS

PREFACE

THIS BIBLIOGRAPHY attempts a comprehensive description of the works of Dorothy L. Sayers. As is evident from her correspondence with James Sandoe, Graham Pollard, Michael Sadleir, and others, Sayers herself was an enthusiastic collector and bibliographer of the works of Wilkie Collins. Her preparation of the Collins bibliography for the *Cambridge Bibliography of English Literature*, her assistance to I. R. Brussel in the investigation of American first editions of Collins (*Anglo-American First Editions*, London: 1935), and her entertaining review of the classic work on detection of bibliographic forgeries by Graham Pollard and John Carter (*An Enquiry into the Nature of Certain Nineteenth Century Pamphlets*) are noteworthy instances of her bibliographic pursuits. However, she seems to have made little effort to keep track of her own work, as James Sandoe discovered in the course of his correspondence with her about his checklist of her writings ("A Contribution Toward a Bibliography of Dorothy L. Sayers," *Bulletin of Bibliography*, vol. 18, May–August 1944, pp. 78–81.).

Sayers' neglect in keeping track of her own writings, not of course unique among authors, and the destruction of some publishers' and agents' records make tracing her early works difficult or impossible. The loss or destruction of many journals by "enemy action" as well as the similarly regrettable shortcomings of the bibliographer has resulted in failure to find and record some items. I suspect that many contributions to newspapers, journals, and parish magazines have yet to be discovered, and it is unfortunate that some of the first printings of the Wimsey stories cannot be found.

A problem of an opposite kind is that of works attributed to Sayers which do not exist or which she did not write. "A Devotional Anthology" by Dorothy L. Sayers, announced by Longmans in *Life and Letters To-day*, February 1941, never appeared, nor has a thorough search turned up evidence of a manuscript. "A School for Detective Yarns Needed," *The Literary Digest*, 23 September 1922, p. 33, is a synopsis of an article written by G. K. Chesterton. There is no evidence that Sayers wrote this synopsis. Sayers did write a *letter* to John Cournos in 1925 commenting on the Chesterton article. The letter to Cournos was erroneously cited as an article in one of the reviews of Janet Hitchman's biography of Sayers (*Such a Strange Lady*); eventually the synopsis in *Literary Digest* was confused with the letter quoted by Hitchman. *The Golden Cockerel* (a play, broadcast on BBC 27 December 1941) was announced as a "Forthcoming Literary Broadcast" by Dorothy L. Sayers in *The Bookseller* (no. 1876, 20 November 1941, p. 457); however, *The Listener* (18 December 1941, p. 834) states that *The Golden Cockerel* is Frances Dillon's translation of Pushkin's fairy tale, with no mention of Sayers. *The Bookseller's* error may be due to the fact that on 21 December 1941 Sayers' play, *Kings in Judea*, the first of the twelve plays comprising *The Man Born to Be King*, was broadcast. *The Library of Congress-National Union Catalog Pre-1956 Imprints*, vol. 522, p. 689, attributes to Sayers a book *Fifty Years in Western Canada: Being the Abridged Memoirs of Rev. A. G. Morice O. M. I.*

by D. L. S., Toronto: The Ryerson Press, 1930; there is no evidence that Sayers is the "D. L. S." responsible for the abridgement.

In this bibliography, Sayers' works are arranged chronologically within seven sections:

A. Books, Pamphlets, Cards and Ephemera by Dorothy L. Sayers Alone or in Collaboration.

This section includes works edited and translated by Sayers. Full bibliographic information is recorded on first English and first American editions. The arrangement and the reference numbers assigned to entries distinguish clearly editions from issues. Issues are sometimes described in detail in order to throw light on modern publishing practice. For example, several of the Harcourt, Brace issues of the Wimsey novels are produced from earlier English settings. Some Harcourt, Brace tandem or omnibus volumes consist of one novel which has been reset and one or more other novels which have been produced from another publisher's typesetting. The publishing histories of most of the novels is further complicated by the fact that in June 1954 Harper and Brothers purchased the plates, dies, jackets, etc., from Harcourt, Brace. In providing descriptive detail, I have tried to follow the principles set forth by Fredson Bowers, tempered by advice given in essays in *Papers of the Bibliographical Society of America* and in *Studies in Bibliography* as well as by the nature of the book in question and by my own idiosyncrasies. In most cases a quasi-facsimile transcription of the title page is followed by a statement of collation, then by the pagination; the description of the format begins with the length and width in centimeters, followed by the bulk, sheets and endpapers without the binding, then with binding, in centimeters. The paper, endpapers, and binding are then described in some detail. The price, number of copies, and official date of publication are given next; in some instances this information was supplied by the publisher; otherwise it was obtained from *The English Catalogue, Whitaker's*, or *The Library of Congress Catalog of Copyright Entries*. Dust jackets are described when they have been seen. Information regarding translations derives from agents' records and *Index Translationum*. Entries marked with a dagger † were not available for examination, and such details as are given were garnered from publishers' or agents' records unless otherwise stated.

B. Contributions to Books, Pamphlets, and Miscellanea.

Only the first book publications have been recorded; descriptive detail is given as for items in Section A. Essays, stories, and poems reprinted in anthologies or collections are not recorded because they are too numerous. The author's own collections of stories, essays, and plays are included in Section A. Contributions to reference works and the publication of excerpts of Sayers' letters are noted under Miscellanea.

C. Contributions to Newspapers and Periodicals.

Only the first publications are recorded. The index should be consulted for information about subsequent book publication.

D. Book Reviews.

Sayers' reviews of detective fiction for the *Sunday Times* 1933–1935 provide a valuable record of the period for students of detective fiction; her other book reviews, especially of Charles Williams' works, are often full length essays.

E. Broadcasts, Play Productions, Films, and Records.

F. Lectures.

This section is included as an account of Sayers' wide range of interests as well as of her popularity as a writer and lecturer.

G. Manuscript Collections.

The most substantial collections of Sayers' manuscripts are held by the Humanities Research Center (University of Texas, Austin, Texas) and the Marion E. Wade Collection (Wheaton College, Wheaton, Illinois). Many of Sayers' manuscripts are of course privately owned; among them are numerous cards and letters, autograph books of early poems, notes, translations, essays on Dante, unpublished typescripts, fragments such as "Cat O' Mary" (announced by Gollancz in 1935), "The Priest's Chamber," "My Edwardian Childhood." All the manuscripts listed in this bibliography are available to scholars.

Although I have been given generous assistance during the five years I have spent preparing this bibliography, I am aware that it leaves some problems unsolved and perhaps creates new ones. The shortcomings and errors in it are my own. I shall welcome additions, corrections, and notes to this bibliography.

ACKNOWLEDGEMENTS

I AM GRATEFUL to many persons who have assisted me. To Anthony Fleming, Sayers' literary executor, I am much indebted. He has graciously answered my troublesome questions and provided me with items otherwise unavailable. I wish to thank him also for permission to include the frontispiece photograph of Sayers and the photographs of title-pages and bindings of her works. David Higham, Anthony Crouch, Anthea Tatton-Brown and Patricia Dean at David Higham Associates Ltd. patiently helped me discover information about the publication history of Sayers' work. Stanhope Coxon and George M. Webster at Curtis Brown Associates Ltd. assisted me in discovering information about Sayers' works before 1935. Ralph L. Clarke, Secretary of the Dorothy L. Sayers Society, has provided me with enthusiastic support and has taken many pains to trace materials for me and to answer my endless questions. He and other members of the Dorothy L. Sayers Society have made my task enjoyable. I am also grateful to many private collectors who have allowed me to examine items in their collections.

Jeannette Blanco, Margaret Burger, J. R. Christopher, Trevor Hall, and Ruth Youngberg exchanged bibliographical information with me and responded to many questions.

Notable among the librarians who have taken a great deal of time and trouble to answer my questions and who have allowed me to examine materials are Barbara Griffin and Clyde S. Kilby of the Marion E. Wade Collection at Wheaton College, Illinois; Barbara Griffin has been especially helpful to me. Ellen Dunlap, Sally Leach, and the staff at the Humanities Research Center in Austin, Texas, cheerfully helped me sift through the wealth of books and manuscripts there. Other librarians who have been helpful are Chad J. Flake, Brigham Young University; Jane Kleiner and Olar Bell, Inter-Library Loan, Louisiana State University; Michael C. Sutherland, Guymon Collection, Occidental College.

I am also grateful to the staffs of the following libraries for supplying information or assisting me with the examination of materials: The British Library in Bloomsbury and the Newspaper Library at Colindale; Cambridge University Library; General Theological Seminary; Library and Archives of the Episcopal Church Historical Society; the Library of Congress; Reader's Services at the Lily Library; McNeese State University Library; National Book League; San Diego Public Library; University of California at Los Angeles Library; University of North Carolina at Chapel Hill Library; University of Texas Libraries; and many others which sent materials via inter-library loan.

Others to whom I am grateful for sending materials or answering my questions include Bell, Book and Radmall; Blackwell's; James Brabazon; R. H. Butcher of Reckitt and Colman; Sandra Cunningham; Vivienne Dickson; John A. Ford at William Collins & Sons Co. Ltd.; C. W. Scott-Giles; E. R. Gregory; Alan Hancox; Ben Kane; Jacqueline Kavanaugh at BBC Written Archives Centre; Anne Marie

Køllgaard; Norah Lambourne; Christie McMenomy of *The Sayers Review*; Timothy Pitt-Miller; Frances Perry; John V. Price of R. &. J. Balding; Barbara Reynolds; Bertram Rota Ltd.; Thomas Thorp; Donald Saunders; Michael Sherratt; Rosamond Kent Sprague; C. B. Wimsey Inc.

The following publishers have responded to questions: Arthur Barker Ltd.; Ernest Benn Ltd.; B. H. Blackwell Publishers Ltd.; William Collins & Sons Co. Ltd.; J. M. Dent & Sons Ltd.; Doubleday, Doran Inc.; William B. Eerdmans; Faber and Faber Ltd.; Hamish Hamilton Ltd.; Harcourt, Brace, Jovanovich; George G. Harrap & Co. Ltd.; Hodder & Stoughton; Hutchinson Publishing Group; Liveright Publishers Inc.; Longman Group Ltd.; Macmillan; Methuen Publishers Ltd.; Thomas Nelson & Sons, Ltd.; Oxford University Press; Sheed and Ward; Sidgwick & Jackson; Victor Gollancz Ltd.

Finally, I wish to thank Katherine C. Crochet and Catherine M. Edmonston and Betty J. Malina for preparing the typescript.

A

BOOKS, PAMPHLETS, CARDS, AND EPHEMERA BY DOROTHY L. SAYERS ALONE OR IN COLLOBORATION

A1   OP. I   1916

[Within a lavish frame of ships, stars, etc., 10·7 × 17 cm., enclosing a white rectangle 5·8 × 11 cm. also framed with single thin rules:] OP. I. | BY | DOROTHY L. SAYERS | [leaf] | Oxford | B. H. Black-well, Broad St. | 1916

Collation: [A]⁸ B–D⁸ E⁴ [\$1 signed] 36 leaves.
p. [1] "ADVENTURES ALL" SERIES. | No. 9. | [drawing of a ship with number 9 on sail] | OP. I.; p. [2] illustrated series title-page, format similar to title-page [frame of Ulyssean adventures, scroll with quotation from II Maccabees, etc., enclosing a white rectangle also framed with heavy single rules:] [hand-lettered:] ADVENTURERS | ALL [followed by designs, "A Series of Young Poets Unknown to Fame", and a quotation from *Ulysses*]; p. [3] title-page; p. [4] dedication; p. [5] untitled poem; p. [6] untitled poem; p. [7] CONTENTS; p. [8] note about previous printings of three poems; pp. 9–71 text (printer's notice at bottom of p. 71); p. [72] advertisement.

19·2 × 13·7 cm. Bulk: ·9 cm. Heavy white wove paper; no endpapers; un-trimmed; brown paper covers; back blank; spine [white paper label, 6·3 × 7 cm., printed in black, within a thin ruled rectangle, bottom to top:] OP. I – DOROTHY L. SAYERS; front [white label, 6·2 × 4·4 cm., within thin black rules, printed in black:] OP. I. | DOROTHY L. SAYERS | [drawing of a ship] | *Oxford* | Blackwell

Price: 2s; number of copies: 350. Published 28 December 1916.
Printed by Vincent, Printer, Oxford for B. H. Blackwell; Dolphin old style print.

Contents: Two untitled prefatory poems (I will build up my house from the stark foundations; There is no remedy for this) – Alma Mater – Lay (Mummers! let love go by) – The Last Castle: War-Time, Pipes, Carol (O know

OP. I.

BY

DOROTHY L. SAYERS

Oxford

B. H. BLACKWELL, BROAD ST.

1916

ADVENTURERS ALL

A Series of Young Poets

Come, my friends—
'Tis not too late to seek
a newer world—it may
be that the gulfs will wash
us down—it may be we
shall touch the Happy
Isles—of our purpose
holds—to sail beyond
the sunset.

ULYSSES

Title-page of *OP.I* (A1)

you how Queen Mary sits), Reckoning, Womanliness, Harvest, Snap-dragons, Self-defence, Symbol – The Gates of Paradise – The Three Kings – Matter of Brittany – A Man Greatly Gifted – The Elder Knight – Hymn in Contemplation of Sudden Death – Epitaph for a Young Musician – Rondels: Going-down Play, To M. J. – Last Morning in Oxford.

Notes: "Lay" was first printed in OXFORD POETRY 1915 (B1). "Hymn in Contemplation of Sudden Death," and "Epitaph for a Young Musician" were first printed in *Oxford Magazine* (C11, C14); "Matter of Brittany" was first printed in *The Fritillary* (C12). Catchwords p. 41 "Dead", p. 45 "The", p. 47 "and", p. 51 "I", p. 63 "Pray". Distributed in America by Longmans, Green in 1916. "A Man Greatly Gifted" and "The Elder Knight" were reprinted in *Songs for Sale: An Anthology of Recent Poetry*, ed. E. B. C. Jones, Oxford: Blackwell, 1918, pp. 38–42.

A2   CATHOLIC TALES AND CHRISTIAN SONGS   1918

[At top of page, initial "C" is a large capital placed to left of three closely spaced lines and is equal in height to all three:] CATHOLIC TALES AND CHRISTIAN | SONGS [leaf] BY DOROTHY LEIGH | SAYERS, AUTHOR OF "OP. I."

Collation: [A]⁸ B–D⁸ [$1. 2 signed] 32 leaves.
p. [1] title-page; p. [2] four lines of verse by H. Belloc; p. [3] untitled poem, p. [4] blank; p. [5] CONTENTS; p. [6] note on previous printing of *Rex Doloris*; pp. 7–63 text; p. [64] colophon: THESE CATHOLIC TALES WERE PRINTED | AT THE VINCENT WORKS, OXFORD, AND | FINISHED IN SEPTEMBER IN THE YEAR OF | OUR LORD JESUS CHRIST, MDCCCCXVIII [leaf]. | PUBLISHED BY B. H. BLACKWELL, BROAD | STREET, OXFORD, AND SOLD IN AMERICA | BY LONGMANS, GREEN & CO., NEW YORK. | [publisher's device]

19 × 14 cm. Bulk: ·7/1·0 cm. Heavy white wove paper; heavy white wove endpapers; untrimmed. Stiff white paper covers; front, back, spine blank. Dust wrapper: white printed in black; back blank; front [8·8 × 8·8 cm. drawing of Christ signed "G P"] | [mediaeval hand letters:] CATHOLIC TALES | BY DOROTHY L. SAYERS [swash "R"] | OXFORD [leaf] B. H. BLACK-WELL. [swash "A"] | Three Shillings net.; spine [mediaeval hand letters:] Cath- | olic | Tales | [leaf] | SAYERS

Price: 3s; number of copies: 1,000. Published 26 October 1918.

Contents: Untitled poem (Jesus, if against my will,) – Desdichado – The Triumph of Christ – Christ the Companion – πάγτας 'Ελκύσω – The Wizard's Pupil – The Dead Man – The Carpenter's Son – The Drunkard – Justus Judex –

17

CATHOLIC TALES
BY DOROTHY L. SAYERS

OXFORD ❧ B.H. BLACKWELL.
Three Shillings net.

Dust Jacket of *Catholic Tales* (A2)

White Magic – Lignum Vitae – Christus Dionysus – Dead Pan – Rex Doloris – Sacrament – Sion Wall – Byzantine – Epiphany Hymn – Carol – Fair Shepherd – A Song of Paradise – Carol for Oxford – The Mocking of Christ: A Mystery – The House of the Soul: Lay

Notes: "Epiphany Hymn" was first published as a Christmas Card, 1917 (A67·1). "Rex Doloris" was first published in *The New Witness* (C19). Gabriel Pippit drew the illustration for the dust wrapper.

A3 WHOSE BODY? 1923

*a.*1. *First edition, first state:*

WHOSE BODY? *BY* | DOROTHY L. SAYERS | [publisher's device] | BONI AND LIVERIGHT | PUBLISHERS :: NEW YORK

Collation: [A–S]⁸ 144 leaves.

p. [i] [to the right:] WHOSE BODY?; p. [ii] blank; p. [iii] title-page; p. [iv] Copyright, 1923 | by | BONI & LIVERIGHT, INC. | [rule] | Printed in the United States of America; p. [v] dedication; p. [vi] blank; p [vii] *The Singular Adventure of the* | *Man with the Golden Pince-Nez*; p. [viii] blank; pp. 1–278 text with running title WHOSE BODY? underlined by a thick rule and a thin rule, on every page except pp. 1, 19, 41, 59, 89, 121, 157, 179, 189, 207, 231, 245, 255, which have Roman numeral chapter headings, and pp. [18, 58, 88, 120, 206, 254], which are blank; pp. [279–280] blank.

18·6× 12·25 cm. Bulk: 2·7/3·3 cm. Cream wove paper, trimmed; cream wove endpapers. Bound in coarse-grained slate-blue cloth; back blank; front [stamped in dark blue, within thick rules and thin rules, 18·5× 11·7 cm.; within the frame at top a rectangle of thin rules 4·8× 8·9 cm. enclosing:] WHOSE | BODY? [vertical double rules, on right and left, from rectangle at the top to a rectangle at the bottom, 1·55× 8·9 cm., which encloses:] DOROTHY L. SAYERS; spine [within a frame of thick and thin rules 18·6× 2·9 cm.:] WHOSE | BODY? | [rule] | [two vertical rules] | [rule] | DOROTHY | L. | SAYERS | [publisher's device] | BONI AND | LIVERIGHT

Price: $2; number of copies: 3,503 total for A3*a.*1. and A3*a.*11. Published 11 May 1923.

Notes: p. 10 lines 24–26 text transposed, line 24 "got a good, decent girl to do for me and Mother," should follow line 26 "myself very fortunate these days to have".
p. 67 between lines 25 and 26, a stray apostrophe above "Mr. Bunter".
p. 81 "the Duke" for "a peer".
p. 82 lines 9–10 "bar-blin'" for "bur-blin'"
p. 89 chapter heading "V" is smudged

p. 94 error in letterhead; "Salisbury" should read "Crimplesham and Wicks,"

p. 124 line 15 "send" for "sent"

p. 145 line 4 "been." for "been?"

p. 166 line 22 "daressay" for "daresay"

p. 184 line 28 "*er.*" for "*cr.*" twice in the Who's Who entry for Freke

p. 185 line 2 "*son,*" for "*son*"

p. 192 line 3 "than" for "thank"

p. 195 line 1, quotation mark should follow first parenthesis.

p. 209 line 1 "o nthe" for "on the"

p. 224 footnote begun on 223 is continued at the top of p. 224

p. 224 line 25 "I think" for "to think"

p. 233 line 21 "jrie" for "prie"

p. 245 line 16 "thee" for "the"

p. 256 line 22 "sceond" for "second"

p. 271 line 1 "tracted" for "traced"

The copy in The Humanities Research Center at Austin, Texas, (Queen 4131) not only is inscribed by the author to "Mother and Dad" but also has corrections written in the author's hand, in pencil. All of the corrections marked by the author in the HRC copy were made in the first English edition (A3*b*.).

a.II. *First edition, second state:*

WHOSE BODY? | *By* | DOROTHY L. SAYERS | [publisher's device] BONI AND LIVERIGHT, INC. | PUBLISHERS :: NEW YORK

Collation: (A–H)^{16} [J]^8 [K]^4 140 leaves.

pp. [i–viii] as A3*a*.I. except the setting of the title page; pp. 1–272 text with running title WHOSE BODY?, and page number, underscored by thick rule and thin rule on all pages except 1, 18, 40, 57, 86, 117, 153, 175, 185, 202, 226, 240, 249, which have Roman numeral chapter headings.

18·6 × 12·25 cm. Bulk: 2·6/3·2 cm. Cream wove paper; trimmed; cream wove endpapers. Bound as A3*a*.I.

Notes: The errors in A3*a*.I. are not corrected, but the pagination is altered to save four leaves by omitting the eight blank pages in A3*a*.I.

b.I. *First English edition* 1923:

WHOSE BODY? | *By* DOROTHY L. SAYERS | T. FISHER UNWIN LTD. | LONDON: ADELPHI TERRACE

Collation: [1]^8 2–18^8 [$1 signed] 144 leaves.

p. [1] WHOSE BODY?; p. [2] list of novels published by Unwin; p. [3] title-page; p. [4] *First published in England 1923* | (*All rights reserved*); p. [5] dedica-

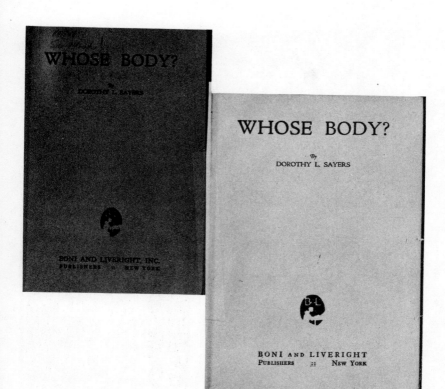

Variant title-pages of *Whose Body?* (A3)
(Photo: Humanities Research Center, University of Texas)

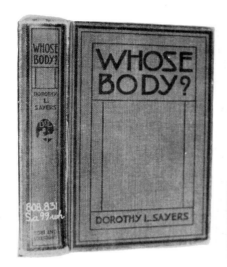

Bindings of *Whose Body?* (A3) and *The Unpleasantness at the Bellona Club* (A6)

tion; p. [6] blank; p. [7] *The Singular Adventure of the | Man with the Golden Pince-Nez*; p. [8] blank; pp. [9]–287 text, with chapter-headings numbered at bottom, printer's notice at bottom p. 287; p. [288] blank.

18·4 × 12·3 cm. Bulk: 3·1/3·4 cm. White wove paper, white wove endpapers, trimmed. Bound in blue cloth (fades to beige); back blank; front [within blind ruled rectangle 18·5 × 11·2, stamped in black] WHOSE BODY? | DOROTHY L. SAYERS; spine [blind rule] | [stamped in black:] WHOSE | BODY? | [short rule] | DOROTHY | L. SAYERS | T. FISHER UNWIN | [blind rule]

Price: 7s6d; number of copies not known. Published October 1923.
Printed by Ebenezer Baylis & Son, Worcester.

Notes: Errors from A3a.I. are corrected. Second impression, 2s6d April 1925. Collins, (A3c.), Gollancz (A3e., A3f.), Avon (A3g., A3h., A3j.), Landsborough (A3k.) editions lack the subtitle *The Singular Adventure of the Man with the Golden Pince-Nez*.

b.II. *Benn's 3s6d Library (London) issue* 1929: 287 pp.

Stated as being produced "from new type," but apparently from the same typesetting as A3b.I.

c.I. *Collins edition* 1932:

WHOSE BODY? | *by* | DOROTHY L. SAYERS | Author of "Un-natural Death," "Clouds of Witness," etc. | [publisher's device] | LONDON 48 PALL MALL | W. COLLINS SONS & CO LTD | GLASGOW SYDNEY AUCKLAND

Collation: [A]¹⁶ B–H¹⁶ [$1 signed] 128 leaves; A1 and H16 are pastedown endpapers. p. [1] WHOSE BODY?; p. [2] blurb, list of books by Sayers; p. [3] title-page; p. [4] printer's notice; p. [5] dedication; p. [6] blank; pp. 7–251 text; p. [252] advertisement.

17·8 × 11 cm. Bulk: 2·5/2·8 cm. Cream wove paper, no endpapers. Bound in blue cloth; front blank; back [stamped in gold:] [an advertisement for Kolynos dental cream]; spine [stamped in dark blue:] [decoration] | WHOSE | BODY? | [solid circle] | DOROTHY L. | SAYERS | [decoration] | [rule] | COLLINS | [rule]

Price: 1s; number of copies not known. Published February 1932.

†*c*.II. *Collins "Crime Club" (London) issue* 1936:251 pp.

Text produced from A3c.I.

†*c*.III. *Collins "6d Mysteries" (London) issue* 1937: 251 pp.

Text produced from A3*c*.1.

d.I. *Harcourt* DOROTHY L. SAYERS OMNIBUS *re-set edition* 1934:

[rule] | DOROTHY L. SAYERS | OMNIBUS | [rule] | *containing* | WHOSE BODY? | THE UNPLEANSANTNESS | AT THE BELLONA CLUB | SUSPICIOUS | CHARACTERS | [publisher's device] | HARCOURT, BRACE AND COMPANY | NEW YORK

Collation: [A–Z, Aa–Hh],[16] [Ii][4] 500 leaves.
p. [1] [rule] | DOROTHY L. SAYERS | OMNIBUS | [rule]; p. [2] list of books by Sayers; p. [3] title-page; p. [4] rights reservation, printer's notice; p. [5] [rule] | WHOSE BODY? | [rule]; p. [6] copyright notice; p. [7] *The Singular Adventure of the | Man with the Golden Pince-Nez*; p. [8] dedication; pp. 9–252 text; sig. H15[a] [rule] | THE UNPLEASANTNESS | AT THE BELLONA CLUB | [rule]; sig. H15[b] copyright notice; sig. H16[a–b] CONTENTS: pp. [1]–345 text; p. [346] blank; sig. T14[a] [rule] | SUSPICIOUS | CHARACTERS | [rule]; sig. T14[b] British title notice and copyright notice; sig. T15[a] CONTENTS; sig. T15[b] blank; sig. T16[a] FOREWORD: sig. T16[b] MAP OF GALLOWAY; pp. 9–398 text; pp. [399–400] blank.

20·4 × 14 cm. Bulk: 4·2/4·8 cm. Cream wove paper; cream wove endpapers. Bound in orange cloth, front and back blank; spine [stamped in gold:] [rule] | DOROTHY L. SAYERS | OMNIBUS | [rule] | HARCOURT, BRACE | AND COMPANY

Price: $2; number of copies not disclosed. Published September 1934.

Notes: WHOSE BODY? is re-set, making this the second American edition. Irregular pagination in this volume is due to the use of plates from A6*b*. for THE UNPLEASANTNESS AT THE BELLONA CLUB and plates from A12*b*. for SUSPICIOUS CHARACTERS (THE FIVE RED HERRINGS). Moreover, the format is such that the first page of text for each novel begins a complete signature. DOROTHY L. SAYERS OMNIBUS was reissued in 1937 with the title THREE MYSTERY NOVELS by HarBrace; and in 1965 with the title 3 LORD PETER MYSTERIES by Harcourt, Brace.

d.II. *Harper and Row (New York) issue* 1955: 252 pp.

Text produced from the plates of A3*d*.1., pp. 9–252.

WHOSE BODY? | by | DOROTHY L. SAYERS | LONDON | VICTOR GOLLANCZ LTD

Collation: [A]⁸ B–S⁸ [$1 signed] 144 leaves.

p. [1] [within single rules:] This re-issue of WHOSE BODY? | (which has received *some corrections* | and *amendments* from MISS SAYERS) | has for a Preface *a short biography* of | *Lord Peter Wimsey*, brought up to | date (May 1935) and communicated | by his uncle PAUL AUSTIN | DELAGARDIE.; p. [2] WIMSEY, PETER DEATH BREDON, D. S. O.; *born* | 1890, *2nd son* of Mortimer Gerald Bredon Wimsey, 15th | Duke of Denver, and of Honoria Lucasta, *daughter of* | Francis Delagardie of Bellingham Manor, Hants. | *Educated*: Eton College and Balliol College, Oxford (1st | class honours, Sch. of Mod. Hist. 1912); served with | H. M. Forces 1914/18 (Major, Rifle Brigade). *Author of*: | "Notes on the Collecting of Incunabula," "The Mur- | derer's Vade-Mecum," etc. *Recreations*: Criminology; | bibliophily; music; cricket. | *Clubs*: Marlborough; Egotists'. *Residences*: 110A Picca- | dilly, W.; Bredon Hall, Duke's Denver, Norfolk. | *Arms*: Sable, 3 mice courant, argent; crest, a domestic | cat crouched as to spring, proper; motto: As my Whimsey | takes me.; p. [3] BI 'GRAPH-ICAL NOTE | *Communicated by* PAUL AUSTIN DELAGARDIE; pp. [4]–9 BIO-GRAPHICAL NOTE; p. [10] a list of books by Sayers; p. [11] title-page; p. [12] *First published in England 1923* | *First 2/6 edition 1935* | [printer's notice]; p. [13] dedication; p. [14] blank; p. [15] CONTENTS; p. [16] blank; pp. [17]–288 text, with pp. [17, 34, 56, 73, 102, 133, 168, 191, 201, 218, 242, 256, 265] chapter headings and text.

18·4× 12·3 cm. Bulk: 3·0/3·3 cm. White wove paper; trimmed; white wove endpapers. Bound in red cloth; front and back blank; spine [stamped in black:] WHOSE | BODY? | BY | DOROTHY L. | SAYERS | GOLLANCZ

Price: 2s6d; number of copies: 10,000. Published 11 July 1935. Dust jacket: yellow printed in black and magenta.

Printed at the Camelot Press London and Southampton.

Notes: Corrections and amendments claimed on p. [1] not found.

A novel, *Cat O'Mary* by "Joanna Leigh" (a pseudonym for Sayers), is announced after a list of her books on p. [10]; this novel has not been published; an unfinished manuscript is privately owned.

Format for the Gollancz 1935 editions of CLOUDS OF WITNESS (A4*d*.1.), UNNATURAL DEATH (A5*d*.1.), THE UNPLEASANTNESS AT THE BELLONA CLUB (A6*d*.1.) are similar to this edition of *WHOSE BODY?* All were published on the same day along with the Gollancz edition of THE DOCUMENTS IN THE CASE (A10); all announce *Cat O'Mary*. All but THE DOCUMENTS IN THE CASE have the biographical notice for Wimsey and the "Biographical Note Communicated by Paul Austin Delagardie".

These are the first biographical notices for Wimsey published in England. The first biographical notice was published in America in 1931 in *Sleuths*, edited by Kenneth Macgowan (B45·1); it has a few more details and some variations (i.e., the Wimsey motto in *Sleuths* reads "I hold by my Whimsy"). See also the biographical notices in THE DAWSON PEDIGREE (UN-NATURAL DEATH) published by Harcourt, Brace in 1938 (A5d.II.) and in UNNATURAL DEATH published by Harper in 1956 (A5d.IV.).

*e.*II. *Gollancz re-issue, Volume I in the "Collected Edition" 1971:*

WHOSE BODY? | by | DOROTHY L. SAYERS | LONDON | VICTOR GOLLANCZ LTD | 1971

Collation: [A]¹⁶ B–I¹⁶ [$1 signed, $5 signed with added star] 144 leaves.
p. [1] WHOSE BODY; p. [2] list of books by Sayers; p. [3] title-page; p. [4] publication, re-issue, ISBN, and printer's notices; p. [5] BIOGRAPHICAL NOTE | *Communicated by* PAUL AUSTIN DELAGARDIE | [same fifteen lines of biographical information as on p. [2] A3*e.*I. | [same five line notice of re-issue as on p. [1] A3*e.*I.; pp. [6]–11 BIOGRAPHICAL NOTE; p. [12] blank; p. [13] dedication; p. [14] blank; p. [15] CONTENTS; p. [16] blank; pp. [17]–288 text as A3*e.*I.

18·4 × 12·3 cm. Bulk: 2·2/2·5 cm. White wove paper; trimmed; white wove endpapers. Bound in red cloth; front and back blank; spine [stamped in gold:] WHOSE | BODY? | BY | DOROTHY L. | SAYERS | GOLLANCZ

Price: £1·25; number of copies not disclosed. Published May 1971. Dust jacket: bright yellow printed in black and magenta.
Printed by Lowe and Brydone (Printers) Ltd., London

Notes: Type damage on pp. 5, 102, 162, 170, 175, 179. On p. [4] *"First published 1932"* should read *"First published 1923"*. Appears to be a photographic reproduction of A3*e.*I.

*f.*I. *Gollancz re-set war edition 1942: 139 pp.*

Includes biographical notice for Wimsey and "Biographical Note by Paul Austin Delagardie", pp. [1]–6; text pp. 13–139.

†*f.*II. *Second Gollancz Detective Omnibus issue 1952:*

Text of WHOSE BODY? pp. 11–137, may have been derived from A3*f.*I.

g. New Avon Library (New York) edition 1943: 158 pp.

h. Avon (New York) re-set edition 1948: 190 pp.

i. Harper and Row (New York) THREE FOR LORD PETER WIM-SEY re-set edition 1960:

WHOSE BODY?, pp. 3–137; CLOUDS OF WITNESS (A4), pp. 141–336; UNNATURAL DEATH (A5), pp. 339–530.

j. Avon (New York) re-set edition 1961: 192 pp.

k.I. Landsborough Four Square Books (London) re-set edition 1965: 191 pp.

k.II. New English Library (London) issue 1968: 191 pp.

Text produced from A3*k*.I.

Translations: Dutch, French, German, Portuguese, Japanese, Swedish, Hebrew, Czechoslovakian.

A4   CLOUDS OF WITNESS   1926

a.I. First edition:

CLOUDS OF WITNESS | BY DOROTHY L. SAYERS | T. FISHER UNWIN LTD. | LONDON: ADELPHI TERRACE

Collation: [A]⁸ B–U⁸ [$1 signed] 160 leaves.

pp. [1–2] paste-down; pp. [3–4] endpaper; p. [5] CLOUDS OF WITNESS; p. [6] advertisement for WHOSE BODY?; *inset:* frontispiece "The BLOTTING PAPER"; p. [7] title-page; p. [8] *First Published in* 1926 | (*All Rights Reserved*); p. [9] THE SOLUTION OF | THE RIDDLESDALE MYSTERY | WITH | A REPORT | OF THE TRIAL OF | THE DUKE OF DENVER | BEFORE THE HOUSE OF LORDS | FOR MURDER | [rule] | [six line quotation from *The Wallet of Kai-Lung*]; p. [10] blank; p. [11] CONTENTS; p. [12] blank; pp. 13–315 text, p. 29 text and diagram, p. 315 text with printer's notice; p. [316] blank; pp. [317–318] endpaper; pp. [319–320] paste-down.

18·5 × 12·5 cm. Bulk: 3·3/3·6 cm. White wove paper; endpapers part of first and last gatherings; trimmed. Bound in blue cloth; back blank; front [stamped in black:] CLOUDS | OF WITNESS | DOROTHY L. SAYERS; spine [stamped in black:] CLOUDS | OF | WITNESS | DOROTHY L. | SAYERS | T. FISHER UNWIN

Price: 7s6d; number of copies not known. Published 8 February 1926. Made and printed by The Camelot Press Limited Southampton.

†*a*.II. T. *Fisher Unwin "Popular edition" (London)* 1927: 315 pp.

Text produced from A4*a*.I.

†*a*.III. Benn's *"3s6d Library edition" (London)* 1929: 315 pp.

Text produced from A4*a*.I.

b. First American edition 1927:

CLOUDS OF | WITNESSES | BY | DOROTHY L. SAYERS |
[publisher's device] | New York | LINCOLN MAC VEAGH | THE
DIAL PRESS | 1927

Collation: [A–S]⁸ 144 leaves.
p. [1] CLOUDS OF WITNESSES; p. [2] blank; p. [3] title-pages; p. [4] copyright, manufacture notices; p. 5 CONTENTS; p. [6] blank; p. [7] THE SO-
LUTION OF | THE RIDDLESDALE MYSTERY | WITH | A REPORT
| OF THE TRIAL OF | THE DUKE OF DENVER | BEFORE THE HOUSE
OF LORDS | FOR | MURDER | [rule] | [five line quotation from *The
Wallet of Kai-Lung*]; p. [8] blank; pp. 9–288 text.

18 × 12·2 cm. Bulk: 2·5/3 cm. Cream wove paper; trimmed; cream wove
endpapers. Bound in green cloth; back blank; front [stamped in yellow:]
CLOUDS | *of* [large leaning swash "f"] | WITNESSES; spine [stamped in
yellow:] CLOUDS | *of* [large leaning swash "f"] | WITNESSES | [small
triangle] | SAYERS | LINCOLN MAC VEAGH | THE DIAL PRESS

Price: $2; number of copies not disclosed. Published 28 March 1927. Printed
by the Vail-Ballou Press, Inc., Binghampton, New York.

Notes: Half-title, title-page, running titles and advertisements for this edition
all read "Clouds of Witnesses."

†*c*.I. *Collins (London)* 1s edition 1931: 286 pp.

†*c*.II. *Collins (London) "6d Mysteries" issue* 1938: 286 pp.

Text produced from A4*c*.I.

d.I. *Gollancz edition* 1935:

CLOUDS OF WITNESS | by | DOROTHY L. SAYERS | LON-
DON | VICTOR GOLLANCZ LTD

Collation: [A]⁸ B–U⁸ [$1 signed with added W], 160 leaves.

p. [1] [within single rules:] This re-issue of CLOUDS OF | WITNESS (which has received | *some corrections* and *amendments* from | MISS SAYERS) has for a Preface *a* | *short biography* of *Lord Peter Wimsey,* | brought up to date (May 1935) | and communicated by his uncle | PAUL AUSTIN DELAGARDIE.; p. [2] biographical information same format as A3*e*.I.; p. [3] BIOGRAPHICAL NOTE | *Communicated by* PAUL AUSTIN DELAGARDIE; pp. [4]–9 BIOGRAPH-ICAL NOTE; p. [10] list of novels by Sayers; p. [11] title-page; p. [12] *First published in 1926* | *First 2/6 edition 1935* | [printer's notice]; p. [13] THE SO-LUTION OF | THE RIDDLESDALE MYSTERY | WITH | A REPORT | OF THE TRIAL OF | THE DUKE OF DENVER | BEFORE THE HOUSE OF LORDS | FOR | MURDER | [rule] | [six line quotation from *The Wallet of Kai-Lung*]; p. [14] blank; p. [15] CONTENTS; p. [16] blank; pp. [17]–320 text, p. 32 diagram with text, pp. [17, 46, 72, 99, 117, 135, 150, 165, 170, 188, 205, 225, 244, 254, 275, 282, 289, 297, 314] unnumbered chapter headings with text.

18·4× 12·3 cm. Bulk: 2·8/3·2 cm. White wove paper; trimmed; white wove endpapers. Bound in red cloth; front and back blank; spine [stamped in black;] CLOUDS | OF | WITNESS | BY | DOROTHY L. | SAYERS | GOL-LANCZ

Price: 2*s*6*d*; number of copies: 10,000. Published 11 July 1935. Dust jacket: yellow printed in black and magenta.
Printed at the Camelot Press, London and Southampton.

Notes: Corrections and amendments claimed on p. [1] not found. See notes for A3*e*.I.

*d.*II. *Gollancz re-issue, Volume 2 in the "Collected Edition"* 1969:

CLOUDS OF WITNESS | by | DOROTHY L. SAYERS | LON-DON | VICTOR GOLLANCZ LTD | 1969

Collation: [A]¹⁶ B–K¹⁶ [$1 signed, $5 signed with added star] 160 leaves.
p. [1] CLOUDS OF WITNESS; p. [2] list of books by Sayers; p. [3] title-page; p. [4] publication, re-issue, ISBN, and printer's notices; pp. [5]–11 BIO-GRAPHICAL NOTE as described for A3*e*.II.; p. [12] blank; p. [13] THE SOLUTION OF | THE RIDDLESDALE MYSTERY | WITH | A RE-PORT | OF THE TRIAL OF | THE DUKE OF DENVER | BEFORE THE HOUSE OF LORDS | FOR | MURDER | [rule] | [six line quotation from *The Wallet of Kai-Lung*]; p. [14] blank; p. [15] CONTENTS; p. [16] blank; pp. [17]–320 text, as A4*d*.I.

18·4 × 12·3 cm. Bulk: 2·4/2·6 cm. White wove paper; white wove endpapers; trimmed. Bound in bright red cloth; front and back blank; spine [stamped in gold:] CLOUDS | OF | WITNESS | BY | DOROTHY L. | SAYERS | GOLLANCZ

Price: 25s; number of copies not disclosed. Published 16 October 1969. Dust jacket: bright yellow printed in black and magneta.
Printed by Lowe and Brydone (Printers) Ltd. London. Appears to be a photographic reproduction of A4d.1.

d.III. Book Club Associates (London) LORD PETER WIMSEY'S CASEBOOK issue 1975:

Text of CLOUDS OF WITNESS produced from A4d.11; text of UNNATURAL DEATH produced from A5d.V.

e.I. Harcourt (New York) re-set edition in tandem with THE DOCUMENTS IN THE CASE 1938:

CLOUDS | OF WITNESS | by DOROTHY L. SAYERS | and | THE DOCUMENTS IN THE CASE | by DOROTHY L. SAYERS | and ROBERT EUSTACE | NEW YORK | HARCOURT, BRACE AND COMPANY

Collation: [A–S]¹⁶ 288 leaves.
p. [i] title-page; p. [ii] rights reservation; p. [1] blank; p. [2] list of books by Sayers; p. [3] CLOUDS OF WITNESS; p. [4] copyright notice; p. [5] subtitle and quotation from *The Wallet of Kai-Lung*; p. [6] blank; p. [7] CONTENTS; p. [8] blank; pp. 9–288 re-set text of CLOUDS OF WITNESS; sig. Kl^a THE DOCUMENTS IN THE CASE; sig. Kl^b copyright notice; pp. [5]–285 text produced from the plates of A10c.1.; pp. [286–288] blank.

19·4 × 12·6 cm. Bulk: 3·7/4·3 cm. White wove paper; original endpapers not seen. Original binding not seen.

Price: $1·98; number of copies not disclosed. Published August 1938.

e.II. Harper (New York) issue 1956:

Text of CLOUDS OF WITNESS produced from the plates of A4e.1.

†*f. PocketBooks (New York) edition* [c. 1940]:

Announced in the PocketBook edition of THE UNPLEASANTNESS AT
THE BELLONA CLUB (16*b*.III.) as PocketBook Number 85.

†*g. Zephyr (Stockholm) continental re-set edition* 1943: 288 pp.

h.I. *Gollancz (London) re-set war edition* 1947: 198 pp.

Includes biographical notice for Wimsey and "Biographical Note by Paul
Austin Delagardie" pp. [4]–9; subtitle p. 13; text pp. 15–198.

h.II. *Gollancz (London) LORD PETER OMNIBUS issue* 1964:

Text of CLOUDS OF WITNESS produced from A4*h*.I. with UNNATURAL
DEATH (A5) and THE UNPLEASANTNESS AT THE BELLONA CLUB
(A6).

i. Harper and Row (New York) re-set edition 1960:

See A3*i*., THREE FOR LORD PETER WIMSEY; text of CLOUDS OF
WITNESS pp. 141–336; lacks subtitle.

j. New English Library (London) edition 1962: 245 pp.

k. Avon Books (New York) edition 1966: 244 pp.

l. Harper and Row (New York) re-set edition 1972:

Includes a brief biographical notice of Wimsey and the subtitle; text pp. 3–218;
in tandem with THE UNPLEASANTNESS AT THE BELLONA CLUB
(A6).

†*m. New American Library (Toronto) edition* 1974:

Announced in *Publisher's Trade List Annual 1974*, New York: Bowker, p. 24.

Translations: French, Italian, Finnish, Swedish, Dutch, Portuguese, Japanese,
Flemish, German, Danish, Spanish, Norwegian, Czechoslovakian.

a.i. First edition:

Unnatural Death | *Dorothy L. Sayers* | 1927 | Ernest Benn Limited

Collation: [1]¹⁶ 2–9¹⁶ [$1 signed, $5 signed with added star] 144 leaves.
p. [1] UNNATURAL DEATH; p. [2] list of works by Sayers; p. [3] title-page; p. [4] printer's notice; p. [5] *The Chapters* [Contents]; p. [6] blank; pp. [7]–285 text, pp. [7, 101, 209] section headings, p. [101] with a note about the Genealogical Table, pp. [8, 102, 210] blank; p. [9] unnumbered chapter heading with text; p. 113 diagram with text; pp. [286–287] Genealogical Table; p. [288] blank.

18·3 × 12·4 cm. Bulk: 2·7/3·0 cm. White wove paper; white wove endpapers, trimmed. Bound in bright yellow cloth; back blank; front [stamped in black:] [frame of icicles pointing in] [two guns facing each other pointing toward the center] | [fat, stylized letters]: Unnatural | Death; spine [stamped in black:] [icicles pointing down] | [fat, stylized letters:] Unnatural | Death | Dorothy | L. Sayers | Benn | [icicles pointing up]

Price: 7s6d; number of copies: 1,000 (agent's records). Published 16 September 1927.
Printer by Ebenezer Baylis & Son, Ltd., The Trinity Press, Worcester.

Note: p. 130, line 7, "Alan Quartermaine" for "Allan Quatermain."

†*a.ii. Benn's (London) 3s6d "edition"* 1927: 287 pp.

Text produced from A5*a.i.*; reprinted 1929.

b. First American edition 1928:

[within double rules:] *The* DAWSON | PEDIGREE | *By* DOROTHY L. SAYERS | *Author of "Clouds of Witnesses"* | [publisher's device] | LINCOLN MAC VEAGH | THE DIAL PRESS | NEW YORK | [dot] | MCM XXVIII

Collation: 152 leaves.
p. [1] THE DAWSON PEDIGREE; p. [2] [upper left, within single rules:] *By the Same Author* | CLOUDS OF WITNESSES | AN ADVENTURE OF LORD PETER | WIMSEY | $2·00 | LINCOLN MAC VEAGH | THE DIAL PRESS | NEW YORK; p. [3] title-page; p. [4] copyright and printer's notices; p. [5] THE CHAPTERS; p. [6] blank; p. [7] To | MAC; p. [8] blank; pp. [9]–299 text, pp. [9, 109, 221] section headings, each with short quotation, pp. [10, 108, 110, 222, 302, 303, 304] blank, p. 121 diagram with text; pp. [300–301] genealogical table; pp. [302–304] blank.

18·6 × 12·6 cm. Bulk: 2·9/3·5 cm. Cream wove paper; cream wove endpapers; top edge dark green; trimmed. Bound in yellow-green cloth; back blank; front [blind stamp of publisher's device]; spine [stamped in red:] *The* [swash "T"] | DAWSON | PEDIGREE | [French rule] | SAYERS | LINCOLN MACVEAGH | THE DIAL PRESS

Price: $2; number of copies not disclosed. Published 17 January 1928. Manu-factured and printed by the Vail-Ballou Press, Inc., Binghamton, New York.

†*c.*I. *Collins (London) Is edition* 1931 : 280 pp.

†*c.*II. *Collins (London) 6d Mysteries issue* 1937: 280 pp.

Text produced from A5*c.*I.

*d.*I. *Gollancz edition* 1935:

UNNATURAL DEATH | by | DOROTHY L. SAYERS | LONDON | VICTOR GOLLANCZ LTD

Collation: [A]⁸ B–S⁸ [$1 signed with added D] 144 leaves.

p. [1] [within a rectangle 4·5 × 5·8 cm:] This re-issue of UNNATURAL | DEATH (which has received *some* | *corrections* and *amendments* from MISS | SAYERS) has for a Preface *a short* | *biography* of *Lord Peter Wimsey,* | brought up to date (May 1935) | and communicated by his uncle | PAUL AUSTIN DELAGARDIE; p. [2] biographical information same as A3*e.*I. p. [3] BIOGRAPHICAL NOTE | *Communicated by* PAUL AUSTIN DELAGARDIE; pp. [4]–9 BIOGRAPHICAL NOTE; p. [10] list of books by Sayers; p. [11] title-page; p. [12] *First published in 1927* | *First 2/6 edition 1935* | [printer's notice]; p. [13] CONTENTS; p. [14] blank; pp. [15]–385 text, pp. [15, 107, 213] section headings, pp. [16, 108, 214] blank; pp. [17, 26, 33, 44, 54, 63, 80, 91, 101, 109, 125, 142, 153, 161, 173, 183, 190, 201, 215, 231, 240, 254, 270] chapter headings with text; pp. [286–287] GENEALOGICAL TABLE; p. [288] blank.

18·4 × 12·3 cm. Bulk: 3/3·4 cm. Cream wove paper; cream wove endpapers; trimmed. Bound in red cloth; front and back blank; spine [stamped in black:] UNNATURAL | DEATH | BY | DOROTHY L. | SAYERS | GOL-LANCZ

Price: 2*s*6*d*; number of copies: 10,000. Published 11 July 1935. Dust jacket: yellow printed in black and magenta.
Printed at the Camelot Press London and Southampton.

Notes: p. 162 type damaged; p. 135 line 28 "Alan Quartermaine" for Allan Quatermain". See notes for A3*e.*I.

*d.*II. *Harcourt, Brace issue in tandem with LORD PETER VIEWS THE BODY* 1938:

THE DAWSON PEDIGREE | *and* | LORD PETER VIEWS THE BODY | *by* | DOROTHY L. SAYERS | NEW YORK | HARCOURT, BRACE AND COMPANY

Collation: [A–T]^{16} 304 leaves.
p. [1] blank; p. [2] list of books by Sayers; p. [3] title-page; p. [4] rights reservation and printing notices; p. [5] BIOGRAPHICAL NOTE | *Communicated by* PAUL AUSTIN DELAGARDIE; p. [6] revised biographical notice for Lord Peter Wimsey; pp. 7–12 "Biographical Note Communicated by Paul Austin Delagardie"; sig. A7^a THE DAWSON PEDIGREE | [Unnatural Death]; sig. A7^b British title notice and copyright notice; pp. [13]–[285] text as A5*d.*I., without running titles; pp. [286–287] genealogical table; p. [288] blank; p. [3] LORD PETER VIEWS THE | BODY: p. [4] THE STORIES; pp. 5–317 text as A8*a.*I.; pp. [318–319] as A8*a.*I.; p. [320] blank.

20·3 × 13·9 cm. Bulk: 3·6/4 cm. Cream wove paper; cream wove endpapers; top edge yellow; top and bottom edges trimmed. Bound in green cloth; front and back blank; spine [stamped in gold:] THE | DAWSON | PEDIGREE | [rule] | LORD PETER | VIEWS | THE BODY | [dot] | SAYERS | HARCOURT, BRACE | AND COMPANY

Price: $1·98; number of copies not disclosed. Published 25 August 1938.

Notes: The revised biographical notice p. [6] includes "*Married* 1935 Harriet Deborah Vane, *daughter of* Henry Vane M. D.; one *son* (Bredon Delagardie Peter) *born* 1936." Among the clubs listed is "Bellona," but the residence is not updated from 110A Piccadilly to 2 Audley Square, nor is "Talboys" included. This is the second biographical notice for Lord Peter Wimsey to be published in America. The first notice appeared in *Sleuths: Twenty-three Great Detectives of Fiction and Their Best Stories* (B 45·1). The biographical notice in *Sleuths* has more detail regarding Wimsey's military service, his detective work (including Climpson's) etc.

*d.*III. *Zephyr (Stockholm) continental issue* 1946:

Text, pp. 9–277, produced from A5*d.*I., does not include biographical notice for Wimsey.

*d.*IV. *Harper and Brothers issue* 1956:

Unnatural | DEATH | (*The Dawson Pedigree*) | BY | DOROTHY L. SAYERS | [publisher's device] | HARPER & BROTHERS | PUBLISHERS NEW YORK

Collation: [A–I]¹⁶ 144 leaves.

p. [1] Unnatural DEATH; p. [2] Wimsey arms; p. [3] title; p. [4] copyright, "This book is published in England under the title of THE DAWSON PEDIGREE.", Library of Congress call number; p. [5] section heading for biographical note; p. [6] biographical notice as in A5*d*.II.; pp. 7–12 and pp. [13]–[287] as A5*d*.I.; p. [288] blank.

Notes: p. [285] at bottom reads "GENEALOGICAL TABLE FOLLOWS" rather than "GENEALOGICAL TABLE OVERLEAF" as p. [285] A5*d*.I. The text was produced from the Harcourt Brace plates (A5*d*.II.), purchased by Harper in June 1954; the title was changed to that used in England. The note on p. [4] is obviously erroneous.

d.v. *Gollancz re-issue, Volume 3 in the "Collected Edition"* 1969:

UNNATURAL DEATH | by | DOROTHY L. SAYERS | LONDON | VICTOR GOLLANCZ LTD | 1969

Collation: [A]¹⁶ B–H¹⁶ [$1 signed, $5 signed with added star] 144 leaves.

p. [1] UNNATURAL DEATH; p. [2] list of books by Sayers; p. [3] title-page; p. [4] publication, re-issue, ISBN and printer's notices; pp. [5]–11 BIOGRAPHICAL NOTE as described for A3*e*.II.; p. [12] blank; pp. [13]–[288] as A5*d*.I.

18·4× 12·3 cm. Bulk: 2·3/2·5 cm. White wove paper; trimmed; white wove endpapers. Bound in bright red cloth; front and back blank; spine [stamped in gold:] UNNATURAL | DEATH | BY | DOROTHY L. | SAYERS | GOLLANCZ

Price: 25*s*; number of copies not disclosed. Published October 1969. Dust jacket: bright yellow printed in black and magenta.
Printed by Lowe and Brydone (Printers) Ltd., London. Appears to be a photographic reproduction of A5*d*.I.

d.VI. *Book Club Associates (London) LORD PETER WIMSEY'S CASE BOOK issue* 1975:

Text of UNNATURAL DEATH produced from A5*d*.v.; text of CLOUDS OF WITNESS produced from A4*d*.II.

e.I. *Gollancz (London) re-set war edition* 1942:

Includes biographical notice for Wimsey and "Biographical Note Communicated by Paul Austin Delagardie" pp. [1]–6; text pp. 13–188; genealogical table pp. 190–191.

*e.*II. *Gollancz (London) LORD PETER OMNIBUS issue* 1964:

> See A4*h*.II; text of UNNATURAL DEATH pp. 205–380, genealogical table pp. 382–383; produced from the plates of A5*e*.I.

f. Gollancz (London) re-set edition in The Gollancz Detective Omnibus 1951:

> Test of UNNATURAL DEATH, including the "Biographical Note Communicated by Paul Austin Delagardie" pp. 307–501, genealogical table pp. 502–503.

g. Harper and Row (New York) THREE FOR LORD PETER WIMSEY re-set edition 1960:

> See A3*i*.; text of UNNATURAL DEATH pp. 339–530, genealogical table pp. 532–533.

h. Avon Books (New York) edition 1964: 290 pp.

i. New English Library edition 1964: 253 pp.

Translations: Swedish, German, Danish, French, Italian, Norwegian, Dutch, Finnish, Spanish, Hebrew, Czechoslovakian, Portuguese.

A6 THE UNPLEASANTNESS AT THE 1928
BELLONA CLUB

*a.*I. *First edition:*

The | Unpleasantness at the | Bellona Club | *by* Dorothy L. Sayers | LONDON | Ernest Benn Limited

Collation: [A]⁸ B–S⁸ [$1 signed] 144 leaves.
p. [1] THE UNPLEASANTNESS AT THE | BELLONA CLUB: p. [2] list of works by Sayers; p. [3] title-page; p. [4] [publisher's device: drawing of a horse] | First Published in | 1928 | Printed | in | Great Britain; p. [5] CONTENTS; p. [6] blank; pp. [7]–287 text, pp. [7, 12, 17, 32, 40, 51, 66, 84, 101, 113, 124, 135, 144, 159, 169, 181, 194, 210, 236, 251, 265, 277, 283] chapter headings and text; p. [288] printer's notice.

18·5 × 12·2 cm. Bulk: 2·8/3·2 cm. White wove paper; white wove endpapers; trimmed. Bound in black cloth; back blank; front [stamped in orange:] [border of icicles pointing toward the center] | [two guns pointing toward each other and the center] | [fat, stylized, letters:] The | UNPLEASANTNESS | at the | Bellona Club; spine [stamped in orange:] [icicles pointing down] | [fat, stylized letters:] The Un- | pleasant- | ness at the | Bellona | Club | Dorothy | Sayers | [triangle] | Ernest Benn | [icicles pointing up]

Price: 7s6d; number of copies: 1,000 (agent's records). Published 6 July 1928. Dust jacket: cream printed in black, with black borders.
Printed by Wyman & Sons Ltd. London, Reading and Fakenham.

a.II. *Benn's (London) 3s6d issue* 1930: 287 pp.

Text produced from A6*a*.1; reprinted in 1934.

b.I. *First American edition* 1928:

[rule] | [all type set from the left margin:] THE | UNPLEASANT-NESS | AT THE BELLONA CLUB | [rule] | BY | DOROTHY L. SAYERS | [rule] | [blank area] | [rule] | PAYSON & CLARKE LTD | NEW YORK | [rule]

Collation: [A–Y]⁸ 176 leaves.
p. [i] [rule] | THE | UNPLEASANTNESS | AT THE BELLONA CLUB | [rule]; p. [ii] blank; p. [iii] title-page; p. [iv] COPYRIGHT, 1928 BY | *Payson & Clarke Ltd.*; pp. v–vi CONTENTS; pp. 1–345 text with running title: *The Unpleasantness at the Bellona Club* on even numbered pages, and chapter titles on odd numbered pages; p. [346] THIS BOOK HAS BEEN SET ON THE LINOTYPE | IN | 2 PT. GARAMOND, PRINTED AND | BOUND IN THE UNITED STATES OF | AMERICA BY J. J. LITTLE & IVES | [publisher's device]

18·5 × 12·5 cm. Bulk: 2·7/3·1 cm. White laid paper; trimmed; white wove endpapers. Bound in purple cloth; front and back blank; spine [stamped in yellow:] DOROTHY L. | SAYERS | [rule] | [top to bottom:] THE UNPLEASANT-NESS AT THE BELLONA CLUB | [rule] | [upright:] PAYSON & | CLARKE LTD.

Price: $2; number of copies not determined. Published 12 August 1928.

b.II. *Harcourt (New York) DOROTHY L. SAYERS OMNIBUS issue* 1934:

See A3*d*.1; text of THE UNPLEASANTNESS AT THE BELLONA CLUB, pp. 1–345, produced from A6*b*.1.

b.III. *Pocket Books (New York) issue* 1940: 345 pp.

> Text produced from A6*b*.I.; page size is smaller (16·5×10·5 cm.), but type area is the same (14×8·8).

b.IV. *Harper and Row (New York) issue* 1957: 345 pp.

> Text produced from A6*b*.I.

c. Penguin (Harmondsworth, England) edition 1935: 284 pp.

d.I. *Gollancz edition* 1935:

THE UNPLEASANTNESS | AT THE BELLONA CLUB | by DOROTHY L. SAYERS | LONDON | VICTOR GOLLANCZ LTD

> *Collation:* [A]⁸ B–S⁸ [$1 signed with added u] 144 leaves.
> p. [1] [within single rules:] This re-issue of THE UN- | PLEASANTNESS AT THE | BELLONA CLUB (which has | received *some corrections* and *amend-* | *ments* from MISS SAYERS has for | a Preface *a short biography* of Lord | *Peter Wimsey*, brought up to date | (May 1935) and communicated | by his uncle PAUL AUSTIN | DELAGARDIE; p. [2] biographical information same as A3*e*.I.; p. [3] BIOGRAPHICAL NOTE| *Communicated by* PAUL AUSTIN DELAGARDIE; pp. [4]– 9 BIOGRAPHICAL NOTE; p. [10] list of books by Sayers; p. [11] title- page; p. [12] *First published in 1928* | *First 2/6 edition 1935* | [printer's notice]; p. [13] CONTENTS; p. [14] blank; pp. [15]–285 text, pp. [15, 20, 24, 39, 46, 57, 71, 88, 105, 116, 126, 137, 146, 160, 169, 181, 194, 209, 234, 249, 263, 275, 281] chapter headings and text; pp. [286–288] blank.
>
> 18·4× 12·3 cm. Bulk: 3·0/3·3 cm. White wove paper; trimmed; white wove endpapers. Bound in red cloth; front and back blank; spine [stamped in black:] THE | UNPLEASANTNESS | AT THE | BELLONA | CLUB | BY | DOROTHY L. | SAYERS | GOLLANCZ
>
> *Price:* 2s6d; number of copies: 10,000. Published 11 July 1935. Dust jacket: yellow printed in black and magenta.
> Printed at the Camelot Press London and Southampton
>
> *Notes:* Corrections and amendments claimed on p. [1] not found.
> See notes for A3*e*.I.

d.II. *Gollancz re-issue, Volume 4 in the "Collected edition"* 1969:

THE UNPLEASANTNESS | AT THE BELLONA CLUB | by | DOROTHY L. SAYERS | LONDON | VICTOR GOLLANCZ LTD | 1969

Collation: [A]^{16} B–I^{16} [$1 signed, $5 signed letter plus star] 144 leaves.
p. [1] THE UNPLEASANTNESS | AT THE BELLONA CLUB; p. [2] list of books by Sayers; p. [3] title-page; p. [4] publication, re-issue, ISBN and printer's notices; pp. [5]–11 BIOGRAPHICAL NOTE as A3*e*.II.; p. [12] blank; p. [13] CONTENTS; p. [14] blank; pp. [15]–285 text, as A6*d*.I.; pp. [286–288] blank.

18·4 × 12·3 cm. Bulk: 2·2/2·5 cm. White wove paper; trimmed; white wove endpapers. Bound in bright red cloth; front and back blank; spine [stamped in gold:] THE | UNPLEASANTNESS | AT THE | BELLONA | CLUB | BY | DOROTHY L. | SAYERS | GOLLANCZ

Price: 25*s*; number of copies not disclosed. Published October 1969. Dust jacket: bright yellow printed in black and magenta.
Printed by Lowe and Brydone (Printers) Ltd., London. Appears to be a photographic reproduction of A6*d*.I.

*e.*I. *Gollancz (London) re-set war edition* 1947: 172 pp.

Includes biographical notice for Wimsey and "Biographical Note Communicated by Paul Austin Delagardie", pp. [1]–6; text pp. 13–172.

*e.*II. *Gollancz (London) LORD PETER OMNIBUS issue* 1964:

See A4*h*.II.; text of THE UNPLEASANTNESS AT THE BELLONA CLUB, pp. 391–550, produced from A6*e*.I.

f. Longman's (London) edition 1962: 118 pp.

One of the "Simplified English Series".

g. New English Library (London) edition 1963: 222 pp.

h. Avon Books (New York) edition 1963: 192 pp.

i. Harper and Row re-set edition in tandem with CLOUDS OF WIT-NESS 1972:

See A4*l*.; text of THE UNPLEASANTNESS AT THE BELLONA CLUB, pp. 221–409.

Translations: French, Danish, Swedish, German, Dutch, Finnish, Spanish, Czechoslovakian, Flemish, Greek, Portuguese, Norwegian, Italian.

a.1. First edition:

EDITED BY | DOROTHY L. SAYERS | GREAT SHORT
STORIES | OF DETECTION, MYSTERY | AND HORROR |
LONDON | VICTOR GOLLANCZ LTD | 14 Henrietta Street
Covent Garden | 1928

Collation: [A]^{16} B–Z^{16} Aa–Mm^{16} Nn^8 Oo–Pp^{16} [$1 signed] 616 leaves.
p. [1] GREAT SHORT STORIES | OF DETECTION, MYSTERY, AND
| HORROR; p. [2] Quotation from Arthur Machen (5 lines); p. [3] title-
page; p. [4] printer's and binder's notices; pp. [5]–8 CONTENTS; pp. [9]–47
INTRODUCTION; p. [48] blank; p. [49] Section I | STORIES OF |
DETECTION AND MYSTERY; p. [50] blank; pp. [51]–617 text, pp. [56,
118, 163, 178, 345, 380, 396, 457, 520, 584, 606] unnumbered story title-pages
with text; p. [618] blank; p. [619] SECTION II | STORIES OF | MYSTERY
AND HORROR; p. [620] blank; p. [621]–1229 text, pp. [621, 660, 677, 705,
816, 834, 863, 881, 934, 993, 1099, 1187, 1201] unnumbered story title-pages
with text; p. [1230] blank; p. [1231] Appendix; p. [1232] blank.

18·5 × 12·2 cm. Bulk: 4·3/4·6 cm. Cream wove paper, trimmed; cream wove
endpapers. Bound in black cloth; front and back blank; spine [stamped in
orange:] DETECTION | MYSTERY | HORROR | SAYERS | GOL-
LANCZ

Price: 8s6d; number of copies not disclosed. Published September 1928. Dust
jacket: yellow printed in black and magenta.
Printed by the Camelot Press Ltd., London and Southampton; paper by
Spalding & Hodge; and bound by Leighton-Straker Bookbinding Co. Ltd.

Contents: The History of Bel – *The History of Susanna* – *The Story of Hercules
and Cacus* – *The Story of Rhampsinitus* – Mrs. Henry Wood, *The Ebony Box* –
Hedley Barker, *The Ace of Trouble* – Edgar Allan Poe, *The Mystery of Marie
Rogêt* – Baroness Orczy, *The Mysterious Death in Percy Street* – Conan Doyle,
The Adventure of the Priory School – J. Storer Clouston, *Coincidence* – Ernest
Bramah, *The Ghost at Massingham Mansions* – F. A. M. Webster, *The Secret of
the Singular Cipher* – Bechhofer Roberts, *The English Filter* – E. C. Bentley,
The Clever Cockatoo – Eden Phillpotts, *Prince Charlie's Dirk* – Robert Barr,
The Absent-minded Coterie – L. T. Meade and Robert Eustace, *The Face in the
Dark* – Austin Freeman, *The Blue Sequin* – Edgar Jepson and Robert Eustace,
The Tea-Leaf – Anthony Wynne, *The Cyprian Bees* – Raymund Allen, *A
Happy Solution* – Percival Wilde, *The Adventure of the Fallen Angels* – Victor
Whitechurch, *Sir Gilbert Murrell's Picture* – G. K. Chesterton, *The Hammer of
God* – H. C. Bailey, *The Long Barrow* – Sir Basil Thomson, *The Hanover Court*

Murder – Aldous Huxley, *The Giaconda Smile* – Mrs. Belloc Lowndes, *Her Last Adventure* – E. W. Hornung, *The Wrong Horse* – Mrs. Oliphant, *The Open Door* – Charles Dickens, *Story of the Bagman's Uncle* – Charles Collins and Charles Dickens, *The Trial for Murder* – M. R. James, *Martin's Close* – Oliver Onions, *Phantas* – Robert Hichens, *How Love Came to Professor Guildea* – "Saki", *The Open Window* – Arthur Machen, *The Black Seal* – Sax Rohmer, *Tchériapin* – W. W. Jacobs, *The Monkey's Paw* – A. J. Alan, *The Hair* – E. F. Benson, *Mrs. Amworth* – Ambrose Bierce, *Moxon's Master* – Jerome K. Jerome, *The Dancing Partner* – R. L. Stevenson, *Thrawn Janet* – R. H. Benson, *Father Meuron's Tale* – Marjorie Bowen, *The Avenging of Ann Leete* – J. F. Sullivan, *The Man with a Malady* – W. F. Harvey, *August Heat* – Morley Roberts, *The Anticipator* – Joseph Conrad, *The Brute* – May Sinclair, *Where Their Fire Is Not Quenched* – J. S. LeFanu, *Green Tea* – J. D. Beresford, *The Misanthrope* – John Metcalfe, *The Bad Lands* – A. M. Burrage, *Nobody's House* – A. C. Quiller-Couch, *The Seventh Man* – N. Royde-Smith, *Proof* – Walter de la Mare, *Seaton's Aunt* – Michael Arlen, *The Gentleman from America* – R. Ellis Roberts, *The Narrow Way* – Traditional Tales of the Lowlands, *Sawney Bean* – Bram Stoker, *The Squaw* – Violet Hunt, *The Corsican Sisters* – Barry Pain, *The End of a Show* – H. G. Wells, *The Cone* – Ethel Colburn Mayne, *The Separate Room*.

Notes: Percival Wilde, *The Adventure of the Fallen Angels* begins on p. [457] not on p. 455, as stated in the CONTENTS on p. 6; on p. 8 there is a bit of broken type between the "M" and "I" in MICROCOSMOS.

The CONTENTS (pp. [5]–8) classifies each story according to type within the genres of Detection and Mystery, or Mystery and Horror. Some of the stories are not included in the American edition (A7*b*.1.) *The Trial for Murder* is listed as written by Charles Collins and Charles Dickens; Sayers notes in A13*a*.1. that it is by Dickens alone.

The introduction, a classic essay on detective fiction, has been reprinted many times. This volume was printed ten times by 1937. †Issued in Canada by Longmans.

*a.*II. *Gollancz (London) two-volume issue* 1939:

Text produced from A7*a*.1., with the exception of lines 38 and 39 in the Introduction on p. 9 (A7*a*.1.) which are re-set in A7*a*.II. as line 38 on p. 9 and line 1 on page 10; from there the type settings for both issues are the same. Volume I contains the stories of Detection and Mystery; Volume II contains the stories of Mystery and Horror. The pagination of the text in Volume II begins anew; thus p. [621] of A7*a*.1. becomes p. [11] of A7*a*.II.

*a.*III. *Gollancz (London) two volume re-issue* 1952:

Text produced from A7*a*.1. as Parts I and II of the six-part issue of GREAT SHORT STORIES OF DETECTION, MYSTERY AND HORROR [see also A13a.II. and A20a.II.]. The pagination of the text runs consecutively from Part I to Part II as in A7a.I.

b.I. First American edition 1929:

THE | OMNIBUS | OF | CRIME | EDITED BY | DOROTHY L. SAYERS | [rule] | PAYSON AND CLARKE LTD | NEW YORK MCMXXIX

Collation: [A–Z; Aa–Oo]^{16} 592 leaves.

p. [1] [extreme right:] THE | OMNIBUS | OF | CRIME; p. [2] list of books by Sayers; p. [3] title-page; p. [4] INTRODUCTION COPYRIGHT, 1929 | DOROTHY L. SAYERS | *First printing August 1929*; pp. [5–8] CONTENTS; pp. 9–47 INTRODUCTION; p. [48] blank; pp. [49]–1177 text, pp. [49, 587, 1011] section title-pages, pp. [50, 586, 588, 1010, 1012] blank; pp. [51, 56, 117, 215, 223, 339, 355, 589, 672, 714, 769, 787, 816, 887, 918, 959, 996, 1013, 1030, 1044, 1060, 1136, 1150] story title-pages with text; p. [1178] This book has been set in ten point Garamond on the linotype, | electrotyped, printed and bound by J. J. Little & Ives Co. | in the United States of America. The paper has been | specially made and watermarked by the Ticon- | deroga Pulp and Paper Company, furnished | through Herman Scott Chalfant, Inc.; pp. [1179–1184] blank.

21 × 14 cm. Bulk: 4·7/5·2 cm. White laid paper; trimmed; white wove end-papers. Bound in black cloth; front and back blank; spine [stamped in orange:] [rule] | THE | OMNIBUS | OF | CRIME | [rule] | [design 13 cm. long] | [rule] | PAYSON AND | CLARKE LTD | [rule]

Price: $3·00; number of copies not known. Published 10 August 1929.

Contents: The History of Bel – The History of Susanna – The Story of Hercules and Cacus – The Story of Rhampsinitus – Mrs. Henry Wood, *The Ebony Box* – Hedley Barker, *The Ace of Trouble* – Edgar Allan Poe, *The Mystery of Marie Rogêt* – Conan Doyle – *The Adventure of the Priory School* – Ernest Bramah, *The Ghost At Massingham Mansions* – F. A. M. Webster, *The Secret of the Singular Cipher* – Bechhofer Roberts, *The English Filter* – E. C. Bentley, *The Clever Cockatoo* – Eden Phillpotts, *Prince Charlie's Dirk* – Robert Barr, *The Absent-minded Coterie* – L. T. Meade and Robert Eustace, *The Face in the Dark* – Edgar Jepson and Robert Eustace, *Mr. Belton's Immunity* – Anthony Wynne, *The Cyprian Bees* – F. Britten Austin, *Diamond Cut Diamond* – Raymund Allen, *A Happy Solution* – Percival Wilde, *The Adventure of the Fallen Angels* – Victor Whitechurch, *Sir Gilbert Murrell's Picture* – G. K. Chesterton, *The Hammer of God* – H. C. Bailey, *The Long Barrow* – Sir Basil Thomson, *The Hanover Court Murder* – Aldous Huxley, *The Gioconda Smile* – Mrs. Belloc Lowndes, *Her Last Adventure* – E. W. Hornung, *The Wrong House* – Mrs. Oliphant, *The Open Door* – Charles Dickens, *Story of the Bagman's Uncle* – Charles Collins and Charles

42

Dickens, *The Trial for Murder* – Robert Hitchens, *How Love Came to Professor Guildea* – "Saki," *The Open Window* – Arthur Machen, *The Black Seal* – Sax Rohmer, *Tchériapin* – W. W. Jacobs, *The Monkey's Paw* – A. J. Alan, *The Hair* – E. F. Benson, *Mrs. Amworth* – Ambrose Bierce, *Moxon's Master* – Jerome K. Jerome, *The Dancing Partner* – R. L. Stevenson, *Thrawn Janet* – Marjorie Bowen, *The Avenging of Ann Leete* – W. F. Harvey, *August Heat* – Morley Roberts, *The Anticipator* – Joseph Conrad, *The Brute* – May Sinclair, *Where Their Fire Is Not Quenched* – J. S. LeFanu, *Green Tea* – J. D. Beresford, *The Misanthrope* – John Metcalfe, *The Bad Lands* – A. M. Burrage, *Nobody's House* – A. C. Quiller-Couch, *The Seventh Man* – N. Royde Smith, *Proof* – Walter de la Mare, *Seaton's Aunt* – Edward Lucas White, *Lukundoo* – Michael Arlen, *The Gentleman From America* – R. Ellis Roberts, *The Narrow Way* – Traditional Tales of the Lowlands, *Sawney Bean* – Bram Stoker, *The Squaw* – Violet Hunt, *The Corsican Sisters* – Barry Pain, *The End of a Show* – H. G. Wells, *The Cone* – Ethel Colburn Mayne, *The Separate Room.*

Notes: Contents vary from GREAT SHORT STORIES OF DETECTION MYSTERY AND HORROR (A7a.1). Introduction is the same. †Issued in Canada by McCleod.
Stories of the Supernatural from The Omnibus of Crime, New York: McFadden-Bartell, 1963, and *Human and Inhuman Stories*, New York: Manor Books, 1974, consist of selected stories from THE OMNIBUS OF CRIME.

*b.*II. *Garden City (Garden City, New York) issue* 1931: 1177 pp.

Text produced from A7*b.*I.

*b.*III. *HarBrace (New York) issue* 1941: 1177 pp.

Text produced from A7*b.*I.

c. Harcourt (New York) re-set edition 1961: 920 pp.

A8　　　LORD PETER VIEWS THE BODY　　　1928

*a.*I. *First edition:*

LORD PETER | VIEWS THE BODY | *by* | DOROTHY L. SAYERS | Author of "Whose Body?" "Unnatural Death," | etc. | LONDON | VICTOR GOLLANCZ LTD | 14 Henrietta Street Covent Garden | 1928

Collation: [A]⁸ B–U⁸ [$1 signed with added B] 160 leaves.

p. [1] LORD PETER VIEWS THE | BODY; p. [2] THE STORIES [contents]; p. [3] title-page; p. [4] printer's notice; pp. 5–317 text with pp. [40, 150, 222, 248] blank; [53] crossword square with text; p. 106 map; p. 215 illustration with text; pp. [318–319] NOTES, solution of crossword puzzle; p. [320] blank.

18·4 × 12·5 cm. Bulk: 2·5/2·9 cm. Cream laid paper; cream laid endpapers; trimmed. Bound in black cloth; front and back blank; spine [stamped in orange]: LORD PETER | VIEWS THE | BODY | BY | DOROTHY L. SAYERS | GOLLANCZ

Price: 7s6d; number of copies: 5,000. Published 12 November 1928. Dust jacket: cream printed in brown and orange similar to A6a.I.
Printed by the Camelot Press on paper by Spalding & Hodge Ltd., and bound by Leighton-Straker Bookbinding Co., Ltd.

Contents: The Abominable History of the Man with Copper Fingers – The Entertaining Episode of the Article in Question – The Fascinating Problem of Uncle Meleager's Will – The Fantastic Horror of the Cat in the Bag – The Unprincipled Affair of the Practical Joker – The Undignified Melodrama of the Bone of Contention – The Vindictive Story of the Footsteps that Ran – The Bibulous Business of a Matter of Taste – The Learned Adventure of the Dragon's Head – The Piscatorial Farce of the Stolen Stomach – The Unsolved Puzzle of the Man with No Face – The Adventurous Exploit of the Cave of Ali Baba.

a.II. Payson and Clarke (New York) issue:

LORD PETER | VIEWS THE BODY | *by* | DOROTHY L. SAYERS | Author of | *"Whose Body?" "Unnatural Death,"* | etc. | NEW YORK | PAYSON & CLARKE LTD.

Collation: As A8a.I.

Pagination: As A8a.I.

18·4 × 12·5 cm. Bulk: 2·5/2·9 cm. Cream laid paper; cream laid endpapers; top edge dark blue. Bound in green cloth; front and back blank; spine [stamped in blue:] LORD | PETER | VIEWS | THE | BODY | [two crosses] | SAYERS | PAYSON | & | CLARKE | LTD

Price: $2; number of copies not known. Published March 1929. Dust jacket: illustrated by Stuart Eldridge in shades of blue, emerald and rust.

Note: Appears to be made up from the sheets of A8a.I.

a.III. Gollancz (London) Prime Minister's Detective Library issue 1929: 319 pp.

Text produced from A8a.I.

a.IV. *Gollancz (London) DOROTHY L. SAYERS OMNIBUS issue*
1933:

> Text of LORD PETER VIEWS THE BODY produced from A8*a*.I. with
> THE FIVE RED HERRINGS (A12) and STRONG POISON (A11).

a.V. *Harcourt (New York) issue in tandem with THE DAWSON
PEDIGREE* 1938: 319 pp.

> See A5*d*.II.; text of LORD PETER VIEWS THE BODY produced from the
> plates of A8*a*.I.

a.VI. *Zephyr Books Continental Book Company (Stockholm) issue* 1944:
319 pp.

> Text produced from the plates of A8*a*.I., for distribution outside the British
> Empire and the U.S.A.

a.VII. *Gollancz re-issue, Volume 5 in the "Collected Edition"* 1970:

LORD PETER | VIEWS THE BODY | by | DOROTHY L.
SAYERS | LONDON | VICTOR GOLLANCZ LTD | 1970

> *Collation:* [A]¹⁶ B–K¹⁶ [$1 signed] 160 leaves.
> p. [1] LORD PETER VIEWS THE | BODY; p. [2] a list of works by Sayers;
> p. [3] title-page; p. [4] publication, reissue, ISBN notices, "THE STORIES"
> (Contents), printer's notice; pp. 5–319 text as A8*a*.I.; p. [320] blank.
>
> 18·4× 12·3 cm. Bulk: 2·9/2·4 cm. White wove paper, trimmed; white wove
> endpapers. Bound in bright red cloth; front and back blank; spine [stamped
> in gold:] LORD | PETER | VIEWS | THE | BODY | BY | DOROTHY L. |
> SAYERS | GOLLANCZ.
>
> *Price:* 25*s*; number of copies not disclosed. Published May 1970. Dust jacket:
> bright yellow printed in black and magenta.
> Printed by Lowe & Brydone (Printers) Ltd., London.
>
> *Notes:* p. 145 has KB signature from A8*a*.I. Appears to be a photographic
> reproduction of A8*a*.I.

b.I. *Gollancz (London) re-set war edition* 1942: 212 pp.

> Text pp. 5–210, pp. [211–212] notes and solution to the puzzle.

b.II. *Gollancz (London) TREASURY OF SAYERS STORIES issue*
1958:

Includes HANGMAN'S HOLIDAY (A18) (pp. 7–140) followed by the text of LORD PETER VIEWS THE BODY, pp. 143–348, pp. [349–350] notes and solution of crossword puzzle, produced from the plates of A8b.1.

c. Best Seller Mystery (New York) edition, n.d. [circa 1946]: 126 pp.

Does not include five storeis: "The Abominable History of the Man with Copper Fingers", "The Entertaining Episode of the Article in Question", "The Fascinating Problem of Uncle Meleager's Will", "The Learned Advanture of the Dragon's Head", "The Adventurous Exploit of the Cave of Ali Baba".

d. Penguin (Harmondsworth, England) edition 1962: 280 pp.

e. Avon Books (New York) edition 1969:

[stylised, heavy print:] DOROTHY | L. SAYERS | LORD PETER | VIEWS THE BODY | [publisher's device] | AN AVON BOOK

Collation: 128 leaves.

p. [1] advertisement; p. [2] list of books by Sayers; p. [3] title-page; p. [4] publisher's notices, p. [5] LIST OF STORIES (contents); p. [6] blank; pp. 7–253 text; p. [254] blank; p. 255 Solution of Crossword puzzle; p. [256] advertisement for Avon books.

17.7 × 10.5 cm. Bulk: 10.8 cm. Cream wove paper; no endpapers. Red illustrated paper cover printed in yellow and white; back [printed blurb, statues and woman's corpse being dipped in bronze]; front [AN AVON MYSTERY V2289/75¢ [publisher's device] | [fat, stylized letters:] DOROTHY | L. SAYERS | [illustration as on back] | LORD PETER | VIEWS THE BODY | One dozen mystery gems featuring the | internationally famous LORD PETER WIMSEY. | "Fantastic grotesque, and macabre." | NEW YORK HERALD TRIBUNE; spine [publisher's device] | [top to bottom:] SAYERS LORD PETER VIEWS THE BODY [upright:] 9 | AVON | V2289 | 75¢

Price: 75¢; number of copies undisclosed. Published June 1969.

Notes: This appears to be the first complete American edition. The publisher's notice states "Reprinted by arrangement with Harper & Row, Publishers." In June 1954 Harper purchased the plates, dyes, jackets, etc. of Dorothy L. Sayers' detective books from Harcourt, Brace. (Harcourt, Brace had taken over the plates of Sayers books from Payson & Clarke and Brewer and Warren in 1930). No evidence has been found of an earlier, complete, American edition of this title.

f. New English Library (London) edition 1973: 288 pp.

Note: See LORD PETER (A61) which includes all the stories from LORD PETER VIEWS THE BODY.

Translations: French, Dutch, Flemish, Danish, Spanish, German, Czechoslovakian, Swedish, Hebrew, Burmese.

A9 TRISTAN IN BRITTANY 1929

a.1. First edition:

[Within single rules, with decoration at each corner]: BENN'S ESSEX LIBRARY | *Edited by Edward G. Hawke, M. A.* | [rule] | [flanked by vertical rules:] TRISTAN IN BRITTANY | Being fragments of The | Romance of Tristan, written | in the XII century, by Thomas | the Anglo-Norman. Drawn | out of the French into the | English by Dorothy Leigh | Sayers, M. A., sometime scholar | of Somerville College, Oxford. With an Introduction by | George Saintsbury. | [rule] | LONDON: ERNEST BENN LTD. | *Bouverie House, Fleet Street.*

> *Collation:* [A]⁸ B–D⁸ E–I¹⁶ [$1 signed] 112 leaves.
> p. [i] TRISTAN IN BRITTANY; p. [ii] list of Benn's Essex Library titles; p. [iii] title-page; p. [iv] *First Published . . . . . . July 1929*; p. [v] CONTENTS; p. [vi] *To M. K. P.*; pp. vii–xxvii INTRODUCTION p. [xxviii] blank; pp. xxix–xxxiv TRANSLATOR'S NOTE; p. xxxv THE MANUSCRIPTS; p. [xxxvi] blank; pp. 37–220 text; p. 220 printer's notice; pp. [221–222] list of Benn's Essex Library books; pp. [223–224] blank.

> 16·7× 10·5 cm. Bulk: 1.1/1.3 cm. Cream wove paper; trimmed; top edge brown; cream wove endpapers. Bound in brown leather-like cloth; back blank; front [blind stamped design in center]; spine [stamped in gold; ornate, compartment-like decorations; multiple decorative rules at top and bottom; sides: thin decorative rule] [within top rectangle:] TRISTAN | IN | BRITTANY | [design] | SAYERS | [diamond] | [four sets of decorative rules alternating with three net-like designs] | ERNEST | BENN | [decorative rules]
> Variant binding: brown cloth stamped in black as described above.
> *Note:* See "The Tristan of Thomas" (C30) for the first printing of part of TRISTAN IN BRITTANY.

> *Price:* 3s6d; number of copies not known. Published July 1929.
> Printed and made by The Crypt House Press Ltd., Gloucester and London.

TRISTAN IN BRITTANY | *being* | the fragments of the Romance of | TRISTAN | written in the XII century by | Thomas the Anglo-Norman. | Drawn out of the French into the | English by Dorothy Leigh Sayers, | M.A., sometime scholar of | Somerville College, Oxford, | with an | Introduction by George Saintsbury. | PAYSON & CLARKE LTD | NEW YORK

Collation: [A]⁸ B–O⁸ [$1 signed] 112 leaves.
p. [i] TRISTAN IN BRITTANY; p. [ii] blank; p. [iii] title-page; p. [iv] PRINTED IN GREAT BRITAIN; p. [v] CONTENTS; p. [vi] *To* | *M.K.P.*; pp. vii–xxvii INTRODUCTION; p. [xxviii] blank; p. xxix–xxxiv TRANSLATOR'S NOTE; p. xxxv THE MANUSCRIPTS; p. [xxxvi] blank; pp. 37–220 text; pp. [221–224] blank.

22·6 × 15·3 cm. Bulk: 1·8/2·4 cm. White wove paper; trimmed; top edge violet; white wove endpapers. Bound in violet cloth; front and back blank; spine [stamped in gold:] [top to bottom:] Tristan IN BRITTANY | [upright:] SAYERS | PAYSON | & | CLARKE | LTD

Price: $2; number of copies not known. Published September 1929. Dust jacket: cream printed in green.

Note: This issue, printed in Great Britain and bound and distributed in America by Payson & Clarke, appears to be an enlarged reproduction of A9*a*.I.

A10   THE DOCUMENTS IN THE CASE   1930

a.I. *First edition:*

THE | DOCUMENTS IN THE CASE | Dorothy L. Sayers | and | Robert Eustace | LONDON | ERNEST BENN LIMITED

Collation: [A]⁸ B–S⁸ [$1 signed] 144 leaves.
p. [i] THE DOCUMENTS IN THE CASE; p. [ii] list of books by Sayers; p. [iii] title-page; p. [iv] [publisher's device] | First Published in | 1930 | Printed | in | Great Britain; p. [v] CONTENTS; p. [vi] author's statement of fictitiousness of characters; pp. vii–viii INTRODUCTION; p. [9]–287 text, with pp. [9, 165] section headings, pp. [10, 164, 166] blank; p. [288] printer's notice.

18·4 × 12·2 cm. Bulk: 3·1/3·5 cm. Cream wove paper, trimmed; cream wove endpapers. Bound in black cloth; back blank, front [stamped in orange:] [border of icicles pointing toward the center] | [two guns pointing toward the center] | [fat, stylized letters:] The | Documents | in the Case | [star]; spine [stamped in orange:] [icicles pointing down] | [fat, stylized letters:] The | Documents | in the Case | [triangle] | Dorothy | L. Sayers | and | Robert | Eustace | Ernest Benn | [icicles pointing up]

Price: 7s6d; number of copies: 1,000 (agent's records). Published 4 July 1930. Printed by Purnell and Sons, Paulton (Somerset) and London.

a.II. *Benn's 3s6d issue* 1932: 287 pp.

Text produced from A10*a*.I.

b. *First American edition:*

[rule] | THE | DOCUMENTS | IN THE CASE | [rule] | BY | DOROTHY L. SAYERS | AND | ROBERT EUSTACE | [rule] | [blank area] | [rule] | BREWER & WARREN INC | NEW YORK | [rule]

Collation: [A–T]⁸ 152 leaves.
p. [1] [rule] | THE DOCUMENTS | IN THE CASE | [rule]; p. [2] blank; p. [3] title-page; p. [4] copyright, rights reservation and printer's notices; p. [5] [upper right:] [rule] | SECTION I. | SYNTHESIS | [rule]; p. [6] blank; pp. 7–304 text, pp. [172, 174] blank, p. [173] [upper right:] [rule] | SECTION II. | ANALYSIS | [rule]

19 × 12.7 cm. Bulk: 2.9/3.2 cm. Cream wove paper, cream wove endpapers, trimmed. Bound in tan cloth; back blank; front [stamped in green, stylized letters:] THE | DOCUMENTS | IN THE | CASE | [green illustration of a skull and graveyard]; spine [stamped in green, stylized letters:] [diagonally, left to right, upwards:] THE | DOCUMENTS | IN THE | CASE | SAYERS | & | EUSTACE | [upright:] A | [publisher's device, stylized "B" over a "W"] | MYSTERY | BREWER & WARREN INC

Price: $2; number of copies not known. Published 24 October 1930. Printed by Chas. H. Bohn & Co. Inc., New York.

Notes: The Introduction is printed in this edition as part of the text on pp. 7–8, rather than separately, as in A10*a*.I.
p. 23 line 16 "Mr. H." for "Mrs. H.";
p. 107 line 27 "stupified" for "stupefied";
p. 122 line 16 "your" for "you".

c.I. *Gollancz edition* 1935:

THE | DOCUMENTS IN THE CASE | by | DOROTHY L. SAYERS | and | ROBERT EUSTACE | LONDON | VICTOR GOLLANCZ LTD

Collation: [A]⁸ B–S⁸ [$1 signed with added C] 144 leaves.
p. [1] THE DOCUMENTS IN THE CASE; p. [2] list of novels by Sayers;
p. [3] title-page; p. [4] *First published July 1930* | *First 2/6 edition 1935* | [printer's
notice]; p. [5] CONTENTS; p. [6] blank; pp. [7]–8 INTRODUCTION;
pp. [9]–285 text, with pp. [9, 163] section headings, pp. [10, 162, 164] blank;
pp. [11, 165] unnumbered pages of text; pp. [286–288] blank.

18·5 × 12·2 cm. Bulk: 3·0/3·3 cm. White wove paper; trimmed; white wove
endpapers. Bound in red cloth; front and back blank; spine [stamped in black:]
THE | DOCUMENTS | IN THE | CASE | BY | DOROTHY L. | SAYERS
| AND | ROBERT | EUSTACE | GOLLANCZ

Price: 2s6d; number of copies: 10,000. Published 11 July 1935. Dust jacket:
yellow printed in black and magenta.
Printed at The Camelot Press, London and Southampton.

*c.*II. *Harcourt (New York) issue in tandem with CLOUDS OF WIT-*
NESS 1938:

See A4*e.*I.; THE DOCUMENTS IN THE CASE, pp. [5]–285, is produced
from A10*c.*I.

*c.*III. *Gollancz re-issue, Volume 6 in the "Collected Edition"* 1970:

THE | DOCUMENTS IN THE CASE | by | DOROTHY L.
SAYERS | and | ROBERT EUSTACE | LONDON | VICTOR
GOLLANCZ LTD | 1970

Collation: [A]¹⁶ B–I¹⁶ [$1, 5 signed] 144 leaves.
p. [1] THE DOCUMENTS IN THE CASE; p. [2] list of books by Sayers;
p. [3] title-page; P. [4] publication, reissue, ISBN, and printer's notice; pp.
[5]–285 as A10*c.*I.; pp. [286–288] blank.

18·5 × 12 cm. Bulk: 2·3/2·6 cm. White wove paper, white wove endpapers,
trimmed. Bound in red cloth, front and back blank; spine [stamped in gold:]
THE | DOCUMENTS | IN THE | CASE | BY | DOROTHY L. | SAYERS
| & | ROBERT | EUSTACE | GOLLANCZ

Price: 25s; number of copies not disclosed. Published May 1970. Dust jacket:
bright yellow printed in black and magenta.
Printed by Lowe & Brydone (Printers) Ltd., Thetford, Norfolk. Appears to be
a photographic reproduction of A10*c.*I.

d. Penguin (Harmondsworth, England) edition 1937: 255 pp.

e. Gollancz (London) re-set war edition 1942: 174 pp.

f.i. Four Square (London) edition 1965: 204 pp.

f.ii. New English Library reissue 1969: 204 pp. Text reproduced from A10*f.i.*

g. Avon Books (New York) edition 1968: 221 pp.

Translations: Swedish, Dutch, Danish, Spanish, French, German, Portuguese, Italian.

A11   STRONG POISON   1930

a.1. First edition:

DOROTHY L. SAYERS | STRONG POISON | *"Where gat ye your dinner, Lord Rendal, my son? | Where gat ye your dinner, my handsome young man?"* | " *– O I dined with my sweetheart, Mother; make my bed soon,* | *For I'm sick to the heart and I fain wad lie down."* | *"O that was strong poison, Lord Rendal, my son.* | *O that was strong poison, my handsome young man."* | " *– O yes, I am poisoned,* Mother; make my bed soon, | *For I'm sick to the heart, and I fain wad lie down."* | [right:] OLD BALLAD | LONDON | VICTOR GOLLANCZ LIMITED | 14 Henrietta Street Covent Garden | 1930

Collation: [A]⁸ B–S⁸ [$1 signed] 144 leaves.
p. [i] STRONG POISON; p. [2] full page advertisement for LORD PETER VIEWS THE BODY; p. [3] title-page; p. [4] printer's notice; pp. [5]–288 text, pp. [5, 25, 36, 45, 58, 69, 81, 89, 111, 120, 137, 146, 173, 185, 194, 213, 225, 241, 248, 270, 275, 285] unnumbered chapter headings with text.

18·5 × 12·4 cm. Bulk: 2·8/3·1 cm. White laid paper, white laid endpapers, trimmed. Bound in black cloth, front and back blank; spine [stamped in orange:] STRONG | POISON | BY | DOROTHY L. SAYERS | GOLLANCZ

Price: 7s6d; number of copies: 5,000. Published 18 September 1930. Dust jacket: yellow printed in black and magenta.
Printed by Purnell and Sons Ltd., Paulton (Somerset) and London.

Note: Thirteen impressions by October, 1940.

a.II. *Gollancz (London) DOROTHY L. SAYERS OMNIBUS issue*
1933:

See A8*a*.IV.; text of STRONG POISON produced from A11*a*.II.

a.III. *Gollancz (London) re-issue, Volume 7 in the "Collected Edition"*
1970:

STRONG POISON | by | DOROTHY L. SAYERS | *"Where gat
ye your dinner, Lord Rendal, my son? | Where gat ye your dinner, my
handsome young man?" | " – O I dined with my sweetheart, Mother;
Make my bed soon, | For I'm sick to the heart and I fain wad lie down."
| " – O that was strong poison, Lord Rendal, my son, | O that was strong
poison, my handsome young man." | " – O yes, I am poisoned, Mother;
make my bed soon, | For I'm sick to the heart, and I fain wad lie down."*
| [right:] OLD BALLAD | LONDON | VICTOR GOLLANCZ
LTD | 1970

> *Collation:* [A]¹⁶ B–I¹⁶ [$1, 5 signed; 5 with letter plus added star, except F5,
> which is signed F] 144 leaves.
>
> p. [1] STRONG POISON; p. [2] list of books by Sayers; p. [3] title-page;
> p. [4] publication, re-issue, ISBN, and printer's notices; pp. [5]–288 text as
> A11*a*.I.
>
> 18·3 × 12·4 cm. Bulk: 2·3/2·5 cm. Bound in red cloth; front and back blank;
> spine [stamped in gold:] STRONG | POISON | BY | DOROTHY L. |
> SAYERS | GOLLANCZ
>
> *Price:* £1·25; number of copies not disclosed. Published October 1970. Dust
> jacket: bright yellow printed in black and magenta.
> Printed at The Camelot Press, London and Southhampton.
>
> *Notes:* p. 273 "SP" signature from A11*a*.I. Type damage throughout. Pro-
> duced from A11*a*.I.

b.I. *First American edition* 1930:

[rule] | [extreme left:] STRONG | POISON | [rule] | BY |
DOROTHY L. SAYERS | [rule] | [blank area] | [rule] | BREWER
& WARREN INC | NEW YORK | [rule]

> *Collation:* [A–Y]⁸ 176 leaves.
> p. [i] [rule] | STRONG | POISON | [rule]; p. [ii] list of books by Sayers;
> p. [iii] title-page; p. [iv] copyright, rights reservation, printer's notice; p. [v]

eight lines from OLD BALLAD (Lord Rendal); p. [vi] blank; p. [vii] [rule] | STRONG | POISON | [rule]; p. [viii] blank; pp. 1–344 text.

18·5 × 12·5 cm Bulk: 3·2/3·7 cm. White wove paper; white wove endpapers; trimmed. Bound in red cloth; back blank; front: [stamped in black:] STRONG | POISON | [drawing of a poison bottle clutched by a hand, a half-seen face in the background]; spine [stamped in black:] [diagonally, lower left to upper right:] STRONG | POISON | [drawing of a skull, cross-bones, and a hand held up] | [in a semi-circle beneath the drawing:] SAYERS | A | [publisher's device of a "B" centered over a "W"] | MYSTERY | BREWER & | WARREN INC.

Price: $2; number of copies not known. Published 30 September 1930. Printed and manufactured by Chas. H. Bohn & Co. Inc., New York City.

b.II. *Garland (New York) re-issue* 1976: 344 pp.

Produced from A11*b*.I.

c.I. *Harcourt, Brace edition, in tandem with HAVE HIS CARCASE* 1936:

STRONG POISON | *and* | HAVE HIS CARCASE | *by Dorothy L. Sayers* | HARCOURT, BRACE AND COMPANY | NEW YORK

Collation: [A–Y]¹⁶ 352 leaves.
p. [i] blank; p. [ii] list of books by Sayers; p. [iii] title-page; p. [iv] rights reservation, printer's notice; p. [v] [rule] | STRONG | POISON | [rule]; p. [vi] copyright notice, eight line quotation from Old Ballad (Lord Rendal); pp. 1–252 text of STRONG POISON: sig. I2ᵃ [rule] | HAVE HIS | CARCASE | [rule]; sig. I2ᵇ "NOTE", copyright, "Printed in the United States of America"; p. [5]–6 CONTENTS; pp. [7]–448 text of HAVE HIS CARCASE produced from A15a.II.

18·6 × 12·7 cm. Bulk: 3·5/3·8 cm. Cream wove paper; cream wove endpapers; trimmed. Bound in black cloth; back, blank; front [stamped in red:] STRONG POISON | & | HAVE HIS | CARCASE; spine [stamped in red:] *Sayers* | STRONG | POISON | & | HAVE HIS | CARCASE | *Harcourt, Brace* | *and* *Company*

Price: $2; number of copies not known. Published 20 August 1936. Printed by The Polygraphic Company of America, New York.

Notes: Irregular pagination after the first novel is due to use of plates from A15a.II.

*c.*II. *Triangle Books (New York) issue* 1938: 252 pp.

Text produced from A11*c.*I., pp. 1–252.

*c.*III. *Tower Books (Cleveland) issue* 1945: 252 pp.

Text produced from A11*c.*I., pp. 1–252.

*c.*IV. *Harper (New York) issue* 1958: 252 pp.

Text produced from A11*c.*I., pp. 1–252.

*c.*V. *Franklin Watts (New York) large type issue* 1963: 252 pp.

Text produced from A11*c.*I., pp. 1–252.

*d.*I. *Gollancz (London) re-set war edition* 1941: 170 pp.

Text pp. 5–170.

*d.*II. *Gollancz (London)* THE SAYERS HOLIDAY BOOK *re-issue* 1963:

Contains GAUDY NIGHT (A21); text of STRONG POISON, pp. 353–518, produced from the plates of A11*d.*I.; and IN THE TEETH OF THE EVIDENCE (A32).

†*e. Shakespeare Press (Sydney, Australia) edition* 1945.

*f.*I. *Landsborough Four Square Books (London) edition* 1960: 192pp.

*f.*II. *New English Library (London) issue* 1962: 192 pp.

Text produced from A11*f.*I.

*f.*III. *New English Library (London) re-issue* 1967: 192 pp.

Text produced from A11*f.*I.

g. Ulverscroft (Leicester, England) large print edition 1966: 244 pp.

h. Avon Books (New York) edition 1967: 192 pp.

†i. *New American Library* (*Toronto*) *edition* 1974:

Announced in *Publisher's Trade List Annual 1974*, New York: Bowker, p. 24.

Translations: French, Swedish, Norwegian, Polish, Portuguese, Turkish, Dutch, Danish, Japanese, German, Hebrew, Spanish, Czechoslovakian, Italian.

A12   THE FIVE RED HERRINGS   1931

a.i. First edition:

THE | FIVE RED HERRINGS | by | DOROTHY L. SAYERS | author of | *Strong Poison, Lord Peter Views the Body* | etc., etc. | LONDON | VICTOR GOLLANCZ LTD | 14 Henrietta Street Covent Garden | 1931

Collation: [A]⁸ B–X⁸ [$1 signed] 176 leaves.
p. [1] THE FIVE RED HERRINGS; p. [2] advertisements for STRONG POISON, and LORD PETER VIEWS THE BODY; p. [3] title-page; p. [4] printer's notice; p. [5] CONTENTS; p. [6] blank; p. [7] FOREWORD; p. [8] blank; pp. [9]–351 text, pp. [9, 20, 35, 42, 48, 60, 70, 86, 95, 101, 112, 126, 135, 152, 162, 172, 179, 185, 193, 201, 222, 241, 258, 268, 283, 300, 311, 331, 345] chapter headings with text; p. [352] blank.

18·5 × 12·4 cm. Bulk: 2·6/3·0 cm. White laid paper; white wove endpapers illustrated with a "MAP OF GALLOWAY FOR USE WITH THE FIVE RED HERRINGS"; trimmed. Bound in black cloth; front and back blank; spine: [stamped in orange:] FIVE RED | HERRINGS | BY | DOROTHY L. SAYERS | GOLLANCZ

Price: 7s6d; number of copies: 4,000. Published 26 February 1931. Dust jacket: yellow printed in black and magenta.
Printed by The Camelot Press Ltd. on paper by Spaulding & Hodge Ltd., bound by The Leighton-Straker Bookbinding Co., Ltd.

a.ii. Gollancz (*London*) *DOROTHY L. SAYERS OMNIBUS issue* 1933:

See A8*a.*IV.; text of THE FIVE RED HERRINGS produced from A12.*a.*I.

a.iii. Gollancz re-issue, Volume 8 in the "Collected Edition" 1970:

THE | FIVE RED HERRINGS | by | DOROTHY L. SAYERS | LONDON | VICTOR GOLLANCZ LTD | 1970

Collation: [A]¹⁶ B–L¹⁶ [$1, 5 signed] 176 leaves.
p. [1] THE FIVE RED HERRINGS; p. [2] list of books by Sayers; p. [3] title page; p. [4] publication, reissue, ISBN, and printer's notices; p. [5] CONTENTS; p. [6] blank; p. [7] FOREWORD; p. [8] blank; pp. [9]–351 text as A12a.I.; p. [352] blank.

18·5 × 12 cm. Bulk: 2·8/3·4 cm. White wove paper; white wove illustrated endpapers; trimmed. Bound in red cloth; front and back blank; spine [stamped in gold:] THE | FIVE | RED | HERRINGS | BY | DOROTHY L. | SAYERS | GOLLANCZ

Price: 25s; number of copies not disclosed. Published October 1970. Dust jacket: bright yellow printed in black and magenta. Printed by Lowe & Brydone (Printers) Ltd. Thretford, Norfolk.

Notes: Appears to be a photographic reproduction of A12a.I.

b.I. *First American edition* 1931:

[rule] | [extreme left:] SUSPICIOUS | CHARACTERS | *The New Lord Peter Mystery* | [rule] | BY DOROTHY L. SAYERS | [rule] | [blank area] | [rule] | BREWER, WARREN & PUTNAM | NEW YORK, 1931 | [double rule]

Collation: [A–Z, Aa–Bb]⁸ 200 leaves.
p. [1] [rule] | SUSPICIOUS | CHARACTERS | *The New Lord Peter Mystery* | [rule]; p. [2] list of books by Sayers; p. [3] title-page; p. [4] copyright, rights reservation, "PUBLISHED IN GREAT BRITIAN UNDER THE TITLE 'THE FIVE RED HERRINGS'", printer's and binder's notices; p. [5] CONTENTS; p. [6] blank; p. [7] FOREWORD; p. [8] Map of Galloway; pp. 9–398 text; pp. [399–400] blank.

18·5 × 12·5 cm. Bulk: 3·0/3·6 cm. White wove paper, trimmed; top edge black; cream wove endpapers. Bound in orange cloth, back blank; front [stamped in black:] SUSPICIOUS | CHARACTERS; spine [stamped in black:] SUSPICIOUS | CHARACTERS | SAYERS | BREWER | WARREN | & PUTNAM

Price: $2; number of copies not known. Published 4 September 1931.

Notes: Running title: *Suspicious Characters* on even numbered pages; chapter title on odd numbered pages.

b.II. *Harcourt (New York) DOROTHY L. SAYERS OMNIBUS issue* 1934;

See A3d.I.; text of SUSPICIOUS CHARACTERS (THE FIVE RED HERRINGS) produced from A12b.I.

†c. *Modern Age (New York) SUSPICIOUS CHARACTERS edition* 1937: 306 pp.

d.i. *Gollancz (London) re-set war edition* 1942: 244 pp.

d.ii. *Gollancz (London) THE NEW SAYERS OMNIBUS issue* 1957:

> Text of THE FIVE RED HERRINGS pp. 7–244, produced from A12d.i. with HAVE HIS CARCASE (A15) and MURDER MUST ADVERTISE (A16).

e. *New Avon Library (New York) SUSPICIOUS CHARACTERS edition* 1943: 336 pp.

f. *Harper and Brothers (New York) edition* 1958:

THE FIVE | RED HERRINGS | (*Suspicious Characters*) | BY | DOROTHY L. SAYERS | [Wimsey Coat of Arms] | HARPER & BROTHERS | PUBLISHERS NEW YORK

> *Collation:* [A–K]¹⁶ 160 leaves.
> p. [i] THE FIVE RED HERRINGS; p. [ii] "MAP OF GALLOWAY"; p. [iii] title-page; p. [iv] copyright, "*Printed in the United States of America*", rights reservations, "This book was published in England under the title of *The Five Red Herrings*. It was first published in this country under the title, *Suspicious Characters*.", Library of Congress number; p. [v] CONTENTS; p. [vi] blank; p. [vii] FOREWORD; p. [viii] blank; p. [ix] THE FIVE RED HERRINGS; p. [x] blank; pp. 1–306 text; pp. [307–310] blank.
>
> 18·5 × 12 cm. Bulk: 2/2·5 cm. White wove paper; black and white printed endpapers. Bound in grey and quarter black cloth; front and back blank; spine [stamped in gold:] SAYERS | [top to bottom:] THE FIVE | [parallel with the preceding line:] RED HERRINGS | [upright:] HAR [publisher's device] PER | [rule]
>
> *Price:* $3·50; number of copies not disclosed. Published 1958.
>
> *Notes:* This is the first time the novel is titled THE FIVE RED HERRINGS in America.

g.i. *Landsborough Four Square Books (London) edition* 1959: 283 pp.

g.ii. *New English Library (London) issue* 1962: 283 pp.

> Text produced from A12g.i.; reprinted 1968, 1972.

h. Avon Books (New York) edition 1964: 286 pp.

i. Nelson (London) "Streamline Books" edition 1966: 177 pp. (Abridged).

j. Nelson Doubleday (Garden City, New York) edition in tandem with MURDER MUST ADVERTISE 1977:

> Text of THE FIVE RED HERRINGS pp. 7–300; see A16*i*.

Translations: Dutch, German, French, Danish, Spanish, Czechoslovakian, Portuguese.

A13 GREAT SHORT STORIES OF DETECTION, 1931 MYSTERY AND HORROR—SECOND SERIES

a.1. First edition:

EDITED BY DOROTHY L. SAYERS | GREAT SHORT STORIES OF | DETECTION, MYSTERY | AND HORROR | SECOND SERIES | LONDON | VICTOR GOLLANCZ LTD | 14 Henrietta Street Covent Garden | 1931

> *Collation:* [A]¹⁶ B–Z¹⁶ AA–MM¹⁶ [$1 signed with added M] 576 leaves.
> p. [1] GREAT SHORT STORIES OF DETECTION, | MYSTERY AND HORROR | SECOND SERIES; p. [2] advertisement for first series; p. [3] title-page; p. [4] printer's, paper supplier's, and binder's notices; pp. [5]–7 CONTENTS; p. [8] blank; p. [9] [section heading:] INTRODUCTION; p. [10] blank; pp. [11]–26 INTRODUCTION, p. [27] EDITOR'S ACKNOWLEDGEMENTS; p. [28] blank; p. [29] PUBLISHER'S NOTE; p. [30] blank; p. [31] GREAT SHORT STORIES OF DETECTION, | MYSTERY AND HORROR; p. [32] blank; p. [33] section heading for Stories of Detection and Mystery; p. [34] blank; pp. [35]–476 text, pp. [35, 102, 164, 216, 242, 264, 281, 285, 344, 372, 444] story title pages with text; p. [477] section heading for Stories of Mystery and Horror; p. [478] blank; pp. [479]–1147 text, pp. [479, 500, 525, 633, 691, 713, 730, 752, 808, 833, 927, 986, 1046, 1068, 1080, 1112] story title-pages with text; pp. [1148–1152] blank.

> 18·4 × 12·3 cm. Bulk: 4·4/5·0 cm. Cream wove paper, trimmed; cream wove endpapers. Bound in black cloth, front and back blank, spine [stamped in orange:] DETECTION | MYSTERY | HORROR | [rule] | SECOND SERIES | [rule] | SAYERS | GOLLANCZ

> *Price:* 8*s*6*d*; number of copies not disclosed. Published 13 July 1931. Dust jacket: yellow printed in black and magenta.

Printed by The Camelot Press on paper by Spalding & Hodge, Ltd. and bound by The Leighton-Straker Bookbinding Co. Ltd.

Contents: F. Britten Austin, *Diamond Cut Diamond* – H. C. Bailey, *The Little House* – Robert Barr, *Lord Chizelrigg's Missing Fortune* – E. C. Bentley, *The Inoffensive Captain* – Anthony Berkeley, *The Avenging Chance* – Ernest Bramah, *Who Killed Charlie Winpole?* – G. K. Chesterton, *The Queer Feet* – Agatha Christie, *The Adventure of the Clapham Cook* – G. D. H. and M. Cole, *In a Telephone Cabinet* – William Wilkie Collins, *The Biter Bit* – Freeman Wills Crofts, *The Mystery of the Sleeping Car Express* – J. S. Fletcher, *Blind Gap Moor* – Milward Kennedy, *Mr. Truefitt Detects* – Milward Kennedy, *Death in the Kitchen* – Ronald A. Knox, *Solved by Inspection* – Mrs. Belloc Lowndes, *An Unrecorded Instance* – Baroness Orczy, *The Regent's Park Murder* – John Rhode, *The Elusive Bullet* – Dorothy L. Sayers, *The Cave of Ali Baba* – M. P. Shiel, *The Race of Orven* – J. C. Squire, *The Alibi* – Sir Basil Thomson, *The Vanishing of Mrs. Fraser* – Henry Wade, *Duello* – Victor L. Whitechurch, *How the Captain Tracked a German Spy* – Percival Wilde, *The Pillar of Fire* – A. J. Alan, *My Adventure in Norfolk* – Stacy Aumonier, *Miss Bracegirdle Does her Duty* – R. H. Barham, *The Leech of Folkestone* – Max Beerbohm, *A. V. Laider* – E. F. Benson, *The Room in the Tower* – J. D. Beresford, *Cut-Throat Farm* – Ambrose Bierce, *The Damned Thing* – Algernon Blackwood, *Secret Worship* – Mrs. E. Bland, *No. 17* – Douglas G. Browne, *The Queer Door* – A. M. Burrage, *The Waxwork* – William Wilkie Collins, *Mad Monkton* – Alan Cunningham, *The Haunted Ships* – Clemence Dane, *The King Waits* – Walter de la Mare, *The Tree* – S. L. Dennis, *The Second Awakening of a Magician* – Charles Dickens, *No. 1 Branch Line: The Signalman* – Ford Madox Ford, *Riesenberg* – W. F. Harvey, *The Beast with Five Fingers* – Holloway Horn, *The Old Man* – Violet Hunt, *The Prayer* – W. W. Jacobs, *The Well* – Edgar Jepson, *The Resurgent Mysteries* – J. S. LeFanu, *Mr. Justice Harbottle* – Sir Edward Bulwer – Lytton, Lord Lytton, *The Haunted and the Haunters* – Arthur Machen, *The Great Return* – Frederick Marryat, *The Story of the Greek Slave* – John Masefield, *Anty Bligh* – John Metcalfe, *The Double Admiral* – Mrs. Oliphant, *The Library Window* – Barry Pain, *Rose Rose* – Eden Phillpotts, *The Iron Pineapple* – Edgar Allan Poe, *Berenice* – Sir Arthur Quiller-Couch – *The Roll Call of the Reef* – Naomi Royde-Smith, *Mangaroo* – "Saki" (H. H. Munro), *Sredni Vashtar* – Mary Wollstonecraft Shelley, *The Mortal Immortal* – M. P. Shiel, *The Primate of the Rose* – Henry Spicer, *Called to the Rescue* – Hugh Walpole, *The Enemy* – H. C. Wells, *The Inexperienced Ghost* – E. L. White, *Lukundoo.*

Notes: p. 76 line 34 "mile" for "smile," line 36 "th re" for "there"; p. 493 line 34 "se" for "she"; p. 809 line 21 square-shaped smudge; p. 1001 damaged type first line; p. 1121 signature MMM signed MMM.
Eight printings by 1950. †Issued in Canada by Longmans.

a.II. *Gollancz* (*London*) *two-volume issue* 1952:

Text of A13*a*.I. is produced as Part III and Part IV of the six part GREAT SHORT STORIES OF DETECTION, MYSTERY AND HORROR (see A7*a*.III. and A20*a*.II.) with the same, consecutive, pagination as in A13*a*.I.

b.I. *First American edition* 1932:

[Within single rules:] [thick rule] | [space] | [two thin rules:] | THE SECOND | OMNIBUS OF CRIME | 1932 | EDITED BY | DORO-THY L. SAYERS | [design of two tulips curving toward each other] | COWARD-McCANN, INC. | NEW YORK

Collation: [A–Z, AA–DD]¹⁶ 432 leaves.
p. [i] THE SECOND | OMNIBUS OF CRIME; p. [ii] blank; p. [iii] title-page; p. [iv] copyright, rights reservation, publisher's device of lighted candle in holder, notice of American manufacture; pp. v–vi CONTENTS; p. [vii] [section heading:] INTRODUCTION; p. [viii] blank; pp. [1]–16 INTRO-DUCTION; p. [17] EDITOR'S ACKNOWLEDGEMENTS; p. [18] blank; p. [19] PUBLISHER'S NOTE: p. [20] blank; p. [21] THE SECOND | OMNIBUS OF CRIME; p. [22] blank; pp. [23]–855 text with pp. [23, 357] section headings and pp. [24, 358] blank; p. [856] blank.

20·9 cm. × 13·9 cm. Bulk: 4·5/4·9 cm. White wove paper; trimmed; white wove endpapers. Bound in black cloth; front and back blank; spine [stamped in orange:] THE | SECOND | OMNIBUS | OF | CRIME | [abstract design within single rules] | EDITED | BY | DOROTHY | L. | SAYERS | Coward | McCann

Price: $2·50; number of copies not known. Published January 1932.

Contents: F. Britten Austin, *The Fourth Degree* – Robert Barr, *Lord Chizelrigg's Missing Fortune* – E. C. Bentley, *The Ordinary Hair-Pins* – Anthony Berkeley, *The Avenging Chance* – Ernest Bramah, *Who Killed Charlie Winpole?* – Agatha Christie, *The Adventure of the Clapham Cook* – William Wilkie Collins, *The Biter Bit* – Freeman Wills Crofts, *The Mystery of the Sleeping-Car Express* – J. S. Fletcher, *Blind Gap Moor* – Milward Kennedy, *Death in the Kitchen* – Mrs. Belloc Lowndes, *An Unrecorded Instance* – Baroness Orczy, *The Regent's Park Murder* – John Rhode, *The Elusive Bullet* – Dorothy L. Sayers, *The Cave of Ali Baba* – J. C. Squire, *The Alibi* – Sir Basil Thomson – *The Vanishing of Mrs. Fraser* – Henry Wade, *Duello* – Victor L. Whitechurch, *How the Captain Tracked a German Spy* – Percival Wilde, *The Pillar of Fire* – Stacy Aumonier, *Miss Bracegirdle Does Her Duty* – R. H. Barham, *The Leech of Folkestone* – Max Beerbohm, *A. V. Laider* – J. D. Beresford, *Cut-Throat Farm* – Ambrose Bierce, *The Damned Thing* – Algernon Blackwood, *Secret Worship* – Mrs. E. Bland, *No. 17* – A. M. Burrage, *The Waxwork* – Stephen Crane, *The Open Boat* |

Clemence Dane, *The King Waits* – Walter de la Mare, *The Tree* – Ford Madox Ford, *Riesenberg* – Holloway Horn, *The Old Man* – Violet Hunt, *The Prayer* – W. W. Jacobs, *The Well* – Manuel Komroff, *Ants* – J. S. LeFanu, *Mr. Justice Harbottle* – Sir Edward Bulwer-Lytton, Lord Lytton, *The Haunted and the Haunters* – Arthur Machen, *The Great Return* – Frederick Marryat, *The Story of the Greek Slave* – John Masefield, *Anty Bligh* – Herman Melville, *The Bell-Tower* – John Metcalfe, *The Double Admiral* – Mrs. Oliphant, *The Library Window* – Barry Pain, *Rose Rose* – Eden Phillpotts, *The Iron Pineapple* – Edgar Allan Poe, *Berenice* – Sir Arthur Quiller-Couch, *The Roll-Call of the Reef* – Naomi Royde-Smith, *Mangaroo* – "Saki" (H. H. Munro), *Sredni Vashtar* – Henry Spicer, *Called to the Rescue* – Hugh Walpole, *The Enemy* – H. G. Wells, *The Inexperienced Ghost*.

Notes: The contents vary from those of GREAT SHORT STORIES OF DETECTION, MYSTERY AND HORROR SECOND SERIES (A13*a*.1.) †Issued in Canada by McClelland.

b.II. **Blue Ribbon Books** (*Garden City, New York*) *issue* 1934: 855 pp.

Text produced from the plates of A13*b*.1.; reprinted 1936. Variant title: THE WORLD'S GREAT CRIME STORIES.

A14   THE FLOATING ADMIRAL   1931

a. First edition:

THE | FLOATING ADMIRAL | BY | CERTAIN MEMBERS OF | THE DETECTION CLUB | HODDER AND STOUGHTON | LIMITED [publisher's device] LONDON

Collation: [A]⁸ B–X⁸ [$1 signed] 176 leaves.
p. [1] THE FLOATING ADMIRAL; p. [2] map; p. [3] title-page; p. [4] printer's notice; pp. [5–6] contents; pp. [7]–11 INTRODUCTION BY DOROTHY L. SAYERS; p. [12] blank; pp. [13]–18 PROLOGUE BY G. K. CHESTERTON; pp. [19]–302 text with pp. [19, 31, 48, 64, 73, 90, 110, 151, 191, 215, 222, 232] as chapter headings with text; pp. 303–347 *APPENDIX I SOLUTIONS*; pp. 347–351 *APPENDIX II* (notes); p. [352] blank.

18·5 × 12·4 cm. Bulk: 3·7/4 cm. Cream wove paper, trimmed; cream wove endpapers. Bound in light blue cloth; back blank; front [stamped in black:] THE FLOATING ADMIRAL | *by* | CERTAIN MEMBERS OF | THE DETECTION CLUB | [lower right corner:] G. K. CHESTERTON | DOROTHY L. SAYERS | V. L. WHITECHURCH | G. D. H. & M. COLE | HENRY WADE | AGATHA CHRISTIE | JOHN RHODE | MILWARD

KENNEDY | RONALD A. KNOX | F. WILLS CROFTS | EDGAR
JEPSON | CLEMENCE DANE | ANTHONY BERKELEY; spine [stamped
in black:] THE | FLOATING | ADMIRAL | [rule] | *by* | CERTAIN MEM-
BERS | OF THE | DETECTION CLUB | [publisher's device] | HODDER &
STOUGHTON

Price: 7s6d; number of copies not disclosed. Published 2 December 1931.

Notes: Sayers' contributions are the Introduction (pp. 7–11), Chapter VII
"Shocks for the Inspector" (pp. 110–150), and Appendix I – "Chapter VII",
her solution.

b. First American edition 1932:

THE | FLOATING ADMIRAL | [rule] | BY CERTAIN MEMBERS
OF | THE DETECTION CLUB | G. K. Chesterton | Canon Victor
L. Whitechurch | G. D. H. and M. Cole | Henry Wade | Agatha
Christie | John Rhode | Milward Kennedy | Dorothy L. Sayers |
Ronald A. Knox | Freeman Wills Crofts | Edgar Jepson | Clemence
Dane | Anthony Berkeley | [Publisher's device] | PUBLISHED FOR
| THE CRIME CLUB, INC. | BY DOUBLEDAY, DORAN &
COMPANY, INC. | GARDEN CITY NEW YORK | 1932

Collation: 160 leaves.
p. [i] THE FLOATING ADMIRAL | [lower left corner:] An extraordinary |
detective story | by thirteen great | writers, with two appendices for | mystery
story en- | thusiasts.; p. [ii] map; p. [iii] title-page; p. [iv] printer's notice,
copyright notice, " FIRST EDITION"; pp. v–vi CONTENTS; p. [vii] THE
FLOATING ADMIRAL; p. [viii] blank; pp. [1]–5 INTRODUCTION;
pp. 6–10 PROLOGUE; pp. 11–265 text; pp. 266–305 APPENDIX I: SOLU-
TIONS; pp. 306–309 APPENDIX II: NOTES; pp. [310–312] blank.

19 × 13 cm. Bulk: 3/3·5 cm. Cream wove paper; top edge trimmed; cream
wove endpapers. Bound in black cloth; back blank; front [9·5 × 3·5 cm. yellow
rectangle, to the extreme right; stamped in black:] THE | FLOATING |
ADMIRAL; spine [5·3 × 3·3 cm. yellow rectangle; stamped in black:] THE
| FLOATING | ADMIRAL | [4 × 3 cm. yellow rectangle at bottom of spine
stamped in black:] [publisher's device] | THE CRIME | CLUB, INC.

Price: $2; number of copies not disclosed. Published 11 February 1932.

Notes: Sayers' contributions are the Introduction (pp. 1–5); "Shocks for the
Inspector" (pp. 92–128); and "Solution" (pp. 275–295).

Translation: French.

a.i. First edition:

HAVE HIS CARCASE | by | DOROTHY L. SAYERS | You must produce the body ... | *Habeas Corpus Act* | LONDON | VICTOR GOLLANCZ LTD | 14 Henrietta Street Covent Garden | 1932

Collation: [A]⁸ B–Z⁸ Aa–Dd⁸ [$1 signed with added C] 224 leaves.
p. [1] HAVE HIS CARCASE; p. [2] advertisements for other works by Sayers; p. [3] title-page; p. [4] NOTE, printer's notice; pp. [5]–6 CONTENTS; pp. [7]–448 text with pp. [7, 22, 33, 47, 64, 75, 83, 92, 100, 115, 127, 141, 161, 178, 187, 204, 222, 235, 246, 259, 269, 290, 302, 311, 320, 339, 354, 363, 378, 390, 399, 413, 430, 442] chapter headings with quotations from T. L. Beddoes, and text.

18·5 × 12·4 cm. Bulk: 3·2/3·7 cm. White laid paper; white laid endpapers; trimmed. Bound in black cloth, front and back blank; spine [stamped in orange:] HAVE | HIS | CARCASE | DOROTHY L. SAYERS | GOLLANCZ

Price: 7s6d; number of copies: 5,000. Published 11 April 1932. Dust jacket: yellow printed in black and magenta.
Printed by The Camelot Press on paper by Spalding & Hodge, bound by The Leighton Straker Bookbinding Co. Ltd.

Notes: p. 7, last line, last word, "coast" for "cliffs"; corrected in re-set edition 1948 (A15c.) and in A15a.v. Thirteen impressions by 1941.

a.ii. First American issue 1932:

[rule across page] | [extreme left:] HAVE HIS | CARCASE | [rule across page] | BY | DOROTHY L. SAYERS | [rule across page] | [blank area] | [rule across page] | BREWER WARREN & PUT- NAM | NEW YORK, 1932 | [double rule across page]

Collation: [A]⁸ B–Z⁸ Aa–Dd⁸ [$1 signed with added C] 224 leaves.
p. [1] [extreme right:] [rule] | HAVE HIS | CARCASE | [rule]; p. [2] list of books by Sayers; p. [3] title-page; p. [4] "NOTE", copyright notice, "Printed in the United States of America"; pp. [5]–6 CONTENTS; pp. [7]–448 text, as A15a.i.

19 × 13 cm. Bulk: 3·2/3·7 cm. White wove paper, trimmed; white wove endpapers. Bound in red cloth; back blank; front [stamped in yellow, fat letters:] HAVE | – HIS | – CARCASE; spine [stamped in yellow:] HAVE | – HIS | – CARCASE | SAYERS | BREWER | WARREN & | PUTNAM

Price: $2; number of copies not known. Published 20 May 1932.

a.iii. *Harcourt, Brace (New York) issue in tandem with STRONG POISON* 1936:

See A11c.i. Text of HAVE HIS CARCASE produced from A15a.ii.

a.iv. *Harper (New York) issue* 1959: 448 pp.

Text produced from the plates of A15a.ii.

a.v. *Gollancz (London) re-issue as Volume 9 in the "Collected Edition"* 1971:

HAVE HIS CARCASE | by | DOROTHY L. SAYERS | You must produce the body . . . | LONDON | VICTOR GOLLANCZ LTD | 1971

> *Collation:* [A]¹⁶ B–O¹⁶ [$1 signed, $5 signed with added star, except A5] 224 leaves.
> p. [1] HAVE HIS CARCASE; p. [2] list of books by Sayers; p. [3] title-page; p. [4] publication and reissue notices, "NOTE", printer's notice; pp. [5]–6 CONTENTS; pp. [7]–448 text, as A15a.i. except for correction on p. [7].
>
> 18·3 × 12·3 cm. Bulk: 3·5/3·7 cm. White wove paper; trimmed; white wove endpapers. Bound in red cloth; front and back blank; spine [stamped in gold:] HAVE | HIS | CARCASE | BY | DOROTHY L. | SAYERS | GOLLANCZ
>
> *Price:* £1·50; number of copies not disclosed. Published May 1971. Dust jacket: bright yellow printed in black and magenta.
> Printed by Lowe and Brydone (Printers) Ltd., London.
>
> *Note:* Appears to be a photographic reproduction of A15a.i. with correction on p. [7].

b. First American edition 1942:

[within decorated rules at top and bottom connected by single vertical rules on the right and left:] Have His | CARCASE | A LORD PETER WIMSEY MYSTERY | BY | *Dorothy Sayers* | double rule | *Pocket* BOOKS, Inc. [publisher's device] NEW YORK, N. Y.

> *Collation:* [A–O]¹⁶ 224 leaves.
> p. [i] HAVE HIS CARCASE | [advertisement for Victory Book Campaign]; p. [ii] advertisement for Pocketbooks; p. [iii] title-page; p. [iv] printing history, "NOTE", "*Printed in the U.S.A.*", copyright notice; pp. v–vii *Table of Contents*; pp. 1–440 text; pp. [441–442] advertisements.

16·5 × 10·5 cm. Bulk: 1·7 cm. White wove paper; red wove endpapers; trimmed. Paper covers; back [yellow and white, printed in black:] [blurb and advertisement for Pocketbooks]; front [top: a narrow orange band across the page, printed in black:] A LORD PETER WIMSEY MYSTERY | [black background illustrated in green and purple, printed in yellow and green:] [extreme left:] 163 | HAVE HIS | CARCASE | [lower right, printed in black on an orange rectangle:] DOROTHY | SAYERS | [bottom left, printed in purple and white:] publisher's device [across the bottom, a purple band printed in white:] *Pocket* BOOK *edition* COMPLETE AND UNABRIDGED

Price: 25 cents; number of copies not known. Published June 1942.

Notes: Three impressions in 1942.

c.I. *Gollancz (London) re-set war edition* 1948: 307 pp.

c.II. *Gollancz (London) re-issue in THE NEW SAYERS OMNIBUS* 1957:

See A12*d*.II; text of HAVE HIS CARCASE produced from A15*c*.I.

d. Penguin (Harmondsworth, England) edition 1962: 359 pp.

e. Avon Books (New York) edition 1968: 351 pp.

f. New English Library (London) edition 1974: 444 pp.

Translations: Swedish, Danish, Japanese, Dutch, German, French, Spanish.

A16   MURDER MUST ADVERTISE   1933

a.I. *First edition:*

DOROTHY L. SAYERS | MURDER MUST ADVERTISE | *A DETECTIVE STORY* | LONDON | VICTOR GOLLANCZ LTD | 14 Henrietta Street Covent Garden | 1933

> *Collation:* [A]⁸ B–X⁸ [$1 with added A, except D1 and U1 signed DB and UB] 176 leaves.
> p. [1] MURDER MUST ADVERTISE; [2] advertisement of books by Sayers; p. [3] title-page; [4] Author's Note; pp. 5–6 CONTENTS; pp. [7]–352 text, pp. [7, 25, 37, 52, 78, 95, 111, 126, 151, 164, 186, 203, 221, 237, 247, 270, 284, 304, 322, 335, 347] chapter headings and text.

18·5 × 12 cm. Bulk: 2·7/3·1 cm. Cream laid paper; all edges trimmed; cream wove endpapers. Bound in black cloth; front and back blank; spine [stamped in orange:] MURDER | MUST | ADVERTISE | BY | DOROTHY L. SAYERS | GOLLANCZ

Price: 7s6d; number of copies: 6,000. Published 6 February 1933. Dust jacket: yellow printed in black and magenta.
Printed by The Camelot Press Ltd., paper by Spalding & Hodge, bound by The Leighton-Straker Bookbinding Co. Ltd.

Notes: Thirteen impressions by August 1941. Chapter XVIII "The Unexpected Conclusion of a Cricket Match" was printed in *Best Cricket Stories*, chosen by E. W. Swanton, London: Faber, 1957.

a.II. *Zephur (Stockholm) continental issue* 1943:

Text produced from A16a.I.

a.III. *Gollancz re-issue, Volume 10 in the "Collected Edition"* 1971:

DOROTHY L. SAYERS | MURDER MUST ADVERTISE | *A DETECTIVE STORY* | LONDON | VICTOR GOLLANCZ LTD | 14 Henrietta Street Covent Garden | 1971

Collation: [A]¹⁶ B–L¹⁶ [$1 signed, $5 signed with added star] 176 leaves.
p. [1] MURDER MUST ADVERTISE; p. [2] list of books by Sayers; p. [3] title-page; p. [4] publication, re-issue, ISBN notices, "AUTHOR'S NOTE", printer's notice; pp. [5]–6 CONTENTS; pp. [7]–352 text, as A16.*a.I.*

18·2 × 12·3 cm. Bulk: 2·7/3·1 cm. White wove paper; untrimmed. Bound in red cloth; front and back blank; spine [stamped in gold:] MURDER | MUST | ADVERTISE | BY | DOROTHY L. | SAYERS | GOLLANCZ

Price: £1·50; number of copies not disclosed. Published October 1971. Dust jacket: bright yellow printed in back and magenta.
Printed by Lowe & Brydone (Printers) Ltd.

Notes: Type damage on pp. 129, 191, 193, 319, 320. Appears to be a photographic reproduction of A16a.I

b.I. *First American edition* 1933:

[Within double rules, thick reverse "L" outside frame at the right and bottom:] MURDER | MUST | ADVERTISE | A DETECTIVE STORY | BY | DOROTHY L. SAYERS | [publisher's device] | HARCOURT, BRACE | AND COMPANY | NEW YORK

Collation: [A–Y]⁸ 176 leaves.

p. [i] MURDER | MUST | ADVERTISE; p. [ii] list of books by Sayers; p. [iii] title-page; p. [iv] copyright, rights reservation, *"first edition"*, "AUTHOR'S NOTE", printer's notice; pp. v–vi CONTENTS; p. [1] MURDER | MUST | ADVERTISE; p. [2] blank; pp. 3–344 text; pp. [345–346] blank.

19 × 12·5 cm. Bulk: 3·5/4·0 cm. White wove paper; trimmed; white endpapers. Bound in blue cloth; back blank; front [stamped in orange to the left:] MURDER | MUST | ADVERTISE; spine [stamped in orange:] MURDER | MUST | ADVERTISE | [solid circle] | SAYERS | HARCOURT, BRACE | AND COMPANY
Variant binding: orange stamped in black.

Price: $2; number of copies not disclosed. Published 6 April 1933.
Printed by Quinn & Bodden Company, Inc. Rahway, N. J.; typography by Robert Josephy.

*b.*ii. *Grosset and Dunlap (New York) issue* 1934: 344 pp.

Text produced from A16*b*.i.

*b.*iii. *Harcourt, Brace (New York) tandem issue with HANGMAN'S HOLIDAY* 1938:

Text of MURDER MUST ADVERTISE produced from the plates of A16*b*.i.; see also A18*b*.ii.

*b.*iv. *Harper and Row (New York) issue* 1959:

Text produced from the plates of A16*b*.i.

c. Pocketbooks (New York) edition 1939: 374 pp.

*d.*i. *Gollancz (London) re-set war edition* 1942: 247 pp.

*d.*ii. *Gollancz (London) THE NEW SAYERS OMNIBUS issue* 1957:

See A12*d*.ii.; text of MURDER MUST ADVERTISE produced from the plates of A16*d*.i.

e. Grafish Forlag (Copenhagen) Easy Reader No. 15 edition 1948: 68 pp.

*f.*i. *Landsborough (London) edition* 1959: 255 pp.

f.ii. *New English Library (London) issue* 1962: 255 pp.

Text produced from A16*f*.i.

f.iii. *New English Library (London) re-issue* 1974: 255 pp.

Text produced from A16*f*.i.

g. Avon Books (New York) edition 1967: 288 pp.

†*h. New American Library (Toronto) edition* 1974:

Announced in *Publisher's Trade List Annual* 1974, New York: Bowker, p. 24.

i. Nelson Doubleday (Garden City, New York) edition in tandem with THE FIVE RED HERRINGS 1977:

Text of MURDER MUST ADVERTISE pp. 305–600; see A12*j*.

Translations: Hungarian, French, Swedish, Polish, Italian, Norwegian, German, Portuguese, Dutch, Czechoslovakian, Hebrew, Finnish, Danish, Spanish.

A17   ASK A POLICEMAN   1933

a. First edition:

ASK A POLICEMAN | BY | ANTHONY BERKELEY | MILWARD KENNEDY | GLADYS MITCHELL | JOHN RHODE | DOROTHY L. SAYERS | & | HELEN SIMPSON | LONDON | ARTHUR BARKER LTD. | 21 GARRICK STREET, COVENT GARDEN

Collation: [1]⁸ 2–20⁸ [$1 signed] 160 leaves.
pp. [2] blank; p. [i] ASK A POLICEMAN; p. [ii] map; p. [iii] title-page; p. [iv] printer's notice; p. v CONTENTS; p. [vi] blank; pp. 1–311 text with pp. [66, 68] blank; p. [312] FINAL NOTE.

18·7 × 12·3 cm. Bulk: 3·0/3·3 cm. White wove paper, untrimmed. White wove endpapers. Bound in light blue cloth; back blank; front [stamped in green:] ASK | A | POLICEMAN; spine [stamped in green:] ASK | A | POLICE-MAN | [3·4 cm. dagger] | [·5 cm. drop (of blood?)] | ANTHONY BERKELEY | MILWARD KENNEDY | GLADYS MITCHELL | JOHN RHODE | DOROTHY L. SAYERS | HELEN SIMPSON | BARKER

Price: 7s6d; number of copies not known. Published 13 March 1933.

Notes: Sayers' contributions are "The Conclusions of Roger Sheringham", (pp. 225–276) and the footnotes added by "P[eter] W[imsey]" to Anthony Berkeley's narrative (pp. 172 and 176).

b. First American edition 1933:

[very thick rule] ASK A | POLICEMAN | [extreme left:] by | ANTHONY BERKELEY | MILWARD KENNEDY | GLADYS MITCHELL | JOHN RHODE | DOROTHY L. SAYERS | and | HELEN SIMPSON | WILLIAM MORROW & COMPANY [Morrow Mystery device] | NEW YORK: 1933 [very thick rule]

Collation: 160 leaves.
p. [i] [very thick rule] ASK A | POLICEMAN; p. [ii] map; p. [iii] title-page; p. [iv] copyright, publishers, rights reservations, and printer's notices; p. [1] CONTENTS; p. [2] blank; p. [3] as p. [i]; p. [4] blank; pp. 5–313 text, with pp. [70, 72] blank; p. [314] blank; p. [315] FINAL NOTE; p. [316] blank.

19·0 × 12·9 cm. Bulk: 2·7/3·2 cm. White wove paper, untrimmed, top edge black. Bound in red cloth; back blank; front [stamped in black:] [very thick rule] ASK A | POLICEMAN | [extreme left, bottom:] [publisher's device]; spine [stamped in black:] ASK | A | POLICEMAN | ANTHONY | BERKE-LEY | MILWARD | KENNEDY | GLADYS | MITCHELL | JOHN | RHODE | DOROTHY | L. SAYERS | HELEN | SIMPSON | [publisher's device]

Price: $2·00; number of copies not known. Published 14 June 1933. Dust jacket: red, black and white illustrated.

Notes: Sayers' contributions are *The Conclusions of Mr. Roger Sheringham* (pp. 175–225) and the two footnotes added by "P.[eter] W.[imsey]" to Anthony Berkeley's narrative.

Translation: Spanish.

A18   HANGMAN'S HOLIDAY   1933

a.1. First edition:

HANGMAN'S HOLIDAY | by | DOROTHY L. SAYERS | LON-DON | VICTOR GOLLANCZ LTD | 14 Henrietta Street Covent Garden | 1933

Collation: [A]⁸ B–S⁸ [$1 signed] 144 leaves.

p. [1] HANGMAN'S HOLIDAY; p. [2] list of works by Sayers; p. [3] title-page; p. [4] "AUTHOR'S NOTE", printer's notice; p. [5] CONTENTS; p. [6] blank; pp. [7]–288 text, with pp. [7, 47, 87, 115, 133, 153, 171, 189, 207, 227, 245, 267] story title pages, pp. [8, 48, 116, 134, 152, 154, 172, 190, 208, 228, 246, 268] blank, pp. [9, 49, 89, 117, 135, 155, 173, 191, 209, 247, 269] story title pages and text; p. [88] plan for "The Queen's Square".

18·4 × 12·4 cm. Bulk: 3·0/3·3 cm. White laid paper; white laid endpapers, trimmed. Bound in black cloth; front and back blank; spine [stamped in orange:] HANGMAN'S | HOLIDAY | BY | DOROTHY L. | SAYERS | GOLLANCZ

Price: 7s6d; number of copies: 3,000. Published 1 May 1933. Dust jacket: yellow printed in black and magenta.
Printed by The Camelot Press Ltd., paper by Spalding & Hodge, bound by The Leighton-Straker Bookbinding Co. Ltd.

Contents: The Image in the Mirror – The Incredible Elopement of Lord Peter Wimsey – The Queen's Square – The Necklace of Pearls – The Poisoned Dow '08 – Sleuths on the Scent – Murder in the Morning – One Too Many – Murder at Pentecost – Maher-shalal-hashbaz – The Man Who Knew How – The Fountain Plays

Notes: "Murder in the Morning" begins on p. 171 not on p. 173 as stated in the Contents; p. 177 line 19 "nigh" for "night". This edition was reprinted twelve times by September 1942.

*a.*II. *Gollancz re-issue, Volume 11 in the "Collected Edition"* 1971:

HANGMAN'S HOLIDAY | by | DOROTHY L. SAYERS | LONDON | VICTOR GOLLANCZ LTD | 1971

Collation: [A]¹⁶ B–I¹⁶ [$1 signed, $5 signed with added star] 144 leaves. p. [1] HANGMAN'S HOLIDAY; p. [2] list of books by Sayers; p. [3] title-page; p. [4] publication, reissue, ISBN notices, "AUTHOR'S NOTE", printer's notice; p. [5] CONTENTS p. [6] blank; pp. [7]–288 text, as A18*a.*I.

18·3 × 12·2 cm. Bulk: 2·2/2·5 cm. White wove paper; white wove endpapers. Bound in red cloth; front and back blank; spine [stamped in gold:] HANGMAN'S | HOLIDAY | BY | DOROTHY L. | SAYERS | GOLLANCZ

Price: £1·50; number of copies not disclosed. Published October 1971. Dust jacket: bright yellow printed in black and magenta.
Printed by Lowe & Brydone (Printers) Ltd. London

Notes: Murder in the Morning begins on p. 171 not p. 173 as stated in contents, p. 177 line 19 "nigh" for "night". Appears to be a photographic reproduction of A18*a.*I.

b.I. *First American edition* 1933:

[Within double-rules, thick reverse "L" outside frame at right and bottom:] HANGMAN'S | HOLIDAY | BY | DOROTHY L. SAYERS | [publisher's device] | HARCOURT, BRACE AND COMPANY | NEW YORK

Collation: [A–S]⁸ 144 leaves.

p. [1] HANGMAN'S HOLIDAY; p. [ii] list of books by Sayers; p. [iii] title-page; p. [iv] copyright, rights reservation, *"first edition"*, "AUTHOR'S NOTE", printer's notice; p. [v] CONTENTS; p. [vi] blank; pp. [1]–282 text, pp. [1, 41, 81, 109, 127, 147, 165, 183, 201, 221, 239, 261] story title-pages for each story and pp. [2, 40, 42, 110, 128, 146, 166, 184, 202, 220, 222, 238, 240, 262, blank, and p. [82] plan for "The Queen's Square"

19 × 12·5 cm. Bulk: 3·0/3·5 cm. White wove paper; white wove endpapers; trimmed. Bound in light green cloth; back blank; front [stamped in black:] HANGMAN'S | HOLIDAY; spine [stamped in black:] HANGMAN'S | HOLIDAY | [solid circle] | SAYERS | HARCOURT, BRACE | AND COMPANY

Price: $2; number of copies not disclosed. Published 21 September 1933. Printed by Quinn & Bodden Company, Inc., Rahway, N. J. Green, grey and white dust jacket, illustrated by Arthur Hawkins, Jr.

b.II. *Harcourt, Brace* (*New York*) *tandem issue with* MURDER MUST ADVERTISE 1938:

Text of HANGMAN'S HOLIDAY produced from the plates of A18*b*.I.; See also A16*b*.III.

c.I. *Gollancz* (*London*) *re-set war edition* 1942: 140 pp.

c.II. *Gollancz* (*London*) *A TREASURY OF SAYERS STORIES issue* 1958:

Text produced from the plates of A18*c*.I. in tandem with LORD PETER VIEWS THE BODY (A8).

d. *Bestseller Mystery* (*New York*) *edition* n.d. [circa 1942]: 126 pp.

Does not include two stories: "Sleuths on the Scent" and "Murder in the Morning."

e. *Penguin Books* (*Harmondsworth, England*) *edition* 1962: 191 pp.

f. Avon Books (New York) edition 1969: 191 pp.

g. New English Library (London) edition 1974: 192 pp.

Note: See LORD PETER (A61) which includes some stories from HANGMAN'S HOLIDAY.

Translations: Swedish, Danish, Spanish, German.

A19   THE NINE TAILORS   1934

a.1. First edition:

THE | NINE TAILORS | [short double rule] | CHANGES RUNG ON | AN OLD THEME | in | Two Short Touches and | Two Full Peals | by | DOROTHY L. SAYERS | [short double rule] | LON-DON | VICTOR GOLLANCZ LTD | 14 Henrietta Street Covent Garden | 1934

> *Collation:* [A]⁸ B–X⁸ [$1 signed] 176 leaves.
> p. [1] THE NINE TAILORS; p. [2] blank; *inset:* plate "Parish Church of Fenchurch St. Paul"; p. [3] title-page; p. [4] FOREWORD; pp. [5]–6 CONTENTS; pp. [7]–350 text; with pp. [7, 65, 265, 323] section headings; pp. [8, 66, 266, 324] change rings, pp. [9, 33, 67, 91, 118, 143, 165, 184, 201, 216, 249, 267, 274, 288, 298, 310, 325, 334, 347] chapter headings and text, pp. [37, 55] diagrams, pp. [64, 264, 322] blank; p. [351] ten line song of the bells; p. [352] printer's notice.
>
> 18·4× 12·4 cm. Bulk: 2·7/3·0 cm. White laid paper; white laid endpapers; trimmed. Bound in black cloth; front and back blank; spine [stamped in orange:] THE | NINE | TAILORS | BY | DOROTHY L. | SAYERS | GOLLANCZ
>
> *Price:* 7s6d; number of copies: 6,000. Published 8 January 1934. Dust jacket: yellow printed in black and magenta.
> Printed by The Camelot Press, paper by Spaulding & Hodge, bound by The Leighton-Straker Bookbinding Co. Ltd.
>
> *Notes:* The frontspiece is a sketch of Fenchurch St. Paul with Detail of Roof by "W. J. Redhead, Architect". Reprinted thirteen times by 1941. A booklet prepared in July 1956 by Bass, Ratcliff and Gretton Ltd., advertising Bass beer contains an extract, entitled "Lord Peter Asks for Bass", from line 24, p. 239 to line 18 p. 240 of this novel.

a.II. *Gollancz re-issue, Volume 12 in the "Collected Edition"* 1972:

THE | NINE TAILORS | [short double rule] | CHANGES RUNG
ON | AN OLD THEME | in | Two Short Touches and | Two Full
Peals | by | DOROTHY L. SAYERS | [short double rule] | LON-
DON | VICTOR GOLLANCZ LTD. | 1972

> *Collation:* [A]¹⁶ B–L¹⁶ [$1 signed, $5 signed with added star] 176 leaves.
> p. [1] THE NINE TAILORS; p. [2] list of books by Sayers; *inset:* plate "Parish
> Church of Fenchurch St. Paul"; p. [3] title-page; p. [4] FOREWORD, pub-
> lication, reissue, ISBN, printer's notices; pp. [5]–6 CONTENTS; pp. [7]–
> 351 text as A19*a*.1.; p. [352] blank.
>
> 18·4 × 12·2 cm. Bulk: 2·2/3·0 cm. White wove paper, trimmed; white wove
> endpapers. Bound in red cloth; front and back blank; spine [stamped in gold:]
> THE | NINE | TAILORS | by | DOROTHY L. | SAYERS | GOLLANCZ
>
> *Price:* £1·60; number of copies not disclosed. Published April 1972. Dust
> jacket: bright yellow printed in black and magenta.
> Printed by Lowe & Brydone (Printers) Ltd.
>
> *Note:* The frontispiece is a sketch of Fenchurch St. Paul with Detail of Roof
> by "W. J. Redhead, Architect". Type damage p. 242. Appears to be a photo-
> graphic reproduction of A19*a*.1.

b.I. *First American edition* 1934:

[Within double rules, thick reverse "L" outside frame at right and
bottom:] THE NINE | TAILORS | CHANGES | RUNG ON AN
OLD THEME | *in* | *Two Short Touches* | *and Two Full Peals* | BY |
DOROTHY L. SAYERS | HARCOURT, BRACE | AND COM-
PANY | NEW YORK

> *Collation:* [A–X]⁸ [Y]⁴ 172 leaves.
> p. [i] THE NINE TAILORS; p. [ii] list of books by Sayers; *inset:* plate "Parish
> Church of Fenchurch St. Paul"; p. [iii] title-page; p. [iv] copyright, rights,
> *"first edition,"* typography and printer's notices; p. [v] FOREWORD; p.
> [vi] blank; pp. vii–[viii] CONTENTS; pp. [1]–331 text, with pp. 31, 47
> diagrams, [56, 248] blank, and pp. [1, 2, 57, 58, 249, 250, 305, 306] section
> headings and notes for change-ringing; p. [332] blank; p. [333] song of the
> bells, pp. [334–336] blank.
>
> 19 × 12·2 cm. Bulk: 3·0/3·4 cm. Cream wove paper; trimmed; cream wove
> endpapers. Bound in orange cloth; back blank; front [stamped in black; top,
> left:] THE | NINE | TAILORS; spine [stamped in black:] THE | NINE |

TAILORS | [solid circle] | SAYERS | HARCOURT, BRACE | AND COMPANY

Variant binding: dark blue stamped in orange.

Price: $2·50; number of copies not disclosed. Published March 1934.
Printed by Quinn & Boden Company Inc., Rahway, N. J.; typography by Robert Josephy.

Notes: The frontispiece is a sketch of Fenchurch St. Paul with Detail of Roof by "W. J. Redhead, Architecht." p. 227 line 35 "Thorday" for "Thoday".

*b.*II. *HarBrace (New York) issue* 1938: 333 pp.

Text produced from A19*b*.I.; reprinted in 1945 and 1962.

c. Albatross Continental (Hamburg) edition 1934: 317 pp.

*d.*I. *Gollancz (London) re-set war edition* 1942: 237 pp.

*d.*II. *Gollancz (London) THE SAYERS TANDEM issue* 1957:

Text of THE NINE TAILORS produced from the plates of A19*d*.I. with BUSMAN'S HONEYMOON (A25)

*e.*I. *Landsborough (London) edition* 1959: 255 pp.

Reprinted in 1962.

*e.*II. *New English Library (London) issue* 1968: 255 pp.

Text produced from A19*e*.I.; reprinted in 1970 and 1975.

f. HarBrace Paperback Library (New York) re-set edition 1962: 311 pp.

Translations: Finnish, Dutch, Swedish, French, Japanese, German, Spanish, Danish, Hebrew, Greek, Czechoslovakian, Norwegian.

A20 GREAT SHORT STORIES OF DETECTION,   1934
MYSTERY AND HORROR THIRD SERIES

*a.*I. *First edition:*

EDITED BY DOROTHY L. SAYERS | GREAT SHORT

STORIES OF | DETECTION, MYSTERY | AND HORROR | THIRD SERIES | LONDON | VICTOR GOLLANCZ LTD | 14 Henrietta Street Covent Garden | 1934

Collation: [A]¹⁶ B–Z¹⁶ Aᴀ–Iɪ¹⁶ Kᴋ⁸ [$1 signed with added D] 536 leaves.
p. [1] GREAT SHORT STORIES OF DETECTION, | MYSTERY AND HORROR | THIRD SERIES; p. [2] advertisement for first and second series; p. [3] title-page; p. [4] printer's, paper supplier's, and binder's notices; pp. [5]–7 CONTENTS; p. [8] blank; p. [9] INTRODUCTION; p. [10] blank; pp. [11]–18 Introduction; p. [19] Editor's acknowledgements; p. [20] blank; p. [21] GREAT SHORT STORIES OF DETECTION, | MYSTERY AND HORROR; p. [22] blank; p. [23] SECTION I | STORIES OF | DETECTION AND MYSTERY; p. [24] blank; pp. [25]–505 text, with pp. [25, 44, 150, 283, 389, 411, 435] unnumbered title-pages and text; p. [506] blank; p. [507] SECTION II | STORIES OF | MYSTERY AND HORROR; p. [508] blank; pp. [509]–1069 text, with pp. [509, 663, 672, 680, 749, 753, 828, 840, 854, 883, 954, 1015, 1024, 1063] unnumbered title pages and text; pp. [1070–1072] blank.

18·4 × 12·4 cm. Bulk: 4·2/4·6 cm. Cream wove paper, trimmed; cream wove endpapers. Bound in black cloth; front and back blank; spine [stamped in orange:] DETECTION | MYSTERY | HORROR | [rule] | THIRD SERIES | [rule] | SAYERS | GOLLANCZ

Price: 8s6d; number of copies not disclosed. Published 3 September 1934. Dust jacket: yellow printed in black and magneta.
Printed by The Camelot Press Ltd., paper by Spaulding & Hodge Ltd., bound by The Leighton-Straker Bookbinding Co. Ltd.

Contents: Stacy Aumonier, *The Perfect Murder* – Alex. Barber, *Stain!* – J. J. Bell, *The Bullet* – Leslie Charteris, *The Mystery of the Child's Toy* – Carl Clausen, *Poker-Face* – Freeman Wills Crofts, *The Level Crossing* – St. John Ervine, *The Brown Sandwich* – J. S. Fletcher, *The Judge Corroborates* – R. Austin Freeman, *The Echo of a Mutiny* – Ormond Greville, *The Perfect Crime* – Laurence Kirk, *No Man's Hour* – Ethelreda Lewis, *Blind Justice* – G. R. Malloch, *Saxophone Solo* – H. A. Manhood, *Wilful Murder* – John Millard, *Member of the Jury* – Basil Mitchell, *The Blue Trout* – Anthony Parsons, *A Sleeping Draught* – Robert E. Pinkerton, *Wet Paint* – Melville Davisson Post, *The Wrong Hand* – Garnett Radcliffe, *On the Irish Mail* – Margery Sharp, *Risk* – Frederick Skerry, *Leading Light* – Harold Steevens, *The Leak* – Henry Wade, *The Missing Undergraduate* – E. M. Winch, *Buttons* – Loel Yeo, *Inquest* – Francis Brett Young, *A Busman's Holiday*, A. J. Alan, *The 19 Club* – Martin Armstrong, *Sombrero* – John Betjeman, *Lord Mount Prospect* – Algernon Blackwood, *The Wendigo* – Ann Bridge, *The Song in the House* – D. K. Broster, *Couching at the Door* – Thomas Burke, *The Dumb Wife* – A. M. Burrage, *The Bargain* – A. E. Coppard, *Arabesque: The Mouse* – Oswald Couldrey, *The Mistaken Fury* – E. M. Delafield,

Sophy Mason Comes Back – Lord Dunsany, *Our Distant Cousins* – James Francis Dwyer, *A Jungle Graduate* – Leonora Gregory, *The Scoop* – Alan Griff, *The House of Desolation* – L. P. Hartley, *The Island* – William Fryer Harvey, *Double Demon* – Margaret Irwin, *The Book* – W. W. Jacobs, *The Interruption* – M. R. James, *The Diary of Mr. Poynter* – Cyril Landon, *"You'll Come to the Tree in the End"* – John Metcalfe, *Time-Fuse* – J. C. Moore, *Decay* – Claire D. Pollexfen, *Stowaway* – Sir Arthur Quiller-Couch, *A Pair of Hands* – R. Ellis Roberts, *The Hill* – Naomi Royde-Smith, *The Pattern* – Herbert Shaw, *What Can a Dead Man Do?* Vincent Sheean, *The Virtuoso* – Lady Eleanor Smith, *No Ships Pass* – Sir Frederick Treves, *The Idol with Hands of Clay* – H. Russell Wakefield, *The Frontier Guards* – H. G. Wells, *The Story of the Late Mr. Elvesham* – Ben Ames Williams, *Witch-Trot Pond* – Clarence Winchester, *Anniversary.*

Notes: Six printings by 1950; † Issued in Canada by Longmans.

*a.*II. *Gollancz (London) two-volume re-issue* 1952:

Text of A20*a.*I. is produced as Part V and Part VI of the six part GREAT SHORT STORIES OF DETECTION MYSTERY AND HORROR (See A7*a.*III. and A13*a.*II.) with the same, consecutive pagination as in A20*a.*I.

*b.*I. *First American edition* 1935:

[Within thick rules and double thin rules:] THE THIRD | OMNIBUS OF CRIME | 1935 | EDITED BY | DOROTHY L. SAYERS | [curved line design] | COWARDMcCANN, INC. | NEW YORK

Collation: 410 leaves.
p. [i] THE THIRD | OMNIBUS OF CRIME; p. [ii] blank; p. [iii] title-page; p. [iv] copyright, rights reservation, PRINTED IN THE U.S.A.; p. [v] EDITOR'S ACKNOWLEDGMENTS; p. [vi] blank; pp. [vii–viii] CONTENTS, p. [ix] section heading for INTRODUCTION; p. [x] blank; pp. 1–7 INTRODUCTION; p. [8] blank; pp. [9]–808 text with pp. [9, 345] section headings, pp. [10, 28, 84, 128, 162, 176, 194, 208, 246, 308, 326, 344, 346, 356, 374, 434, 458, 484, 510, 536, 548, 578, 598, 628, 640, 648, 690, 716, 746, 802] blank; pp. [809–810] blank.

20·6 × 14·0 cm. Bulk: 5·0/5·5 cm. White wove paper, trimmed; white wove endpapers. Bound in black cloth; front and back blank; spine [stamped in red-violet:] THE | THIRD | OMNIBUS | OF | CRIME | EDITED | BY | DOROTHY | L. | SAYERS | [abstract design] | Coward | McCann.

Price: $2·50; number of copies not known. Published 20 January 1935.

Contents: Stacy Aumonier, *The Perfect Murder* – J. J. Bell, *The Bullet* – Leslie Charteris, *The Mystery of the Child's Toy* – Carl Clausen, *Poker-Face* – Freeman

Wills Crofts, *The Level Crossing* – St. John Ervine, *The Brown Sandwich* – J. S. Fletcher, *The Judge Corroborates* – R. Austin Freeman, *The Echo of a Mutiny* – Ormond Greville, *The Perfect Crime* – MacKinlay Kantor, *The Grave Grass Quivers* – Laurence Kirk, *No Man's Hour* – H. A. Manhood, *Wilful Murder* – Basil Mitchell, *The Blue Trout* – Robert E. Pinkerton, *Wet Paint* – Melville Davisson Post, *The Wrong Hand* – Garnett Radcliffe, *On the Irish Mail* – Margery Sharp, *Risk* – Henry Wade, *The Missing Undergraduate* – E. M. Winch, *Buttons* – Loel Yeo, *Inquest* – Francis Brett Young, *A Busman's Holiday* – A. J. Alan, *The 19 Club* – Martin Armstrong, *Sombrero* – John Betjeman, *Lord Mount Prospect* – Algernon Blackwood, *The Wendigo* – D. K. Broster, *Couching at the Door* – Thomas Burke, *The Dumb Wife* – A. M. Burrage, *The Bargain* – A. E. Coppard, *Arabesque: The Mouse* – Oswald Couldrey, *The Mistaken Fury* – E. M. Delafield, *Sophy Mason Comes Back* – Lord Dunsany, *Our Distant Cousins* – James Francis Dwyer, *A Jungle Graduate* – Leonora Gregory, *The Scoop* – L. P. Hartley, *The Island* – William Fryer Harvey, *Double Demon* – Helen R. Hull, *Clay-Shuttered Doors* – Margaret Irwin, *The Book* – W. W. Jacobs, *The Interruption* – M. R. James, *The Diary of Mr. Poynter* – Manuel Komroff, *The Head* – A. Merritt, *The People of the Pit* – John Metcalfe, *Time-Fuse* – J. C. Moore, *Decay* – Sir Arthur Quiller-Couch, *A Pair of Hands* – R. Ellis Roberts, *The Hill* – Naomi Royde-Smith, *The Pattern* – Lady Eleanor Smith, *No Ships Pass* – Sir Frederick Treves, *The Idol With Hands of Clay* – H. Russell Wakefield, *The Frontier Guards* – H. G. Wells, *The Story of the Late Mr. Elvesham* – Clarence Winchester, *Anniversary*.

Notes: Contents vary from those of GREAT SHORT STORIES OF DE-
TECTION, MYSTERY AND HORROR THIRD SERIES. † Issued in
Canada by McClelland.

b.II. *Blue Ribbon Books* (*New York*) *issue* 1937: 808 pp.

Text produced from A20*b*.I.

A21   GAUDY NIGHT   1935

a.I. *First edition:*

DOROTHY L. SAYERS | GAUDY NIGHT | The University is
a Paradise, Rivers of Knowledge | are there, Arts and Sciences flow
from thence. | Counsell Tables are *Horti conclusi*, (as it is said | in the
Canticles) *Gardens that are walled in*, and | they are *Fontes signati*,
Wells that are sealed up; | bottomless depths of unsearchable Counsels
there. | JOHN DONNE | LONDON | VICTOR GOLLANCZ LTD |
14 Henrietta Street, Covent Garden | 1935

Collation: [1]⁸ 2–29⁸ 30¹⁰ [$1 signed, 30₂ signed 30 plus star] 242 leaves.
p. [1] GAUDY NIGHT; p. [2] list of detective stories by Sayers; p. [3] title-page; p. [4] printer's imprint; pp. 5–6 AUTHOR'S NOTE; pp. 7–483 text; p. [484] blank.

19·7 × 12·8 cm. Bulk: 4/4·6 cm. White wove paper, trimmed; white wove endpapers. Bound in black cloth; front and back blank; spine [stamped in orange:] GAUDY | NIGHT | BY | DOROTHY L. | SAYERS | GOLLANCZ

Price: 8s6d; number of copies: 17,000. Published 4 November 1935. Dust jacket: yellow printed in black and magenta.
Printed by William Clowes and Sons Ltd. London & Beccles.

Notes: Lettering on binding fades to gold. The second printing, 4 November 1935, is bound in blue cloth with black lettering; a notice stating second printing before publication on p. [2]; otherwise same as first printing. The third printing, 8 November 1933, is bound in the usual black cloth stamped in orange. There were two more printings in 1935, and thirteen printings altogether by 1942. † Issued in Canada by the Ryerson Press. † Issued by Albatross Verlag (Paris) in English for continental distribution.
An excerpt concerning Lord Peter Wimsey's proposals of marriage to Harriet Vane is included in *Man Proposes*, collected by Agnes Furlong, London: Methuen, 1948.

a.ii. Gollancz re-issue, Volume 13 in the "Collected Edition" 1972:

DOROTHY L. SAYERS | GAUDY NIGHT | The University is a Paradise, Rivers of Knowledge | are there, Arts and Sciences flow from thence. | Counsell Tables are *Horti conclusi,* (as it is said | in the Canticles) *Gardens that are walled in,* and | they are *Fontes signati, Wells that are sealed up*; | bottomless depths of unsearchable Counsels there. | JOHN DONNE | LONDON | VICTOR GOLLANCZ LTD | 1972

Collation: [A]¹⁸ B–P¹⁶ [$1 signed, $5 signed with added star] 242 leaves.
pp. [1]–[484] as A21a.i., except p. [2] has all the novels and short stories listed; p. [4] adds publication, re-issue, ISBN notices to the printer's notice.

18·5 × 12 cm. Bulk: 3·6/3·9 cm. White wove paper, trimmed; white wove endpapers. Bound in red cloth; front and back blank, spine [stamped in gold:] GAUDY | NIGHT | by | DOROTHY L. | SAYERS | GOLLANCZ

Price: £1·60; number of copies not disclosed. Published: April 1972. Dust jacket: bright yellow printed in black and magenta.
Printed by Lowe & Brydone (Printers) Ltd.

Notes: Signature for gathering H is faint. Appears to be a photographic reproduction of A21*a*.1.

b.1. *First American edition* 1936:

Gaudy Night | BY DOROTHY L. SAYERS | *The University is a Paradise, Rivers of Knowledge are there,* | *Arts and Sciences flow from thence. Counsell Tables are* Horti | *conclusi, (as it is said in the Canticles)* Gardens that are walled | in, *and they are* Fontes signati, Wells that are sealed up; *bot-* | *tomless depths of unsearchable counsels there.* JOHN DONNE | HARCOURT, BRACE AND COMPANY | NEW YORK

Collation: [A–P]¹⁶ 240 leaves.
p. [i] Gaudy Night; p. [ii] list of novels by Sayers; p. [iii] title-page; p. [iv] copyright, rights reservation, *"first American edition"*, typography and printer's notices; pp. v–vi AUTHOR'S NOTE; p. [1] Gaudy Night; p. [2] blank; pp. 3–469 text; pp. [470–474] blank.

20·3 × 14 cm. Bulk: 3·5/4 cm. Cream wove paper; cream wove endpapers; trimmed. Bound in black cloth; back blank; front [stamped in blue:] GAUDY NIGHT; spine [stamped in blue:] GAUDY | NIGHT | SAYERS | HARCOURT, BRACE | AND COMPANY

Price: $2·50; number of copies not disclosed. Published February 1936.
Printed by Quinn & Boden Company Inc.; typography by Robert Josephy.

b.11. *HarBrace (New York) issue* 1939: 469 pp.

Text produced from A21*b*.1.

b.111. *Harper and Row (New York) issue* 1960: 469 pp.

Text produced from A21.*b*.1.

c.1. *Gollancz (London) re-set war edition* 1942: 346 pp.

c.11. *Gollancz (London) re-issue in THE SAYERS HOLIDAY BOOK* 1963:

See A11d.11; text of GAUDY NIGHT, pp. 7–346, produced from A21*c*.1.

d.1. *New English Library (London) edition* 1963: 447 pp.

d.ɪɪ. *Landsborough (London) issue* 1965: 447 pp.

Text produced from A21*d*.ɪ.

d.ɪɪɪ. *New English Library reissue* 1975: 447 pp.

Text produced from A21*d*.ɪ.

e. Avon Books (New York) edition 1968: 383 pp.

Translations: German, Norwegian, Dutch, Flemish, Danish, Swedish.

A22   TALES OF DETECTION   1936

a.ɪ. *First edition:*

TALES OF DETECTION | [drawing of vines on criss-cross slats] | EDITED BY DOROTHY L. SAYERS | LONDON: J. M. DENT & SONS LTD.

> *Collation:* [A]¹⁶ B–M¹⁶ N⁸ [$1 signed, $5 signed with added star] 200 leaves. p. [i] Everyman motto (2 lines); p. [ii] advertisement for Everyman's Library; p. [iii] EVERYMAN'S LIBRARY | EDITED BY ERNEST RHYS | FICTION | TALES OF DETECTION | EDITED WITH AN INTRODUCTION | BY DOROTHY L. SAYERS; p. [iv] blank; p. [v] title-page; p. [vi] rights reservation, press, decorations, and publisher's notices, publication notice; pp. vii–xiv INTRODUCTION; p. xv CONTENTS; p. xvi ACKNOWLEDGMENTS; pp. 1–382 text with pp. [20, 70, 116, 133, 206] unnumbered story title pages; p. [383] colophon: [words set around a flower with a long stalk and large leaves:] MADE AT THE | TEMPLE PRESS | LETCHWORTH | GREAT BRITAIN; p. [384] blank; *inserted:* 16 pp. Everyman's Library advertisements.

> 17·2 × 10·8 cm. Bulk: 2·0/2·3 cm. White wove paper; light orange and white endpapers; all edges trimmed; top edge red. Trade binding: red cloth; back blank; front [stamped with publisher's design]; spine [stamped in gold:] TALES | OF | DETECTION | EVERYMAN'S LIBRARY
> Variant bindings in leather and library cloth.

> *Price:* 4*s* leather, 3*s* library cloth, 2*s* trade cloth; number of copies not disclosed. Published 14 May 1936.
> Made at The Temple Press, Letchworth and decorated by Eric Ravilious.

> *Contents:* Edgar Allen Poe, *The Purloined Letter* – Wilkie Collins, *The Biter Bit* – Robert Louis Stevenson, *Was It Murder?* – Gilbert Keith Chesterton,

The Man in the Passage – Edmund Clerihew Bentley, *The Clever Cockatoo* – Ernest Brahmah, *The Ghost at Massingham Mansions* – Edgar Jepson and Robert Eustace, *The Tea Leaf* – Richard Austin Freeman, *The Contents of a Mare's Nest* – Thomas Burke, *The Hands of Mr. Ottermole* – Father Ronald Knox, *Solved by Inspection* – Agatha Christie, *Philomel Cottage* – Anthony Berkeley, *The Avenging Chance* – Freeman Wills Crofts, *The Mystery of the Sleeping-Car Express* – John Rhode, *The Elusive Bullet* – Dorothy Leigh Sayers, *The Image in the Mirror* – Henry Wade, *A Matter of Luck* – Milward Kennedy, *Superfluous Murder* – Henry Christopher Bailey, *The Yellow Slugs* – C. Daly King, *The Episode of the Nail and the Requiem.*

Notes: In addition to editing the book, Sayers' contributions are the Introduction (pp. xii–xiv) and *The Image In The Mirror*, pp. (266–290). Distributed in America by E. P. Dutton & Co. Inc.

*a.*II. *J. M. Dent (London) paperback issue* July 1961 : 382 pp.

Text produced from A22*a.*I.

*a.*III. *J. M. Dent (London) hardcover re–issue* November 1961 : 382 pp.

Text produced from A22*a.*I.

A23   PAPERS RELATING TO THE FAMILY OF   1936
WIMSEY

PAPERS | RELATING TO | THE FAMILY OF WIMSEY | Edited by | MATTHEW WIMSEY | [Wimsey coat of arms] | PRIVATELY PRINTED FOR THE FAMILY | HUMPHREY MILFORD

Collation: A⁴ B–D⁸ [$1 signed] 28 leaves.
p. [1] PAPERS RELATING TO | THE FAMILY OF WIMSEY; p. [2] blank; *inset:* portrait of Thomas, 10th Duke of Denver; p. [3] title-page; p. [4] printer's notice; p. [5] dedication; p. [6] blank; pp. 7–9 FOREWORD; p. [10] blank; pp. 11–12 NOTES ON THE ILLUSTRATIONS; pp. 13–55 text; between pp. 30–31 *inset:* plate of Bredon Hall; p. [56] Family tree.

21·7× 14 cm. Bulk: ·6/·7 cm. Cream laid paper, trimmed; cream laid end-papers. Blue paper covers; front [printed in black:] [within thick and thin rules:] PAPERS | RELATING TO | THE FAMILY OF | WIMSEY
Printed at The Westminster Press, London. About 500 copies were published in December 1936 and distributed to Sayers' friends as gifts.

Notes: Tipped-in portrait of Thomas, 10th Duke of Denver between pp. 2–3

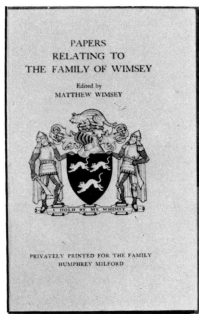

PAPERS
RELATING TO
THE FAMILY OF WIMSEY

Edited by
MATTHEW WIMSEY

I HOLD BY MY WHIMSY

PRIVATELY PRINTED FOR THE FAMILY
HUMPHREY MILFORD

EVEN THE
PARROT

Exemplary Conversations
for Enlightened Children

BY
DOROTHY.L.SAYERS

Illustrated by
SILLINCE
METHUEN & Cº Lᵗᵈ . LONDON
30 ESSEX Sᵗ, STRAND,W.C.2

Title-pages of *Paper. Relating to the Family of Wimsey* (A23)
and *Even the Parrot* (A41)

by Mrs. C. W. Scott-Giles, and tipped-in drawing of Bredon Hall between pp. 30–31 signed "W. J. Redhead". Helen Simpson, Muriel St. Clare Byrne, and C. W. Scott-Giles assisted with the preparation of this pamphlet.

A24   BUSMAN'S HONEYMOON [PLAY]   1937

a.i. First edition:

Dorothy L. Sayers and M. St. Clare Byrne | BUSMAN'S HONEY-MOON | *A Detective Comedy in Three Acts* | LONDON | VICTOR GOLLANCZ LTD | 1937

<blockquote>

Collation: [A]⁸ B–I⁸ [$1 signed] 72 leaves.
p. [1] BUSMAN'S HONEYMOON; p. [2] blank; p. [3] title-page; p. [4] copyright, rights reservations, printer's notice; p. [5] CHARACTERS; p. [6] cast list; pp. [7]–9 AUTHOR'S NOTE; p. [10] blank; pp. [11]–140 text, pp. [11, 48, 90] are unnumbered pages beginning the Acts, pp. [141]–144 NOTE TO PRODUCERS.

18·4 × 10·8 cm. Bulk: ·6/·65 cm. White wove paper; white wove endpapers. Tan paper covers; back blank; spine [printed in black:] BUSMAN'S | HONEY- | MOON | DOROTHY | L. SAYERS | *and* | M. ST. CLARE | BYRNE | VICTOR | GOLLANCZ; front [printed in black:] DOROTHY L. SAYERS *and* | M. ST. CLARE BYRNE | BUSMAN'S HONEYMOON | *A Detective Comedy in Three Acts* | LONDON | VICTOR GOLLANCZ LTD | *14 Henrietta Street Covent Garden* | 1937

Price: 3*s*6*d* paper, 5*s* cloth; number of copies: 20,000. Published February 1937.

Notes: Second impression 1939, third impression 1945, fourth impression 1947, fifth impression 1949, sixth impression 1951.

</blockquote>

a.ii. Gollancz (London) Famous Plays 1937 issue September 1937:

<blockquote>

Text of BUSMAN'S HONEYMOON pp. 289–428, produced from the plates of A24*a.*i.

</blockquote>

b. First American edition 1939:

[extreme left: seven thick vertical rules 9 cm. long] BUSMAN'S HONEYMOON | [left:] [star] | [among seven thick horizontal rules 9 cm. long interrupted where the type appears:] DETECTIVE COMEDY IN THREE ACTS | BY DOROTHY L. SAYERS

AND M. ST. CLARE BYRNE | [right: seven thick vertical rules 3·5 cm. long] [slightly left:] [star] | DRAMATISTS | PLAY | SERVICE | 1939 | INC.

> *Collation:* 72 leaves.
>
> p. [1] title-page; p. [2] copyright, acting rights and other rights notices; p. [3] CHARACTERS, SCENE, ACTS; p. 4 cast-list; pp. 5–6 AUTHOR'S NOTE, pp. 7–134 text; p. [135] scene design; pp. 136-138 NOTE TO PRODUCERS; pp. 139–144 PROPERTY PLOT.
>
> 18·5 × 11·3 cm. Bulk: 1·2 cm. White wove paper; trimmed. No endpapers. Grey paper covers back and spine blank; front, printed in blue, same design as title-page.
>
> *Price:* 75 cents; number of copies not known. Published 1939, no record of the official date.

A25   BUSMAN'S HONEYMOON   1937

a.1. First edition:

Busman's Honeymoon | A LOVE STORY | WITH DETECTIVE INTERRUPTIONS | *by Dorothy L. Sayers* | HARCOURT, BRACE AND COMPANY | NEW YORK

> *Collation:* [1]–[12]^{16} [13]^{8} 200 leaves.
>
> p. [i] BUSMAN'S HONEYMOON; p. [ii] list of works by Sayers; p. [iii] title-page; p. [iv] copyright, printing and printer's notices, *"first American edition"*; p. [v] dedication letter; p. [vi] blank; p. [vii] quotation from Shakespeare; p. [viii] blank; p. [ix] CONTENTS; p. [x] blank; p. [xi] PROTHALAMION; p. [xii] blank; p. [1] Marriage announcement; p. [2] blank; pp. [3]–27 prothalamion; p. [28] blank; pp. 29–380 text, with p. [341] EPITHALAMION; p. [342] blank; pp. [382–388] blank.
>
> 20·3 × 13·6 cm. Bulk: 3·3/3·8 cm. Cream wove paper; trimmed; cream wove endpapers. Bound in black cloth; front [blind rule] | [stamped in purple:] BUSMAN'S HONEYMOON | [blind rule]; spine [stamped in purple:] BUSMAN'S | HONEY- | MOON | [blind rules continued from front cover] | SAYERS | HARCOURT, BRACE | AND COMPANY
>
> *Price:* $2·50; number of copies: 20,000. Published 18 February 1937.
> Printed by Quinn & Boden Company Inc.; typography by Robert Josephy.
>
> *Notes:* pp. 284, 297 "Hermitage" should read "Léoville"; see notes to A26*b*.II.

a.II. *HarBrace (New York) issue* 1942: 381 pp.

Text produced from A25*a*.I.; corrections not made.

a.III. *Harper and Row (New York) issue* 1960: 381 pp.

Text produced from A25*a*.I.; corrections not made.

b.I. *First English edition* 1937:

BUSMAN'S HONEYMOON | A LOVE STORY | WITH
DETECTIVE INTERRUPTIONS | by | DOROTHY L. SAYERS
| LONDON | VICTOR GOLLANCZ LTD | 1937

Collation: [A]⁸ B–Z⁸ 2A–2D⁸ [$1 signed with added B] 224 leaves.
p. [1] BUSMAN'S HONEYMOON; p. [2] list of books by Sayers; p. [3]
title-page; p. [4] printer's imprint; p. [5] quotation from Shakespeare; p. [6]
blank; p. [7] dedication letter; p. [8] blank; p. [9] CONTENTS; p. [10] blank;
p. [11] PROTHALAMION; p. [12] blank; p. [13] marriage announcement;
p. [14] blank; pp. [15]–43 prothalamion, pp. [15, 26] section headings and
text; pp. [44]–[447] text, pp. [44, 61, 73, 82, 100, 126, 139, 166, 183, 209, 230,
246, 260, 278, 301, 322, 335, 346, 363, 386, 405, 415, 432] chapter headings and
text, p. [403] EPITHALAMION; pp. [404, 448] blank.

19·7× 12·8 cm. Bulk: 3·9/4·4 cm. Cream wove paper, trimmed; cream wove
endpapers. Bound in black cloth; front and back blank; spine [stamped in
orange:] BUSMAN'S | HONEYMOON | BY | DOROTHY L. | SAYERS
| GOLLANCZ

Price: 8*s*6*d*; number of copies not disclosed. Published June 1937. Dust jacket:
yellow, printed in black and magenta.
Printed by The Camelot Press Ltd., London.

Notes: Erratum slip, p. [335], corrects "Hermitage" to "Léoville." Other
errors: p. 227, last line, "errific" for "terrific"; p. 378, line 30, "!" for ".".
Nine impressions by 1941. †Issued in Canada by The Ryerson Press. †Issued
in Paris in English by Albatross Verlag for continental distribution.

b.II. *Gollancz (London) re-issue, Volume 14 in the "Collected Edition"*
1972:

BUSMAN'S HONEYMOON | A LOVE STORY | WITH
DETECTIVE INTERRUPTIONS | by | DOROTHY L. SAYERS
| LONDON | VICTOR GOLLANCZ LTD | 1972

Collation: [A]¹⁶ B–O¹⁶ [$1, $5 with added star, except B1 and A9 which are signed Bʙ as in A26 *b*.I.] 224 leaves.

pp. [1]–[448] as A26*b*.I., except p. [4], which has publication, reissue, and ISBN notices in addition to the printer's notice.

18·4 × 12 cm. Bulk: 3·4/3·7 cm. White wove paper, trimmed; white wove endpapers. Bound in red cloth; front and back blank, spine [stamped in gold:] BUSMAN'S | HONEYMOON | by | DOROTHY L. | SAYERS | GOLLANCZ

Price: £1·75; number of copies not disclosed. Published October 1972. Dust jacket: bright yellow printed in black and magenta.

Printed by Lowe & Brydone (Printers) Ltd.

Notes: Appears to be a photographic reproduction of A25.*b*.I., with corrections made on pp. 227, 335, and 350.

c.I. *Gollancz (London) re-set war edition* 1942: 295 pp.

c.II. *Gollancz (London)* THE SAYERS TANDEM *issue* 1957:

Text of BUSMAN'S HONEYMOON produced from A25*c*.I., with THE NINE TAILORS (A19).

d. Penguin (Harmondsworth, England) edition 1962: 378 pp.

e. Avon Books (New York) edition 1968: 318 pp.

f. New English Library edition 1974: 400 pp.

Translations: German, Dutch, Danish, Japanese, Swedish, French.

A26　　　　　THE ZEAL OF THY HOUSE　　　　　1937

a. Acting edition:

THE ZEAL | OF THY HOUSE | *by* | DOROTHY L. SAYERS | Acting Edition | for the Festival of the Friends of Canterbury Cathedral | 1937 | [Gothic type:] Canterbury: | H. J. GOULDEN, LIMITED | (by kind permission of the Author and Victor Gollancz, Ltd.)

Collation: [A–D]⁸ 32 leaves.

pp. [i–ii] blank; p. [iii] title-page; p. [iv] blank; p. [1] DRAMATIS PERSONAE; pp. 2–57 text; pp. [58–60] blank.

18·6×12·4 cm. Bulk: ·6 cm. Cream wove paper, trimmed. No endpapers. Bound in cream paper covers; front [printed in dark blue:] THE ZEAL | OF THY HOUSE | *by* | DOROTHY L. SAYERS | [Seal of the Friends of Canterbury Cathedral] | FRIENDS OF | CANTERBURY CATHEDRAL | EDITION | [Gothic type:] Canterbury: | H. J. GOULDEN, LIMITED; spine and back blank.

Note: A printing of the slightly shortened form of the play for the Canterbury performance, 12–18 June 1937. A 10 pp. music score of incidental vocal music for THE ZEAL OF THY HOUSE, prepared by G. H. Knight for the first performances, was published in Canterbury in 1938.

b. First English trade edition 1937:

THE ZEAL OF THY | HOUSE | by | DOROTHY L. SAYERS | LONDON | VICTOR GOLLANCZ LTD | 1937

Collation: [A]⁸ B–G⁸ [$1 signed with added H] 56 leaves.
p. [1] THE ZEAL OF THY HOUSE: p. [2] blank; p. [3] title-page; p. [4] copyright, dramatic rights, printer's notices; pp. 5–6 PREFACE by Laurence Irving; p. 7 Author's acknowledgements; p. 8 Dramatis Personae; pp. 9–[111] text; p. [112] blank.

21·8×13·7 cm. Bulk: 1/1·6 cm. Cream wove paper; trimmed; cream wove endpapers. Bound in blue cloth; front and back blank; spine [stamped in gold, bottom to top:] THE ZEAL OF THY HOUSE [solid circle] DOROTHY L. SAYERS

Price: 5s; number of copies: 2,000. Published 17 June 1937. Dust jacket: light blue printed in dark blue.
Printed by The Camelot Press Ltd., London and Southampton.

Notes: Seventeen impressions by 1952. †Issued in Canada by The Ryerson Press.

c. First American edition 1937:

THE ZEAL | OF | THY HOUSE | *Dorothy L. Sayers* | Harcourt, Brace and Company | New York

Collation: 64 leaves.
p. [i] THE ZEAL OF THY HOUSE: p. [ii] blank; p. [iii] title-page; p. [iv] copyright, rights reservation, "*first American edition*", printer's notice; pp. v–vii PREFACE; p. [viii] blank; p. [ix] Acknowledgements; p. [x] blank; pp. xi–xii DRAMATIS PERSONAE; p. [1] THE ZEAL OF THY HOUSE; p. [2] blank; pp. 3–115 text; p. [116] blank.

21·6 × 14·0 cm. Bulk: 1·2/2·0 cm. White wove paper, trimmed, top edge blue-grey; white wove endpapers. Bound in brown cloth; front and back blank; spine [stamped in silver:] DOROTHY | L. | SAYERS | [top to bottom:] *The Zeal of Thy House* | [upright:] HARCOURT, | BRACE & CO.

Price: $1·50; number of copies not disclosed. Published 28 June 1937. Dust jacket: light blue printed in white.

d. *Gollancz re-set edition* 1939:

Text of THE ZEAL OF THY HOUSE in *Famous Plays 1938–39*, pp. 9–93.

e. *Living Age Books, Meridian Press (New York) edition* 1957:

Text of THE ZEAL OF THY HOUSE in *Religious Drama Vol. I.*, pp. 267–339.

f. *Second English edition* 1961:

The Zeal of Thy House | DOROTHY L. SAYERS | *With a Preface and Notes by* | C. H. RIEU | *Headmaster,* | *Simon Langston School,* | *Canterbury* | LONDON | METHUEN & CO LTD | 36 ESSEX STREET [solid circle] WC2

Collation: [A]⁸ B–F⁸ [$1 signed] 42 leaves.

p. [i] The Zeal of Thy House; p. [ii] list of Methuen's Modern Classics; *inset:* photograph; pp. [iii] title-page; p. [iv] Publication notices; Preface and Notes copyright, printer's notice, catalogue number, dramatic rights notice; p. [v] contents; p. [vi] blank; pp. [vii]–x Preface; pp. xi–xii A Note on the Author; p. [1] The Zeal of Thy House; p. [2] Dramatis Personae; pp. [3]–74 text, with pp. [19, 35, 53] section headings with text; pp. [75]–78 Historical Notes; pp. [79]–80 Architectural Notes; pp. [81]–84 Translations of Latin Hymns and Prayers, *inset:* photograph between pp. 44–45.

18·5 × 12·2 cm. Bulk: ·8/1·1 cm. Cream wove paper, trimmed; cream wove endpapers. Bound in illustrated purple boards; front [printed in white and red:] THE | ZEAL | OF THY | HOUSE | DOROTHY L. | SAYERS | [an angel above the cathedral and William of Sens falling]; back [cathedral in red, white, black and purple]; spine [top to bottom, printed in white and red:] DOROTHY L SAYERS THE ZEAL OF THY HOUSE | [upright, within red square, in purple:] Methuen

Price: 6s; number of copies not disclosed. Published November 1961.

Note: See FOUR SACRED PLAYS (A46) which includes THE ZEAL OF THY HOUSE.

Translations: Dutch, German, French.

[Gothic:] AN ACCOUNT | OF | Lord Mortimer Wimsey, | THE
HERMIT OF THE WASH, | RELATED IN | A LETTER TO |
Sir H— G— Bart, | BY A CLERGYMAN OF THE CHURCH
OF | ENGLAND. | [waved rule] | GOD having formed us like
Himself, viz.: – as Reasonable | Beings, delights not in irrational
Superstitions, Phrensies, | Extravagancies, &c., &c.; nay, He will
often punish them | by taking away that Reason which they abuse.
Yet we are | not saved by *Reason*, but by *Faith* and *Election*. Thus, |
there is a kind of Despair that, by defect of Reason, may | fall upon
the very Elect: so that (the Reason, which was the | stumbling-
block, being taken away) we must not presume | to say, God cannot
save such a man, in His own time and | by His peculiar grace. –
Rev. JEREMIAH TAPP, D. D.: *Commentary on* ARTICLE XVII. |
[waved rule] | BRISTOL: | Printed by M. BRYAN, Corn-street. |
– | 1816.

Collation: 8 leaves, unsigned, folded from one sheet 56·5 cm. × 45 cm.
p. [1] title-page; p. [2] PRINTED IN GREAT BRITAIN; p. [3]–15 text;
p. [16] blank.

22·3 × 14·3 cm. Bulk: ·1 cm. White wove paper; no endpapers or binding.
Format and typography supervised by Graham Pollard; 250 copies were privately printed by Humphrey Milford at the Oxford University Press in November and December 1937 for Christmas gifts to Sayers' friends.

A28   THE GREATEST DRAMA EVER STAGED   1938

a. First edition:

THE | GREATEST DRAMA | EVER STAGED | BY | DOROTHY
L. SAYERS | LONDON | HODDER AND STOUGHTON

Collation: [A]⁸ B–C⁸ [\$1 signed] 24 leaves.
p. [1] THE | GREATEST | DRAMA | EVER | STAGED; p. [2] blank;
p. [3] title-page; p. [iv] *First Printed – 1938* | [printer's notice]; pp. 5–24 text;
pp. 25–48 THE TRIUMPH OF EASTER.

18·4 × 12·4 cm. Bulk: ·6/·7 cm. Cream wove paper, trimmed; cream wove
endpapers.

Paper covers; back and spine white, blank; front [top and bottom red, gray wavy center, all which bleed beyond thin white frame; at top, a diagonal black rectangle runs up, left to right, with white letters:] Dorothy L. Sayers | [on gray center, in black letters:] The Greatest | Drama | Ever | Staged | [on red, in black letters:] HODDER AND STOUGHTON

Price: 6d; number of copies not known. Published 2 June 1938. Made and printed by Wyman & Sons Ltd. London, Reading and Fakenham.

Contents: The Greatest Drama Ever Staged – The Triumph of Easter.

Notes: "The Greatest Drama Ever Staged" was first printed in *The Sunday Times* 3 April 1938 (C85); this essay also appears in CREED OR CHAOS (A45) and CHRISTIAN LETTERS TO A POST CHRISTIAN WORLD (A60). "The Triumph of Easter" was first published in *The Sunday Times* 17 April 1938 (C86); it also appears in CREED OR CHAOS (A45). †Issued in Canada by Musson.

b. St. Hugh's Press (London) edition 1950: 55 pp.

A 7·6 × 7·6 cm. pocketbook.

c. Church Pastoral Aid Society (London) edition 1964: 16 pp.

Translations: German, Dutch.

A29   DOUBLE DEATH   1939

DOUBLE DEATH | *A Murder Story* | by | DOROTHY L. SAYERS | FREEMAN WILLS CROFTS | VALENTINE WILLIAMS | F. TENNYSON JESSE | ANTHONY ARMSTRONG | DAVID HUME | Supervised and with a Preface | and Prologue by | JOHN CHANCELLOR | LONDON | VICTOR GOLLANCZ LTD | 1939

Collation: [A]⁸ B–S⁸ [$1 signed] 144 leaves.
p. [1] DOUBLE DEATH; p. [2] blank; p. [3] title-page; p. [4] printer's notice; p. 5 CONTENTS; p. 6 NOTE; pp. 7–8 PREFACE; p. [9] PROLOGUE; p. [10] blank; pp. 11–17 text of Prologue; pp. [18] blank; pp. [19] –285 text, pp. [19, 63, 113, 155, 195, 245] section headings; pp. [20, 62, 64, 112, 114, 156, 194, 196, 246] blank; pp. 60, 109 diagrams; pp. [286–288] blank.

18·5 × 12·4 cm. Bulk: 2·8/3·2 cm. White wove paper; white wove endpapers; trimmed. Bound in black cloth, front and back blank; spine [stamped in orange:] DOUBLE | DEATH | BY | DOROTHY L. | SAYERS | FREE-

MAN | WILLS CROFTS | VALENTINE | WILLIAMS | F. TENNYSON
| JESSE | ANTHONY | ARMSTRONG | DAVID | HUME | GOLLANCZ

Price: 7s6d; number of copies not disclosed. Published 19 January 1939. Dust
jacket: yellow printed in black and magenta.
Printed by Purnell and Sons Ltd.

Notes: Sayers wrote PART ONE (pp. 21–61). Four impressions by April
1940. †Issued in Canada by the Ryerson Press, $2, 1940. DOUBLE DEATH
was first printed as a six-part serial, "Night of Secrets", in *The Sunday Chronicle*
May 1937 (C77).

A30   STRONG MEAT   1939

STRONG MEAT | BY | DOROTHY L. SAYERS | "For every
one that useth milk is unskillful in the word | of righteousness; for
he is a babe. | "But strong meat belongeth to them that are of full |
age, even those who by reason of use have their senses | exercised
to discern both good and evil." | – Epistle to the Hebrews | LONDON
| HODDER AND STOUGHTON

Collation: [A]⁸ B–C⁸ [$1 signed] 24 leaves glued at spine.
pp. [1–4] blank; p. [5] STRONG MEAT; p. [6] advertisement for THE
GREATEST DRAMA EVER STAGED; p. [7] title-page; p. [8] *First published
in book form – June 1939* | [rule] | [printer's notice]; pp. 9–44 text; pp. 45–48
blank.

18·4 × 12·4 cm. Bulk: ·6 cm. Cream wove paper, trimmed. Paper covers,
back [white printed in black, within single rules:] Uniform with this book
| THE | GREATEST | DRAMA | EVER STAGED | by Dorothy | L.
Sayers; front [top and bottom blue, grey wavy center, all which bleed beyond
thin white frame; at top, a diagonal black rectangle runs up left to right, with
white letters:] Dorothy L. Sayers | [on grey, in black letters:] Strong Meat
| [on blue, in black letters] HODDER AND STOUGHTON; spine blank.

Price: 6d; number of copies not known. Published 12 June 1939.
Printed by Wyman & Sons Ltd.

Contents: Strong Meat – The Dogma Is the Drama

Notes: Erratum slip p. 9: p. 17, line 14, read "Eternity" for "Time." †Issued
in Canada by Musson. "Strong Meat" was first printed in *The Sunday Times*
9 April 1939, as "The Food of the Full Grown" (C97); "The Dogma Is the
Drama" was first published in *St. Martin's Review*, April 1938 (C84). Both
essays also appear in CREED OR CHAOS? (A45) and CHRISTIAN
LETTERS . . . (A60).

a. Acting edition:

THE DEVIL TO PAY | *by* | DOROTHY L. SAYERS | Acting
Edition | for the Festival of the Friends of Canterbury Cathedral |
1939 | [Gothic:] Canterbury: | H. J. GOULDEN, LIMITED

> *Collation:* [A]² [B–E]⁸ 34 leaves.
> p. [i] title-page; p. [ii] NOTE; p. [iii] PERSONS OF THE DRAMA; p.
> [iv] blank; pp. 1–63 text; p. [64] blank.
>
> 18·6 × 12·5 cm. Bulk: ·6 cm. White wove paper, trimmed. No endpapers.
> Bound in tan paper covers; back and spine blank; front [printed in dark blue:]
> THE DEVIL TO PAY | *by* | DOROTHY L. SAYERS | [emblem of the
> Friends of Canterbury Cathedral] | FRIENDS OF | CANTERBURY
> CATHEDRAL | EDITION | [Gothic:] Canterbury: | H. J. GOULDEN,
> LIMITED
>
> *Notes:* Printed for the first production of the play at Canterbury, 10–17 June
> 1939. A 5 pp. music score of incidental vocal music for THE DEVIL TO PAY,
> prepared by G. H. Knight for the first performances, was published in Canter-
> bury in 1939.

b. First English Trade edition 1939:

THE DEVIL TO PAY | BEING the famous HISTORY OF JOHN
| FAUSTUS the Conjurer of Wittenberg in | Germany; how he
sold his immortal soul | to the Enemy of Mankind, and was served |
XXIV years by Mephistopheles, and ob- | tained Helen of Troy to
his paramour, | with many other marvels; and how GOD | dealt
with him at the last. | A Stage-Play | by DOROTHY L. SAYERS |
LONDON | VICTOR GOLLANCZ LTD | 1939

> *Collation:* [A]⁸ B–G⁸ [$1 signed with added P] 56 leaves.
> p. [1] THE DEVIL TO PAY; p. [2] blank; p. [3] title-page; p. [4] copyright;
> dramatic rights, printer's notices; p. [5] TO THE INTERPRETER | Har-
> court Williams [sonnet with epigraph]; p. [6] blank; pp. 7–13 PREFACE;
> p. [14] blank; p. [15] five line quotation from Donne; p. 16 cast list and pro-
> duction notes; p. 17 PERSONS OF THE DRAMA; [18] diagram of stage;
> pp. 19–112 text.
>
> 21·8 × 13·7 cm. Bulk: 1·2/1·6 cm. Cream wove paper, trimmed; cream wove
> endpapers. Bound in blue cloth, front and back blank; spine [stamped in gold,
> bottom to top:] THE DEVIL TO PAY [solid circle] DOROTHY L. SAYERS

Price: 5*s*; number of copies: 2,000. Published 7 June 1939. Dust jacket: buff printed in red.
Printed by The Camelot Press Ltd.

Notes: †Issued in Canada by The Ryerson Press. THE DEVIL TO PAY also appears in FOUR SACRED PLAYS 1948 (A46). Several excerpts from this play have been reprinted as poems in anthologies.

c. First American edition 1939:

The Devil to Pay | *being* the famous HISTORY OF JOHN FAUSTUS | the conjurer of Wittenberg in Germany; how | he sold his immortal soul to the Enemy of | Mankind, and was served XXIV years by | Mephistopheles, and obtained Helen of Troy | to his paramour, with many other marvels; | and how GOD dealt with him at the last. | A STAGE PLAY | BY DOROTHY L. SAYERS | Harcourt, Brace and Company New York

Collation: 76 leaves.
p. [i] THE DEVIL TO PAY; p. [ii] blank; p. [1] title-page, p. [2] copyright 1939, rights reservation, *"first American edition"*, printer's notices; p. [3] TO THE INTERPRETER | Harcourt Williams [sonnet with epigraph]; p. [4] blank; pp. 5–15 PREFACE; p. [14] blank; p. [15] five line quotation from John Donne; p. [16] cast list; p. [17] PERSONS OF THE DRAMA; p. [18] [diagram, titled:] THE STAGE WITH ITS MANSIONS; pp. 19–147 text; pp. [148–150] blank.

22 × 14.2 cm. Bulk: 1.7/2.4 cm. White wove paper; trimmed; top edge red. White wove endpapers. Bound in black cloth; front and back blank; spine [stamped in silver:] DOROTHY | L. | SAYERS | [top to bottom:] *The Devil to Pay* | [upright:] HARCOURT, BRACE & CO.

Price: $1.50; number of copies not disclosed. Published 19 June 1939. Dust jacket: printed in red and white.

A32   IN THE TEETH OF THE EVIDENCE   1939

a. First edition:

IN THE TEETH OF THE | EVIDENCE | AND OTHER STORIES | by | DOROTHY L. SAYERS | LONDON | VICTOR GOLLANCZ LTD | 1939

Collation: [A]⁸ B–S⁸ [$1 signed with added E] 144 leaves.

p. [1] IN THE TEETH OF THE EVIDENCE | AND OTHER STORIES;
p. [2] advertisement for other books by Sayers; p. [3] title-page; p. [4] printer's
notice; p. [5] CONTENTS; p. [6] blank; p. [7]–286 text, pp. [7, 24, 43, 57,
71, 87, 100, 117, 129, 139, 152, 169, 181, 197, 228, 248, 271] story title pages
and text; [114, 116] blank, [115] section heading; pp. [287–288] blank.

18·4 × 12·3 cm. Bulk: 3·0/3·4 cm. Cream wove paper, trimmed; cream wove
endpapers. Bound in black cloth; front and back blank; spine [stamped in
orange:] IN THE | TEETH | OF THE | EVIDENCE | BY | DOROTHY L. |
SAYERS | GOLLANCZ

Price: 7s6d; number of copies: 10,000. Published 13 November 1939. Dust
jacket: yellow printed in black and magenta.
Printed by Purnell & Sons Ltd. Paulton (Somerset) and London

Contents: LORD PETER WIMSEY STORIES: In the Teeth of the Evidence
– Absolutely Elsewhere – MONTAGUE EGG STORIES: A Shot at Goal –
Dirt Cheap – Bitter Almonds – False Weight – The Professor's Manuscript –
OTHER STORIES: The Milk Bottles – Dilemma – An Arrow o'er the House
– Scrawns – Nebuchadnezzar – The Inspiration of Mr. Budd – Blood Sacrifice
– Suspicion – The Leopard Lady – The Cyprian Cat.

Notes: Only the OTHER STORIES has a section heading in the text; p. 267
imperfect "e" 3rd line from bottom. Four impressions by 1941. †Issued in
Canada by The Ryerson Press. *Seeds of Suspicion,* a drama by John McGreery,
based on the story "Suspicion," was published in Chicago by Dramatic Press
in 1952. For stories listed separately in this bibliography, consult the Index.

b. First American edition 1940:

Dorothy L. Sayers | IN THE TEETH | OF | THE EVIDENCE | *and
other stories* | HARCOURT, BRACE AND COMPANY, NEW
YORK

Collation: 160 leaves.
p. [i] IN THE TEETH OF THE EVIDENCE | *and other stories*; p. [ii] list of
books by Sayers; p. [iii] title-page; p. [iv] copyright, rights reservation, *"first
American edition"*, typography and printer's notices; p. [v] CONTENTS;
p. [vi] blank; p. [1] IN THE TEETH OF THE EVIDENCE | *and other stories*;
p. [2] blank; pp. 3–311 text; pp. [312–314] blank.

20·4 × 13·5 cm. Bulk: 3·0/3·4 cm. White wove paper, trimmed; white wove
endpapers. Bound in blue cloth; back blank; front [stamped in white:] IN
THE TEETH OF THE | EVIDENCE; spine [stamped in white:] IN THE
| TEETH | OF THE | EVIDENCE | SAYERS | HARCOURT, BRACE
| AND COMPANY

Price: $2·50; number of copies not disclosed. Published January 1940. Dust jacket: front and spine, shades of dark blue printed in blue and white; back, white printed in black, advertisement of Sayers' books. Printed by Quinn & Boden Company Inc.; typography by Robert Josephy.

Notes: Second impression January, 1940.

c.i. *Gollancz (London) re-set war edition* 1941: 178 pp.

c.ii. *Gollancz (London) SAYERS HOLIDAY BOOK issue* 1963:

Text of IN THE TEETH OF THE EVIDENCE produced from A32c.i., pp. 225–710, with GAUDY NIGHT (A21) and STRONG POISON (A11).

d. *New Avon Library (New York) edition* 1943: 225 pp.

Does not include "The Milk Bottles," "An Arrow O'er the House," "Scrawns," "The Cyprian Cat."

e. *Best Seller Mystery (New York) edition* n.d. [circa 1943]: 125 pp.

Does not include "A Shot at Goal", "Dirt Cheap", "Bitter Almonds", "False Weight", "The Professor's Manuscript", "Nebuchadnezzar", "Blood Sacrifice".

f. *Avon Books (New York) edition* 1952: 221 pp.

g.i. *Landsborough Four Square Books (London) edition* 1960: 220 pp.

g.ii. *New English Library (London) issue* 1969: 220 pp.

Produced from A32g.i.

h. *Gollancz (London) edition with additional stories, Volume 15 in the "Collected Edition"* 1972:

IN THE TEETH OF THE | EVIDENCE | AND OTHER STORIES | including three final Lord Peter Wimsey Stories | by | DOROTHY L. SAYERS | LONDON | VICTOR GOLLANCZ LTD | 1972

Collation: [A–K]¹⁶ [L]¹⁸ 178 leaves.
p. [1] IN THE TEETH OF THE EVIDENCE | AND OTHER STORIES; p. [2] list of books by Sayers; p. [3] title-page; p. [4] publication, re-issue, ISBN notices, "NOTE" [regarding publication of three final Lord Peter Wimsey

stories], printer's notice; pp. [5–6] CONTENTS; pp. [7]–355 text with pp. [7, 24, 43, 57, 71, 87, 100, 117, 129, 139, 152, 169, 181, 197, 228, 248, 271, 289, 305, 330] story title pages and text, pp. [114, 116, 288] blank; pp. [115, 287] section headings; p. [356] blank.

18·4 × 12·2 cm. Bulk: 2·7/3·0 cm. White wove paper, trimmed; white wove endpapers. Bound in red cloth; front and back blank; spine [stamped in gold:] IN THE | TEETH | OF THE | EVIDENCE | by | DOROTHY L. | SAYERS | GOLLANCZ

Price: £1·75; number of copies not disclosed. Published October 1972. Dust jacket: bright yellow printed in black and magenta.
Printed offset by The Camelot Press Ltd.

Contents: Same as A32a. with the addition of FINAL LORD PETER STORIES: Striding Folly – The Haunted Policeman – Talboys.

Notes: No section headings for Lord Peter Wimsey Stories or Montague Egg Stories; p. 333 line 8 lacks "?". The text from pp. [7]–286 appears to be a photographic reproduction of A32a. This is the first English publication of "Talboys," written in 1942; see LORD PETER (A61) and TALBOYS (A62). Consult the Index for first printings of the other stories.

Translations: Swedish, Spanish, German, Danish, Burmese.

A33   HE THAT SHOULD COME   1939

HE THAT SHOULD | COME | A Nativity Play in One Act | by | DOROTHY L. SAYERS | LONDON | VICTOR GOLLANCZ LTD | 1939

Collation: [A]⁸ B–E⁸ [$1 signed] 40 leaves.
p. [1] HE THAT SHOULD COME; p. [2] other plays by Sayers listed; p. [3] title-page; [4] copyright, dramatic rights, printer's notices; pp. [5]–10 NOTES TO PRODUCERS; p. [11] cast list, performance notes; p. [12] DRAMATIS PERSONAE pp. [13]–80 text.

18·4 × 12·4 cm. Bulk: ·8/·9 cm. Cream wove paper; trimmed. Cream wove endpapers. Cream paper covers, back blank; front [printed in black:] HE THAT | SHOULD COME | [ornament] BY [ornament] | Dorothy L. Sayers; spine [printed in black, bottom to top:] HE THAT SHOULD COME *Dorothy L. Sayers*

Price: 2s; number of copies: 1,000. Published 21 November 1939.
Printed by Richard Clay and Co. Ltd. Bungay, Suffolk.

Notes: Reprinted in 1956 and 1960. †Issued in Canada by The Ryerson Press.

Written for broadcast on Christmas Day 1938 (E15). HE THAT SHOULD COME also appears in FOUR SACRED PLAYS 1948 (A46).

Translation: Dutch.

A34   BEGIN HERE   1940

a. First edition:

BEGIN HERE | A WAR-TIME ESSAY | *by* | DOROTHY L. SAYERS | LONDON | VICTOR GOLLANCZ LTD | 1940

> *Collation:* [A]⁸ B–K⁸ [\$1 signed] 80 leaves.
> p. [1] BEGIN HERE; p. [2] list of works by Sayers; p. [3] title-page; p. [4] printer's notice; p. 5 PREFACE; p. [6] blank; p. 7 CONTENTS; p. 8 blank; pp. [9]–152 text, pp. [9, 27, 47, 75, 93, 129] chapter headings and quotations, pp. [10, 28, 48, 76, 92, 94, 130] blank; pp. 153–156 A NOTE ON CREATIVE READING; pp. 157–160 SOME BOOKS TO READ

> 21.7×13.4 cm. Bulk: $1.7/2.1$ cm. Cream wove paper, trimmed; cream wove endpapers. Bound in black cloth; front and back blank; spine [stamped in gold:] BEGIN | HERE | BY | DOROTHY | L. | SAYERS | GOLLANCZ

> *Price:* 6s; number of copies not known. Published 20 January 1940. Dust jacket: yellow printed in black and magenta.
> Printed by Richard Clay and Co. Ltd.

> *Notes:* Seven impressions by May 1941. †Issued in Canada by The Ryerson Press.

b. First American edition 1941:

BEGIN HERE | *A Statement of Faith* | by | DOROTHY L. SAYERS | [publisher's device] | HARCOURT, BRACE AND COMPANY, NEW YORK

> *Collation:* [A–L]⁸ 88 leaves.
> pp. [2]; p. [i] Begin Here; p. [ii] list of works by Sayers; p. [iii] title-page; p. [iv] copyright, printer's notices, *"first American edition"*; pp. v–xii Preface; p. [xiii] CONTENTS; p. [xiv] blank; pp. [1]–156 text, pp. [1, 21, 43, 73, 91, 131] section headings, pp. [2, 20, 22, 42, 44, 74, 92, 132] blank; pp. [157–160] blank.

> 20.3×13.5 cm. Bulk: $1.8/2.2$ cm. Cream wove paper; trimmed; cream wove endpapers. Bound in red cloth; front and back blank; spine [stamped in white:] [at top, within single rules:] Begin | Here | [rule] | DOROTHY | L. | SAYERS | [at bottom:] HARCOURT, | BRACE and | COMPANY

Price: $2; number of copies not disclosed. Published April 1941. Dust jacket: red printed in red and white.

Notes: A new preface was written for this edition; "A Note on Creative Reading" and "Some Books to Read" from A34*a.* are not included.

A35   CREED OR CHAOS?   1940

CREED OR CHAOS? | Address delivered at the Biennial Festival of the | Church Tutorial Classes Association in | Derby, May 4th, 1940 | BY | DOROTHY L. SAYERS | LONDON | HODDER AND STOUGHTON

Collation: [A]⁸ B–C⁸ [$1 signed] 24 leaves.
p. [1] blank; p. [2] blank; p. [3] CREED | OR | CHAOS?; p. [4] blank; p. [5] title-page; p. [6] quotation of St. John xvi. 8–11, printer's notice; pp. 7–44 text; pp. [45–48] blank.

18·4 × 12·3 Bulk: ·5/·55 cm. Cream wove paper, trimmed. No endpapers. Paper covers, back [white printed in black: advertisement for pamphlet series]; spine white, blank; front [white rectangle with wide blue frame; printed in black:] Creed or | Chaos? | by | Dorothy L. | Sayers | HODDER & STOUGH-TON

Price: 6*d*; number of copies not known. Published 10 June 1940.
Made and printed by Wyman & Sons Lts. Reading and Fakenham.

Notes: †Issued in Canada by Musson. This essay also appears in CREED OR CHAOS (A45) and CHRISTIAN LETTERS (A60). See "The War as a Crusade" (C121), published 10 May 1940, which is an excerpt from this address given 4 May 1940 (F19).

A36   THE MYSTERIOUS ENGLISH   1941

THE MYSTERIOUS | ENGLISH | *By* | DOROTHY L. SAYERS | [Device: a flower] | LONDON | MACMILLAN & CO. LTD. | 1941

Collation: A gathering of 16 leaves stapled at the fold.
p. [1] title-page; p. [2] Introductory paragraph, "COPYRIGHT", "PRINTED IN GREAT BRITAIN"; pp. 3–31 text, with printer's notice at the bottom of p. 31; p. [32] blank.

18·5 × 12·1 cm. Bulk: ·3 cm. Cream wove paper, trimmed. No endpapers.

Orange paper covers, spine [dark blue, blank]; back [a list of Macmillan War Pamphlets printed in blue]; front [top, printed in blue within a blue oval frame:] THE | MYSTERIOUS | ENGLISH | DOROTHY L. SAYERS | [heavy blue rule across cover] | [bottom, a solid blue oval with a thin orange inner frame, printed in orange:] MACMILLAN | WAR PAMPHLETS | [lower left corner, in blue:] NOIO [lower right corner in blue:] 3d NET

Price: 3d; number of copies not known. Published March 1941.
Printed by Purnell and Sons Ltd.

Notes: Distributed in Canada by Macmillan. This essay was originally an address given in London 1940 (F20); it was later printed in UNPOPULAR OPINIONS (A43). See also "The Snob Offensive" (C135).

Translation: German.

A37   THE MIND OF THE MAKER   1941

a.1. First edition:

THE MIND | OF THE MAKER | *by* DOROTHY L. SAYERS | [publisher's device] | METHUEN & CO. LTD. LONDON | *36 Essex Street, Strand, W. C. 2*

Collation: $[\pi]^6$ I–II^8, 12^6 [$1 signed] 100 leaves.
p. [i] announcement of Bridgeheads series, edited by Sayers and M. St. Clare Byrne; p. [ii] list of books by Sayers; p. [iii] title-page; p. [iv] *First published in 1941* | PRINTED IN GREAT BRITAIN; p. [v] dedication; p. [vi] eight-line quotation from John Henry Newman and a four-line quotation from Nicholas Berdyaev; pp. vii–x PREFACE; p. xi CONTENTS; p. [xii] blank; pp. 1–175 text, pp. 1, 15, 25, 37, 49, 69, 75, 87, 101, 119, 145 section headings with quotations, p. 35 and pp. 116–117 NOTES, pp. [36, 48, 68, 100, 118, 176] blank; pp. 177–184 POSTSCRIPT; pp. 185–186 APPENDIX; p. [187] blank; p. [188] printer's notice.

18·4×12·3 cm. Bulk: 2·1/2·4 cm. Cream wove paper, trimmed; cream wove endpapers. Bound in light-orange cloth; front and back blank; spine [stamped in dark blue:] THE | MIND | OF THE | MAKER | DOROTHY L. | SAYERS | METHUEN

Price: 6s; number of copies not disclosed. Published 10 July 1941. Dust jacket: blue and white illustrated.
Printed by Jarrold and Sons Ltd. Norwich.

Notes: Nine impressions by 1947. †Issued in Canada by Saunders. Two chapters, "Image of God" and "Problem Picture" are reprinted in CHRIS-

TIAN LETTERS (A60). Sayers and Muriel St. Clare Byrne acted as general editors for the following Bridgeheads titles: *Masters of Reality* by Una Ellis-Fermor 1942; *The Point of Parliament* by A. P. Herbert 1946; others were announced but not published.

*a.*II. *Religious Book Club (London) issue* 1942: 186 pp.

Text produced from A37*a*.I.

*a.*III. *Greenwood Press (Westport, Connecticut) issue* 1970: 186 pp.

Text produced from A37*a*.I.

b. First American edition 1941:

DOROTHY L. SAYERS | The Mind | of the Maker | [publisher's device] | NEW YORK | HARCOURT, BRACE AND COM-PANY

> *Collation:* 124 leaves.
> p. [i] The Mind of the Maker; p. [ii] blank; p. [iii] title-page; p. [iv] copyright, rights, "*first American edition*", "PRINTED IN THE UNITED STATES OF AMERICA"; p. [v] dedication; p. [vi] blank; p. [vii] nine-line quotation from John Henry Newman and four line quotation from Nicholas Berdyaev; p. [viii] blank; pp. ix–xiv PREFACE, p. [xv] CONTENTS; p. [xvi] blank; pp. [1]–216 text with pp. [1, 19, 33, 47, 61, 85, 93, 109, 125, 147, 179] section headings with quotations, pp. [2, 18, 30, 32, 34, 48, 60, 62, 84, 86, 94, 108, 110, 126, 146, 148, 180] blank, and p. [46] NOTE; pp. 217–225 POSTSCRIPT: p. [226] blank; pp. 227–229 APPENDIX; pp. [230–232] blank.
>
> 20·2 × 13·4 cm. Bulk: 2·2/2·7 cm. Cream wove paper, trimmed; cream wove endpapers. Bound in bright blue cloth; front and back blank; spine [stamped in silver:] [at top, within single rules:] The | Mind | of the | Maker | [rule] | DOROTHY | L. | SAYERS | [at bottom:] HARCOURT, | BRACE and | COMPANY
>
> *Price:* $2; number of copies not disclosed. Published 23 December 1941. Dust jacket: printed in bright yellow and red-brown.

c. Living Age Books – Meridian Press (New York) edition 1956: 220 pp.

Translations: German, Dutch.

WHY WORK? | An Address Delivered at Eastbourne | April 23rd, 1942 | by | DOROTHY L. SAYERS | [publisher's device] | METHUEN & CO., LTD., LONDON | 36 Essex Street, Strand, W.C. 2

Collation: 12 leaves, stapled at fold.

p. [1] title-page; p. [2] *First published in 1942* | [printer's notice]; pp. 3–22 text; pp. 23–24 advertisements for Bridgeheads series edited by Sayers and M. St. Clare Byrne.

18·6 × 12·2 cm. Bulk: ·3/·4 cm. Cream laid paper, trimmed. No endpapers. Light purple paper covers; back blank; front [printed in dark blue:] WHY | WORK? | by | DOROTHY L. SAYERS | METHUEN & CO. LTD. | *One shilling net*

Price: 1s; number of copies not disclosed. Published 1 October 1942. Printed by E. T. Heron & Co. Ltd. London and Silver End, Essex.

Notes: †Issued in Canada by Saunders. WHY WORK? also appears in CREED OR CHAOS? (A45).

A39 THE OTHER SIX DEADLY SINS 1943

The Other Six Deadly Sins | An Address given to the Public Morality Council | at Caxton Hall, Westminster, on | October 23rd, 1941 | by Dorothy L. Sayers | [publisher's device] | METHUEN & CO. LTD., LONDON | 36 Essex Street, Strand, W.C. 2

Collation: 16 leaves, stapled at fold.

p. [1] title-page; p. [2] *First published in 1943* | [printer's notice]; pp. 3–29 text; pp. 30–32 advertisements.

18·3 × 12·2 cm. Bulk: ·3/·4 cm. Cream wove paper, trimmed. No endpapers. Bound in buff paper wraps; back and spine blank; front [printed in red:] THE | OTHER | SIX | DEADLY | SINS | [dot] | DOROTHY L. SAYERS | [dot] | METHUEN | *One shilling net*

Price: 1s; number of copies not disclosed. Published 11 March 1943. Printed by E. T. Heron & Co. Ltd. London and Silver End, Essex.

Notes: †Issued in Canada by Saunders. Reprinted in *Woman's Journal* 1944 (C155), CREED OR CHAOS? (A45), and CHRISTIAN LETTERS . . . (A60).

a. First edition:

THE MAN BORN | TO BE KING | A Play-Cycle on the Life |
of our Lord and Saviour | JESUS CHRIST | *written for broadcasting
by* | DOROTHY L. SAYERS | *Presented by the* | British Broadcasting
Corporation | Dec. 1941–Oct. 1942 | *Producer:* Val Gielgud | LON-
DON | VICTOR GOLLANCZ LTD | 1943

Collation: [A]¹⁶ B–K¹⁶ L¹² [$1 (with added MAN BORN), $5 with added 2,
except L, where L3 is signed L2] 172 leaves.
p. [1] THE MAN BORN TO | BE KING; p. [2] blank; p. [3] title-page;
p. [4] copyright, dramatic rights, printer's notices; p. 5 CONTENTS; p. 6
dedication; pp. 7–8 THE MAKERS; pp. 9–16 FOREWORD (by J. W.
Welch); pp. 17–40 INTRODUCTION; pp. 41–42 PRODUCTION NOTE,
MUSIC; pp. [43]–343 text, with pp. [43, 67, 91, 111, 133, 157, 181, 205, 233,
259, 287, 315] being play title-pages and cast lists and pp. [90, 180, 204, 232,
258, 314] blank; p. [344] blank.

19·6 × 12·5 cm. Bulk: 2·15/3 cm. Cream wove paper, trimmed. Cream wove
endpapers. Bound in blue cloth; front, back blank; spine [stamped in gold:]
THE MAN | BORN | TO BE | KING | BY | DOROTHY L. | SAYERS
| GOLLANCZ
Variant binding: light green cloth, otherwise unchanged.

Price: 10s6d; number of copies: 30,000. Published 24 May 1943. Dust jacket:
light blue printed in dark blue.
Printed by Richard Clay and Co. Ltd. Bungay, Suffolk.

Notes: Reprinted twenty-one times by January 1957. †Issued in Canada by
The Ryerson Press.

b.1. First American edition [1949]:

THE MAN | BORN TO BE KING | A Play-Cycle on the Life |
of our Lord and Saviour | JESUS CHRIST | *written for broadcasting
by* | DOROTHY L. SAYERS | [publisher's device] | PUBLISHERS
| HARPER & BROTHERS | NEW YORK

Collation: [A–L]¹⁶ 176 leaves.
p. [i] THE MAN BORN TO | BE KING; p. [ii] blank; p. [iii] title-page;
p. [iv] copyright, "*Printed in the United States of America*", rights reservations,
"H–Y"; p. [v] dedication; p. [vi] blank; p. [vii] CONTENTS; p. [viii] blank;
pp. ix–[x] THE MAKERS; pp. 1–339 text, with format similar to A39*a*;
pp. [340–342] blank.

21·0 × 14·2 cm. Bulk: 2·5/3·0 cm. White wove paper; not trimmed; white wove endpapers. Bound in black cloth; back blank; front [publisher's device blind stamped on lower right corner]; spine [stamped in gold:] THE | MAN | BORN | TO BE | KING | SAYERS | HARPER

Price: $3·75; number of copies not disclosed. Published 19 August 1949.

*b.*II. *Eerdmans* (*Grand Rapids, Michigan*) *issue* 1970:

Text produced from A40*b*.I.

Translations: German, French, Dutch, Persian, Danish, Urdu.

A41   EVEN THE PARROT   1944

[Illustrated, hand lettered title page in bold display letters with open work; swash letters with decorative tendrils; hand lettering:] EVEN THE | PARROT | Exemplary Conversations | for Enlightened Children | [drawing of a parrot] | BY DOROTHY L. SAYERS | Illustrated by | SILLINCE | METHUEN & Cº Lᵀᴰᐧ LONDON | 36 ESSEX Sᵀᐧ STRAND, W.C. 2 [double rule]

Collation: [1]⁸ 2–4⁸ [$1 signed] 32 leaves.
p. [i] EVEN THE PARROT – ; p. [ii] list of works by Sayers; p. [iii] title-page; p. [iv] publication; War Economy and Printed in Great Britain notices; p. v. CONTENTS; p. [vi] "Let Nature be your teacher." – *Wordsworth* | "Nature is usually wrong." – *Whistler*; p. vii EVEN THE PARROT – [Preface]; p. [viii] blank; pp. 1–55 text, pp. [4, 10, 19, 30, 33, 45, 53] being full-page illustrations, and pp. 2, 7, 8, 16, 27, 28, 41, 55 being text with illustrations; p. [56] printer's notice.

18·6 × 12·3 cm. Bulk: ·4/·8 cm. White wove paper; all edges trimmed; cream wove endpapers. Bound in blue cloth; front and back blank; spine [stamped in yellow, top to bottom, similar to letters on title-page:] EVEN THE PAR-ROT [star] DOROTHY L. SAYERS [star] Methuen

Price: 5s; number of copies not disclosed. Published 13 September 1944. Dust jacket: bright yellow printed in black letters designed as on title page, with a drawing of a nurse in an overstuffed chair and two children; on the back there is an advertisement for the Bridgeheads series.
Printed by Butler & Tanner Ltd., Frome and London.

Notes: Reprinted three times in 1944.

THE JUST VENGEANCE | *The Lichfield Festival Play* | *for 1946* | by | DOROTHY L. SAYERS | LONDON | VICTOR GOLLANCZ LTD | 1946

Collation: [A]⁸ B–C¹⁶ [$1 signed] 40 leaves.
p. [1] THE JUST VENGEANCE; p. [2] blank; p. [3] title-page; p. [4] copyright notices, printer's notice; pp. 5–6 DRAMATIS PERSONAE; p. [7] Performance notice; p. [8] blank; pp. 9–10 INTRODUCTION; pp. 11–80 text.

19·6 × 12·9 cm. Bulk: ·35/·4 cm. White wove paper. No endpapers. Orange paper covers; front [printed in dark blue:] THE JUST | VENGEANCE | by | DOROTHY | L. SAYERS | THE LICHFIELD FESTIVAL PLAY | FOR | 1946; back blank; spine [printed in dark blue; top to bottom:] 3/6 *net* [solid circle] THE JUST VENGEANCE [solid circle] DOROTHY L. SAYERS [solid circle] V [dot] G
Cloth issue: 19·7 × 12·9 cm. Bulk: ·35/·65 cm. White wove paper; white wove endpapers. Bound in black; front and back blank; spine [stamped in gold, bottom to top:] THE JUST VENGEANCE [star] DOROTHY L. SAYERS

Price: 3*s*6*d* paper, 5*s* cloth, number of copies: 3,000. Published 14 June 1946. Dust jacket of cloth issue: light blue printed in dark blue.
Printed by The Camelot Press Ltd.

Notes: Four impressions by October 1946. THE JUST VENGEANCE also appears in FOUR SACRED PLAYS (A46), which see for note of corrections to A42.

A43 UNPOPULAR OPINIONS 1946

a. First edition:

UNPOPULAR OPINIONS | by | DOROTHY L. SAYERS | LONDON | VICTOR GOLLANCZ LTD | 1946

Collation: [A]¹⁶ B–F¹⁶ [$1 signed with added UO] 96 leaves.
p. [1] UNPOPULAR OPINIONS; p. [2] blank; p. [3] title-page; p. [4] copyright, printer's notices; p. 5 CONTENTS; p. [6] blank; pp. 7–8 FOREWORD; pp. 9–190 text; pp. [191–192] blank.

19·7 × 12·6 cm. Bulk: ·9/1·2 cm. Cream wove paper; trimmed; cream wove endpapers. Bound in green cloth; front and back blank; spine [stamped in gold, bottom to top:] UNPOPULAR OPINIONS [star] DOROTHY L. SAYERS

Price: 8*s*6*d*; number of copies: 25,000. Published 30 September 1946. Dust jacket: yellow printed in black.
Printed by The Camelot Press Ltd.

Contents: Christian Morality – Forgiveness – What Do We Believe? – Divine Comedy – A Vote of Thanks to Cyrus – Towards a Christian Aesthetic – Creative Mind – The Gulf Stream and the Channel – The Mysterious English – Plain English – The English Language – They Tried To Be Good – Are Women Human? – The Human-Not-Quite-Human – Living to Work – How Free Is the Press? – Holmes' College Career – Dr. Watson's Christian Name – Dr. Watson, Widower – The Dates in "The Red-Headed League" – Aristotle on Detective Fiction.

Notes: Those essays or speeches in UNPOPULAR OPINIONS which were published elsewhere or given as speeches or broadcast are entered separately in this bibliography; consult the Index. Several of these essays have been reprinted in anthologies. †Issued in Canada by McCleod.

b. First American edition 1947:

[Double rule] | [quadruple rule] | Unpopular Opinions | TWENTY-ONE ESSAYS | BY | DOROTHY L. SAYERS | HARCOURT, BRACE AND COMPANY | NEW YORK

Collation: 124 leaves.
pp. [*2*] blank; p. [i] UNPOPULAR OPINIONS; p. [ii] list of books by Sayers; p. [iii] title-page; p. [iv] copyright, rights, edition, printing notices; pp. v–vi FOREWORD; p. vii CONTENTS; p. [viii] blank; pp. [1]–236 text with pp. [1, 67, 165] being section headings; pp. [2, 68, 166] being blank; pp. [237–238] blank.

20·3 × 13·6 cm. Bulk: 1·6/2·2 cm. Cream wove paper, trimmed; cream wove endpapers. Bound in green cloth, front and back blank; spine [stamped in gold:] [quintuple rule] | [top to bottom:] Unpopular Opinions DOROTHY L. SAYERS | [quintuple rule] | [upright:] *Harcourt, Brace | and Company*

Price: $3·00; number of copies not disclosed. Published 25 September 1947. Dust jacket: black and yellow printed in white.

Notes: Contents same as A43*a*. "Are Women Human?" and "The Human-Not-Quite-Human" were reprinted in *Are Women Human?* Grand Rapids, Michigan: Eerdmans, 1971, 47 pp., with an introduction by Mary McDermott Shideler.

Translations: Dutch, Czechoslovakian, German, Swedish.

MAKING SENSE | OF THE | UNIVERSE | An Address given at the Kingsway Hall | on Ash Wednesday, March 6th, 1946 | by | DOROTHY L. SAYERS

Collation: 8 leaves, stapled at fold.

p. [1] title-page; p. [2] printer's and publisher's notices; pp. 3–15 text; p. [16] blank.

18·2 × 12 cm. Bulk: 1 cm. White wove paper; no endpapers. Beige paper covers; back and spine blank; front [printed in black:] MAKING SENSE | OF THE | UNIVERSE | by | DOROTHY L. SAYERS | Price – – One Shilling

Price: 1s; number of copies not known. Published 1946. Printed by Claridge, Lewis & Jordan Ltd., 68–70 Wardour Street, London, W.1; published by St. Anne's Church House, 57 Dean Street, London, W.1.

<h2>A45   CREED OR CHAOS AND OTHER   1947
ESSAYS</h2>

a. First edition:

CREED OR CHAOS? | *and other Essays in popular Theology* | by | DOROTHY L. SAYERS | [publisher's device] | METHUEN & CO. LTD. LONDON | *36 Essex Street, Strand, W.C. 2*

Collation: [π]⁴, 1–5⁸ 6⁴ [$1 signed] 48 leaves.
p. [i] CREED OR CHAOS?; p. [ii] *By the Same Author* | THE MIND OF THE MAKER; p. [iii] title-page; p. [iv] "*First published in 1947*", catalogue number, economy note, printer's imprint; p. v author's note; p. [vi] blank; p. vii CONTENTS; p. [viii] blank; pp. 1–88 text, pp. 1, 7, 14, 20, 25, 47, 65 section headings and text.

18·2 × 12·3 cm. Bulk: ·9/1·25 cm. White wove paper; all edges trimmed. White wove endpapers. Bound in red cloth; front and back blank; spine [stamped in white, top to bottom:] CREED OR CHAOS? AND OTHER ESSAYS – Dorothy L. Sayers | [upright:] Methuen

Price: 5s; number of copies not disclosed. Published 27 February 1947. Dust jacket: buff printed in red.
Printed by Jarrold and Sons, Ltd. Norwich.

Contents: THE GREATEST DRAMA EVER STAGED – THE TRIUMPH OF EASTER – STRONG MEAT – THE DOGMA IS THE DRAMA –

Notes: Each essay is listed separately in this bibliography; consult the Index.

b.I. *First American edition* 1949:

DOROTHY L. SAYERS | Creed or Chaos? | HARCOURT,
BRACE AND COMPANY | NEW YORK

> *Collation:* 48 leaves.
> p. [i] CREED OR CHAOS? p. [ii] list of books by Sayers; p. [iii] title-page;
> p. [iv] copyright, rights reservation, *"first American edition"*, "PRINTED IN
> THE UNITED STATES OF AMERICA"; p. [v] Author's Note; p. [vi]
> blank; p. [vii] CONTENTS; p. [viii] blank; p. [1] CREED OR CHAOS?;
> p. [2] blank; pp. 3–85 text; pp. [86–88] blank.
>
> 20·5 × 13 cm. Bulk: ·8/1·4 cm. White wove paper, trimmed; white wove end-
> papers. Bound in red cloth; front and back blank; spine [in white, top to
> bottom:] DOROTHY L. SAYERS Creed or Chaos? HARCOURT, BRACE |
> [parallel to the preceeding two words:] AND COMPANY
>
> *Price:* $2·25; number of copies not disclosed. Published 26 May 1949. Dust
> jacket: yellow printed in brown.

b.II. *Religious Book Club (New York) issue* 1949:

> Text produced from A45*b*.I.

Translations: Dutch, Swedish, Czechoslovakian.

A46   FOUR SACRED PLAYS   1948

FOUR SACRED PLAYS | by | DOROTHY L. SAYERS |
LONDON | VICTOR GOLLANCZ LTD | 1948

> *Collation:* [A]¹⁶ B–L¹⁶ [$1 signed with added SP] 176 leaves.
> p. [1] FOUR SACRED PLAYS; p. [2] blank; p. [3] title-page; p. [4] copy-
> right, printer's notices; p. [5] CONTENTS; p. [6] blank; pp. [7]–352 text,
> pp. [7, 105, 213, 275] section headings, pp. [8, 106, 214, 276] copyright notices;
> pp. [14, 104, 222] blank.
>
> 18·3 × 12·4 cm. Bulk: 1·9/2·2 cm. Cream wove paper, trimmed. Cream wove
> endpapers. Bound in blue cloth; front and back blank; spine [stamped in gold:]
> FOUR | SACRED | PLAYS | BY | DOROTHY | L. | SAYERS | GOL-
> LANCZ

Price: 9*s*; number of copies: 10,000. Published 2 March 1948. Dust jacket: white printed in purple.
Printed by The Camelot Press Ltd.

Contents: THE ZEAL OF THY HOUSE – THE DEVIL TO PAY – HE THAT SHOULD COME – THE JUST VENGEANCE

Notes: Errata note for THE JUST VENGEANCE inserted between pp. [278]–279, correction of the first edition (A42): p. 9 line 2, for "St. Theresa of Jesus" read "Thomas à Kempis"; p. 67 line 16 for "...part and part" read "...art and part"; p. 79 between lines 30 and 32 read: "So enter My Father's house, and there take seizure | of the crown laid up and the incorruptable treasure,".
†Distributed in America by W. H. Baker, Boston, $2·50, 1949.

A47 THE LOST TOOLS OF LEARNING 1948

THE LOST TOOLS | OF LEARNING | Paper read at a Vacation Course in | Education, Oxford 1947 | by | DOROTHY L. SAYERS | [publisher's device] | METHUEN & CO. LTD. LONDON | 36 Essex Street, Strand, W.C. 2

Collation: 16 leaves stapled at fold.
p. [i] title-page; p. [ii] *First published in 1948* | The bulk of this pamphlet appeared as an article in the | *Hibbert Journal* | [catalogue number] | [printer's notice]; pp. 1–30 text.

18·3 × 12·4 cm. Bulk: ·2/·3 cm. Cream wove paper, trimmed. Purple paper covers; back blank; front [printed in dark blue:] DOROTHY L. SAYERS | [star] | THE | LOST TOOLS | OF | LEARNING | [star] | METHUEN | *One shilling net*

Price: 1*s*; number of copies not disclosed. Published July 1948.
Printed by E. T. Heron & Co. Ltd.

Notes: An abridged version of this paper was first published in *The Hibbert Journal* (C161). The complete essay also appears in THE POETRY OF SEARCH (A59) and A MATTER OF ETERNITY (A63). The first American publication was in *The National Review* (Orange, Connecticut) Vol. 7, 1 August 1959, pp. 237–244; this version is slightly abridged, with Americanized spelling and punctuation. First American book publication: *Education in a Free Society*, edited by A. H. Burleigh, Indianapolis: Liberty Fund, 1973, pp. 145–167. The Center for Independent Education in Witchita Kansas has also reprinted this essay as a pamphlet.

*a.*I. *First edition:*

THE COMEDY | OF | DANTE ALIGHIERI | THE FLORENTINE
| [star] | CANTICA I | HELL | ⟨L'INFERNO⟩ | [star] | TRANS-
LATED BY | DOROTHY L. SAYERS | [star] | PENGUIN BOOKS
| HARMONDSWORTH · MIDDLESEX

> *Collation:* [A]¹⁶ B–L¹⁶ [$1 signed] 176 leaves.
> p. [i] blank; p. [ii] blank; p. [1] THE PENGUIN CLASSICS | EDITED BY
> E. V. RIEU | L6 | [publisher's device]; p. [2] blank; p. [3] title-page; p. [4]
> Publication, maps and diagrams, and printer's notices; p. [5] dedication; p. [6]
> blank; p. [7] CONTENTS; p. [8] blank; pp. 9–66 INTRODUCTION;
> pp. 67–69 THE GREATER IMAGES; p. 70 diagram; pp. 71–291 text with
> diagrams on pp. 84, 122, 138, 173, 180, 194, 226, 264; pp. 292–298 Appendices;
> pp. 299–345 GLOSSARY OF PROPER NAMES; p. 346 BOOKS TO
> READ; p. [347] advertisement; pp. [348–350] blank.

> 18·2 × 11·3 cm. Bulk: 1·3/1·4 cm. Cream wove paper; no endpapers; trimmed.
> Bound in blue and white paper wraps; back [blue border, white rectangle with
> decorated border, printed in black:] [a list of Penguin Classics]; front [blue
> border, white rectangle with decorated border printed in black:] DANTE |
> THE DIVINE | COMEDY | I: HELL | [drawing of Dante] | TRANSLATED
> BY | DOROTHY L. SAYERS | [blue French rule] | THE PENGUIN |
> CLASSICS | [lower right corner of blue border:] 2/6; spine [blue border, white
> rectangle with decorated rule at top and bottom, printed in black:] [at bottom,
> on blue border, upright:] L6 | [within white rectangle bottom to top:] DANTE |
> [blue publisher's device, upright] | THE DIVINE COMEDY [dot] I [dot] HELL

> *Price:* 2s6d; number of copies not disclosed. Published 10 November 1949.
> Dust jacket: printed just as the wraps.
> Made and printed in Great Britain by R. & R. Clark Ltd. Edinburgh.

> *Notes:* Reprinted 1950, 1951, 1953, 1954. Maps and diagrams by C. W. Scott-
> Giles.

*a.*II. *First American issue* 1949:

> As A48*a.*I. except cover: 2/6 on lower right corner of blue border is replaced
> by 95c on lower right corner of white rectangle; signatures are on the lower

left side of the page rather than on the lower right side of the page.
Made and printed in Great Britain by R. & R. Clark Ltd. Edinburgh.

Note: See A58*b*. for second American issue 1963.

*a.*III. *Penguin Books (Harmondsworth, England) second issue* 1955:

> As A48*a*.I. except that minor revisions were made in the Introduction and
> the Glossary: e.g., p. 33, line 4, "rich and powerful" deleted; p. 33, lines 8–10
> revised; p. 47, lines 34–35 revised; pp. 315–317, alterations in the entry
> "Corybantes" with resultant resetting. Reprinted 1957, 1959 (twice), 1960,
> 1961, 1962, 1963, 1964, 1965, 1966, 1967, 1968, 1969, 1971, 1972, 1973, 1974,
> 1975.

A49   THE EMPEROR CONSTANTINE   1951

*a.*I. *First edition:*

THE EMPEROR CONSTANTINE | A Chronicle | by |
DOROTHY L. SAYERS | LONDON | VICTOR GOLLANCZ
LTD | 1951

> *Collation:* [A]¹⁶ B–F¹⁶ [$1 signed with added C] 96 leaves.
> p. [1] THE EMPEROR CONSTANTINE; p. [2] blank; p. [3] title-page;
> p. [4] copyright, dramatic rights, printer's notices; pp. 5–8 PREFACE; pp. 9–
> 10 DRAMATIS PERSONAE; p. 11 PROLOGUE; p. [12] blank; pp. 13–
> 190 text; p. 191 A BRIEF BIBLIOGRAPHY; p. [192] blank.

> 19·7 × 12·9 cm. Bulk: ·9/1·3 cm. Cream wove paper, trimmed; cream wove
> endpapers. Bound in black cloth, front and back blank; spine [stamped in gold,
> bottom to top:] THE EMPEROR CONSTANTINE [star] DOROTHY L. SAYERS

> *Price:* 8*s*6*d* cloth, 5*s* paper; number of copies: 5,000. Published 20 August
> 1951. Dust jacket: cream, printed in black within brown rules.
> Printed by Purnell and Sons Ltd. Dust jacket printed by The Fanfare Press Ltd.,
> London.
> *Notes:* †Distributed in Canada by Longman. The Preface was first published
> in the Colchester Festival Programme, 2–14 July 1951, as "History, too. . . . "

*a.*II. *First American issue* [1951]:

THE EMPEROR CONSTANTINE | A Chronicle | by |
DOROTHY L. SAYERS | HARPER & BROTHERS PUBLISH-
ERS | NEW YORK

Collation: As A49a.I.

Pagination as A49a.I. except verso title-page, p. [4]: copyright, American agent's rights reservations, "PRINTED IN GREAT BRITAIN".

Format as A49a.I. except bound in tan cloth, front and back blank; spine: [stamped in teal blue, top to bottom:] THE EMPEROR CONSTANTINE [cross] SAYERS [cross] HARPER

Price: $2·50; number of copies not disclosed.
The official distribution date was not disclosed by Harper and Row. Dust jacket: tan printed in teal blue.

*a.*III. *Harper and Brothers* (*New York*) *second issue* [1951]: 190 pp.

Exactly as A49a.II. except the gatherings are not signed and p. [4] reads: copyright, rights reservations, "PRINTED IN THE UNITED STATES OF AMERICA".

*a.*IV. *Eerdmans* (*Grand Rapids, Michigan*), *issue* 1976: 190pp.

Text produced from A49a.III.

A50 THE DAYS OF CHRIST'S COMING 1953

a. First edition Christmas card:

[17·5 × 28·8 cm. blue rectangle with border of black, white and brown illustrations depicting the story of the Christchild; printed in black, stylized, italic letters:] THE DAYS of | CHRIST'S COMING | The Picture painted by FRITZ WEGNER | The Story told by DOROTHY L. SAYERS | [large, decorated T]HE PICTURE inside has twenty-seven numbered doors for you to | open as the story goes along. You can start on the Fourteenth of | December and open one door every day until the Seventh of January. | If you start earlier or later than this, remember that the Stable Door | (Door 12) is the one that opens on CHRISTMAS DAY [3 cm. decorated rule] | Published by Hamish Hamilton, Ltd., 90, Great Russell Street, London, W.C. 1

Collation: Within folded card, one leaf is tipped in at the fold; a sheet of illustrated card is pasted over the illustrated inner side of the back so that the twenty-seven doors open onto decorations.

p. [1] title-page; p. [2–4] text, p. [2] illustrated border as on title page; p. [5] color illustration with 27 doors which open; p. [6] blank.

19·4 × 29 cm. Bulk: ·1 cm. Cardboard covers, white wove leaf, no endpapers.

Price: 2*s*6*d*; number of copies not known. Published 25 October 1953.

*b.*1. *Revised edition* 1960:

The Days of Christ's Coming | BY | DOROTHY L. SAYERS |
ILLUSTRATED BY | FRITZ WEGNER | [drawing of Madonna
and Child] | HAMISH HAMILTON | LONDON

Collation: [A]¹⁶ 16 leaves.
p. [1] title-page; p. [2] edition and publisher's notices, copyright and printer's
notices; pp. [3–30] text, all illustrated, pp. [5, 17, 21, 30] illustrations without
text; pp. [31–32] blank.

18·2 × 14·5 cm. Bulk: ·4/1·0 cm. White wove paper, trimmed; grey and white
endpapers decorated with angels playing string instruments. Bound in glossy
paper boards; back [black] blank; spine [grey] blank; front [full color illustration of the Nativity, a white banner curving across the top, printed in black:]
THE DAYS OF CHRIST'S COMING | [at the bottom of the illustration,
printed in pink:] DOROTHY L. SAYERS

Price: 5*s*; number of copies 40,000. Published 17 August 1960.

Notes: Text slightly altered. Among earthly affairs "making love" is changed
to "making merry" (p. 3). "Before He was born, an Angel told me that He
was to be called 'JESUS.' (Now that name means "Savior')." is changed to
"...'JESUS,' a name that means 'Saviour'." The illustrations altered for the
book format.

*b.*11. *Revised edition, Harper and Row (New York) issue* 1960: 30 pp.

Text as A50*b.*1., except for publisher's imprint on the title-page: HARPER
& BROTHERS | *Publishers* | NEW YORK; edition and publisher's notices
omitted from p. [2]. Format differs in that the spine is red cloth, blank.

A51   INTRODUCTORY PAPERS ON DANTE   1954

*a.*1. *First edition:*

DOROTHY L. SAYERS | [French rule] | Introductory Papers on |
DANTE | with a preface by | BARBARA REYNOLDS | *Lecturer*

in Italian in the University of Cambridge | *Poiche di riguardar pascuito fui,* | *tutto m'offersi pronto al suo servigio,* | *con l'affermar che fa credere altrui.* | *Purg.* XXVI. 103–105 | [publisher's device] | METHUEN & CO. LTD. LONDON | *36 Essex Street, Strand, WC2*

> *Collation:* [1]⁸ 2–14⁸ 15⁸ 16⁸ [$1 signed] 124 leaves.
> p. [i] Introductory Papers on | DANTE; p. [ii] list of works by Sayers; p. [iii] title-page; p. [iv] *First published in 1954* | I.I | [catalogue number, printer's notice]; p. [v] dedication; p. [vi] blank; pp. vii–ix PREFACE; p. [x] blank; p. [xi] CONTENTS; p. [xii] blank; pp. xiii–xix INTRODUCTION; p. [xx] blank; pp. 1–212 text, p. [209] table; pp. 213–225 INDEX; pp. [226–228] blank.

> 21·6 × 13·8 cm. Bulk: 1·5/1·9 cm. White laid paper; white wove endpapers; all edges trimmed; top edge blue. Bound in blue cloth; front and back blank; spine [stamped in gold:] Dorothy L. | Sayers | [French rule] | Introductory | Papers on | DANTE | [star] | METHUEN

> *Price:* 21*s*; number of copies not disclosed. Published 21 October 1954. Dust jacket: cream printed in black; front, decorated border of black and light brown around 18 × 10·4 cm. brown rectangle printed in black. Printed by Butler & Tanner Ltd.

> *Contents:* Dante's Imagery: I–Symbolic – Dante's Imagery: II Pictorial – The Meaning of Heaven and Hell – The Meaning of Purgatory – The Fourfold Interpretation of *The Comedy* – The City of Dis – The Comedy of *The Comedy* – The Paradoxes of *The Comedy*.

> *Notes:* The Index was prepared by Lewis Thorpe; the "blurb" on dust jacket, except for the last paragraph, was written by Barbara Reynolds. Consult the Index for the dates of these lectures. Distributed in Canada by British Book Service.

*a.*II. *First American issue* 1955:

[Title-page exactly as A51*a*.I. except no publisher's device, publishers:] HARPER & BROTHERS | PUBLISHERS | NEW YORK

> *Collation:* [1]⁸⁽±¹⁾ 2–14⁸ 15⁴ 16⁸ [$1 signed] 124 leaves.
> pp. [i–ii] as A51*a*.I.; p. [iii] title page; p. [iv] copyright, rights reservation, "PRINTED IN ENGLAND"; pp. [v]–[228] as A51*a*.I.

> 21·5 × 13·5 cm. Bulk: 1·7/2·4 cm. White laid paper; white wove endpapers; trimmed; (unlike A51*a*.I.:) top edge white. Bound in tan cloth; back blank; front [stamped in blue on lower right corner:] [publisher's device]; spine [stamped in blue:] Introductory | Papers on | DANTE | [star] | Dorothy L. | SAYERS | HARPER

Price: $4·00; number of copies not disclosed. Published 18 November 1955.

Notes: This issue appears to be made up of sheets from the first edition. The watermarks on the paper used are the same as in A51*a*.I., and the type faces are exactly the same. The title page is a cancellans.

*a.*III. *Variant of first American issue* 1955:

The Marion E. Wade Collection holds a curious issue of A51*a*.II. It was printed in America on large laid paper, chain marks horizontal. The type face is the same as A51*a*.I., except for some broken type on p. 3. The volume has been rebound, trimmed, and the 123 leaves stab-sewn; the gatherings are irregular; the half-title is lacking but there is a half-title following the Preface (this second half-title between the Preface and the text is also present in A50*a*.IV.).

*a.*IV. *Later Harper issue* [n.d.]: title-page as A51*a*.II.

Collation: [A–H]¹⁶ 128 leaves.
pp. [i–ii] as A51*a*.I.; p. [iii] title-page; p. [iv] title, copyright, *"Printed in the United States of America,"* rights reservation; pp. [v]–[xx] as A51*a*.I.; p. [xxi] Introductory Papers on | DANTE; p. [xxii] blank; pp. 1–225 as A51*a*.I.; pp. [226–234] blank.

White wove paper; white wove endpapers; trimmed. Bound as A51*a*.II.

*a.*V. *Barnes and Noble (New York) issue* 1969: 225 pp.

Text produced from A51*a*.I.

*a.*VI. *Methuen Library (London) issue* 1970: 225 pp.

Text produced from A51*a*.I.

A52 THE STORY OF EASTER [1955]

[Easter card: front illustrated in rust and blue depicting (top, left to right) The Last Supper, Pilate Washing His Hands, (bottom, left to right) The Crucifixion, and Resurrection, amidst lavish decorations of vines, chalice, crown of thorns, hammer and nails, pieces of silver, etc. In the center is a dome-topped rectangle, outlined in rust, with a blue and white vine border surrounding a white space in which is printed in black Gothic and *italic:* THE | STORY OF EASTER |

Illustrated Card: *The Story of Easter* (A52)

Told by | Dorothy L. Sayers | The Picture painted by B. Biro | *There
are 27 numbered doors to be opened as you follow the story* [bottom, center,
beneath the rectangle:] Published by | Hamish Hamilton Ltd. | 90
Great Russell Street | London W. C. 1 [swash design extending from
the last "n" of "London"]

> *Collation:* Folded card, one leaf tipped in at fold; a sheet of illustrated card is
> pasted over the illustrated inner side of the back so that the twenty-seven doors
> open onto decorations.
>
> p. [1] title-page; pp. [2–4] text; p. [5] color illustration with doors which open;
> p. [6] list of other cards in the series, publisher's and printer's notices.
>
> 19·7 × 29·7 cm. Bulk: ·1 cm.
>
> *Price:* 2s6d; number of copies not known. Published 1 March 1955.
> Printed by The Haycock Press Ltd. London.

A53 THE STORY OF ADAM AND CHRIST [1955]

[printed in black, gold and red on a stone gray background, with
illustrations of mediaeval sculptures of Adam and Eve on the left,
and Christ and Mary on the right, set within illustrations of elaborate
mediaeval friezes:] *The Story of* | ADAM | *and* | CHRIST | *The verses
written by* | DOROTHY L. SAYERS | *The window painted by* |
FRITZ WEGNER | PUBLISHED BY HAMISH HAMILTON LTD
| 90 GREAT RUSSELL STREET LONDON W.C. 1

> *Collation:* 1 leaf, folded twice to make six pages.
> p. [1] title-page; p. [2] text; p. [3 (center)] full color illustration of a stained
> glass window depicting the story of Adam and Christ; p. [4] text; p. [5] blank;
> p. [6 (verso center when folded)] printer's notice at bottom: *Printed in England
> by Harrison & Sons Ltd., London, Hayes, and High Wycombe.*
>
> 26 × 20 cm. Bulk: ·1 cm. Heavy card paper folded in thirds.
>
> *Price:* 2s6d; number of copies not known. Published 25 March 1955.
> Printed by Harrison & Sons Ltd., Hayes and High Wycombe.
>
> *Contents:* Twenty seven stanzas: Adam and Eve – Abraham and Issac – The
> Passover – The Prophets – The Annunciation – The Nativity – The Entry into
> Jerusalem – Christ Sold to Caiaphas – The Last Supper – Christ in Gethsemane
> – The Betrayal – Christ Denied by Peter – Christ Condemned by Caiaphas –
> Christ Before Herod – Christ Before Pilate – Christ Mocked by the Soldiers –
> Christ Shown to the People – Pilate Washing His Hands – Simon of Cyrene –

The Crucifixion – The Entombment – The Harrowing of Hell – The Resurrection – The Women at the Tomb – Christ Appears to Thomas – The Ascension – The Last Judgement.

A54   THE COMEDY OF DANTE ALIGHIERI   1955
THE FLORIENTINE
CANTICA II: PURGATORY

a.1. First edition:

THE COMEDY | OF | DANTE ALIGHIERI | THE FLORENTINE | [star] | CANTICA II | PURGATORY | ⟨IL PURGATORIO⟩ | [star] | TRANSLATED BY | DOROTHY L. SAYERS | [star] | PENGUIN BOOKS

Collation: [A]¹⁶ B–F¹⁶ G⁸ H–N¹⁶ [$1 signed] 200 leaves.
p. [1] THE PENGUIN CLASSICS | EDITED BY E. V. RIEU | L46 | [publisher's device]; p. [2] blank; p. [3] title-page; p. [4] publisher's notice, publication notice, printer's notice; p. [5] dedication; p. [6] illustration notice; p. [7] CONTENTS; p. 8 illustration of Mount Purgatory; pp. 9–71; INTRODUCTION, p. 62 diagram; p. [72] blank; pp. 73–399 text, pp. [100], 202–203, 340 diagrams; pp. 341–349 APPENDIX; pp. 349–350 GLOSSARY OF PROPER NAMES; sigs. M8ᵃ⁻ᵇ and M9ᵃ diagrams for the Universal clock; sig. M9ᵇ blank; pp. 351–388 GLOSSARY; pp. 389–390 SOME BOOKS TO READ: pp. [391–396] advertisements.

18·2 × 11·3 cm. Bulk: 2·1/2·15 cm. Cream wove paper, trimmed. No endpapers. Bound in blue and white paper covers; back [blue frame, white rectangle within decorated rules, printed in black:] [a list of the Penguin Classics]; front [same format as back, printed in black:] DANTE | THE DIVINE | COMEDY | II: PURGATORY | [drawing of Dante] | TRANSLATED BY | DOROTHY L. SAYERS | [blue French rule] | THE PENGUIN | CLASSICS | [lower right corner of frame:] 3/6; spine [blue frame, white rectangle with decorated rule at top and bottom, printed in black:] [at bottom of rectangle, upright:] L46 | [bottom to top:] DANTE [dot] THE DIVINE COMEDY | [blue publisher's device upright] | II [dot] PURGATORY

Price: 3s6d; number of copies not disclosed. Published 7 May 1955. Dust jacket: printed just as the paper covers.
Made and printed in Great Britain by R. & R. Clarke Ltd. Edinburgh

Note: Maps and diagrams by C. W. Scott-Giles.

a.II. *First American issue* 1955:

As A54*a*.I., except front cover has 85c not 3/6 in the bottom right corner. Made and printed in Great Britain by R & R Clark Ltd. Edinburgh.

Note: See A58*b*. for second American issue 1963.

A55   THE STORY OF NOAH'S ARK   [1955]

[Colored pamphlet decorated with an ark and stormy blue sea; lower center is bright yellow with black and large black-and-white, fat, stylized letters:] THE | STORY OF | NOAH'S | ARK | *retold by* | DOROTHY L. SAYERS | *the picture painted by* | FRITZ WEGNER | [small yellow strip beneath the sea, printed in black:] PUBLISHED BY HAMISH HAMILTON LTD [dot] 90 GREAT RUSSEL STREET [dot] LONDON W.C. 1

Collation: Within folded card, one leaf is tipped in at the fold; a sheet of illustrated card is pasted over the illustrated inner side of the back so that the twenty-seven doors open onto decorations.

p. [1] title-page; p. [2] THE STORY OF NOAH'S ARK | [French rule] | . text; p. [3] text | [French rule] | *THE HISTORICAL FLOOD* | italicised text; p. [4] ABOUT THE PICTURE | [French rule] | text; p. [5] illustration; p. [6] [lower right corner:] *Printed in England by Harrison & Sons Ltd., London, Hayes & High Wycombe.*

19·7 × 29 cm. Bulk: ·1 cm. Cardboard covers, white wove leaf; no endpapers.

Price: 2s6d; number of copies not known. Published 12 September 1955. Printed by Harrison & Sons Ltd.

A56   FURTHER PAPERS ON DANTE   1957

a.I. *First edition:*

DOROTHY L. SAYERS | [French rule] | Further Papers on | DANTE | [publisher's device] | METHUEN & CO. LTD. LONDON | *36 Essex Street, Strand WC2*

Collation: [1]⁸ 2–13⁸ 14⁴ 15⁸ [$1 signed] 116 leaves.
p. [i] Further Papers on | DANTE; p. [ii] list of works by Sayers; p. [iii] title-page; p. [iv] *First published in 1957* | I.I | [catalogue number, printer's notice]; pp. v–viii AUTHOR'S PREFACE; p. ix CONTENTS; p. [x] blank; pp. 1–204 text; pp. 205–221 INDEX; p. [222] blank.

21·8 × 13·8 cm. Bulk: 1·2/1·8 cm. White wove paper, trimmed, top edge violet. White wove endpapers. Bound in blue cloth; front and back blank; spine [stamped in gold:] Dorothy L. | SAYERS | [French rule] | Further | Papers on | DANTE | [star] | METHUEN

Price: 25s; number of copies not disclosed. Published 16 May 1957. Dust jacket: cream printed in black with decorated border of black and light blue surrounding blue rectangle.
Printed by Butler & Tanner Ltd.

Contents: "... And Telling You A Story" – The Divine Poet and the Angelic Doctor – Dante's Virgil – Dante's Cosmos – The Eighth Bolgia – The Cornice of Sloth – Dante and Milton – The Poetry of the Image in Dante and Charles Williams.

Notes: Chapters which were lectures are listed elsewhere in the bibliography; consult the Index.

*a.*II. *American issue* 1957:

DOROTHY L. SAYERS | [French rule] | Further Papers on | DANTE | [publisher's device] | HARPER & BROTHERS | *New York*

Collation: [A–G]¹⁶ 112 leaves.
p. [i] Further Papers on | DANTE; p. [ii] list of books by Sayers; p. [iii] title-page; p. [iv] title, copyright, *"Printed in the United States of America"*, rights reservations, Library of Congress catalog card number; pp. v–viii AUTHOR'S PREFACE; p. ix CONTENTS; p. [x] blank; pp. 1–204 text, pp. 205–214 INDEX

21 × 14 cm. Bulk: 1·5/2·2 cm. White wove paper; white wove endpapers; trimmed. Bound in tan cloth; front and back blank; spine [stamped in black:] Further | Papers on | DANTE | [star] | Dorothy L. | SAYERS | HAR [publisher's device] PER | [rule]

Price: $4·00; number of copies not disclosed. Published 24 July 1957.

Notes: Several entries in the index are shortened; entries omitted are "Dante" *"Divina Commedia"*; *"Inferno* quoted"; *"Paradiso* quoted"; *"Purgatorio* quoted"; "Wallingford"; "Wentworth". This issue appears to be a photographic reproduction of A56a.I. with the exception of the shortened Index.

*a.*III. *Barnes and Noble (New York) issue* 1972: 214 pp.

A photographic reproduction of A56a.II.

a.IV. *Methuen Library (London) re-issue* 1973: 221 pp.

A photographic reproduction of A56*a*.I.

A57   THE SONG OF ROLAND   1957

a.I. *First edition:*

THE SONG OF | ROLAND | [star] | A NEW TRANSLATION BY | *Dorothy L. Sayers* | PENGUIN BOOKS

Collation: [A]¹⁶ B–C¹⁶ D⁸ E–G¹⁶ [$1 signed] 104 leaves.
p. [1] THE PENGUIN CLASSICS | EDITED BY E. V. RIEU | L75 | [publisher's device]; p. [2] blank; p. [3] title-page; p. [4] publisher's notice, publication notice, copyright notice, printer's notice, p. [5] CONTENTS; p. [6] note on rondel on the jacket; pp. 7–44 INTRODUCTION; p. 45 ACKNOWLEDGEMENTS; p. [46] blank; p. [47] A NOTE ON COSTUME; pp. 48–49 illustrations and explanations of costumes; p. [50] blank; pp. 51–203 text; p. [204] blank; pp. 205–206 NOTE ON LAISSE 50; pp. [207–208] blank.

18·1 × 11·1 cm. Bulk: 1·0/1·2 cm. Cream, thin, wove paper: no endpapers; all edges trimmed. Green and white paper wraps, back [green frame; white rectangle within decorated rules; printed in black:] [a list of the Penguin Classics]; front [green frame; white rectangle within decorated rules; printed in black:] THE | SONG OF | ROLAND | [rondel from stained glass window] | A NEW TRANSLATION BY | DOROTHY L. SAYERS | [green French rule] | THE PENGUIN | CLASSICS | [lower right corner of rectangle:] 3/6; spine [green frame; white rectangle with decorated rule at top and bottom, printed in black:] [top to bottom] THE SONG | [green publisher's device upright] | OF ROLAND | [at bottom upright] L75

Price: 2s6d; number of copies not disclosed. Published 26 September 1957. Printed by The Whitefriars Press Ltd. London and Tonbridge.

a.II. *American issue* 1957:

Format and text as A57*a*.I. except front cover: instead of 3/6 on the lower right corner: 95c. Issued by Penguin Books, Baltimore, Maryland. Printed by The White Friars Press Ltd. London and Tonbridge.

*a.*1. *First edition:*

THE COMEDY | OF | DANTE ALIGHIERI | THE FLORENTINE
| [star] | CANTICA III | PARADISE | ⟨IL PARADISO⟩ | [star] |
TRANSLATED BY | DOROTHY L. SAYERS | AND | BAR-
BARA REYNOLDS | [star] | PENGUIN BOOKS

> *Collation:* [1]¹² 2–4¹² 5–8¹⁰ 9–10¹² 11–14¹⁰ 15–18¹² [$1 signed] 200 leaves.
> p. [1] THE PENGUIN CLASSICS | EDITED BY E. V. RIEU | L105 |
> [publisher's device]; p. [2] blank; p. [3] title-page; [4] publisher's notice, publica-
> tion notice, copyright notice, printer's notice, publisher's sale conditions; p. [5]
> three line quotation from PARADISO xxx 31–33; p. [6] note on diagrams;
> pp. [7–8] CONTENTS; pp. 9–11 FOREWORD; p. [12] blank; pp. 13–52
> INTRODUCTION; pp. 52–349 text; pp. 350–355 APPENDIX; pp. 356–394
> GLOSSARY; pp. 395–396 BOOKS TO READ; pp. 397–400 GENEA-
> LOGIES; *inset:* fold-out diagram pasted on back cover.

> 18 × 11 cm. Bulk: 1·5/1·6 cm. White wove paper, no endpapers, trimmed.
> Bound in blue and white paper covers; back [blue frame; white rectangle with
> decorated rules, printed in black:] [a list of Penguin Classics]; front [same format
> as back, printed in black:] DANTE | THE DIVINE | COMEDY | III: PAR-
> ADISE | [drawing of Dante] | A NEW TRANSLATION BY | DOROTHY
> L. SAYERS AND | BARBARA REYNOLDS | [blue French rule] | THE
> PENGUIN | CLASSICS | [bottom right of rectangle:] 5'–; spine [blue frame;
> white rectangle with decorated rule at top and bottom; top to bottom:]
> DANTE [dot] THE DIVINE COMEDY | [blue publisher's device upright] |
> III [dot] PARADISE | [upright:] L105

Price: 5*s*; number of copies: 45,000. Published 14 April 1962.
Printed by Hazell Watson & Viney Ltd., Aylesbury and Slough; set in Monotype Bembo.

Notes: The first twenty Cantos and Canto XXXIII were in final form for
publication when Sayers died 17 December 1957. Barbara Reynolds translated
Cantos XXII–XXXII and prepared the introduction and all of the notes, com-
mentaries, etc. Maps and diagrams by C. W. Scott-Giles.

*a.*11. *First American issue* 1962:

As A58*a*.1. except front cover has $1·25 on the bottom right corner. Made

and printed in Great Britain by Hazell Watson & Viney Ltd., Aylesbury and Slough; set in Monotype Bembo.
See A58b. for second American issue.

b. *Three volume second American issue* 1963:

THE COMEDY | OF | DANTE ALIGHIERI | THE FLORENTINE | [leaf and tendril decoration] | CANTICA I | HELL | (L'INFERNO) | [leaf and tendril decoration] | TRANSLATED BY | DOROTHY L. SAYERS | [leaf and tendril decoration] | ILLUSTRATED WITH A SELECTION | OF WILLIAM BLAKE'S DRAWINGS | BASIC BOOKS, INC., PUBLISHERS | NEW YORK

Collation: [A–K]¹⁶ [L]⁸ [M]¹⁶ 184 leaves.

p. [1] THE COMEDY | OF | DANTE ALIGHIERI; p. [2] blank; p. [3] title-page; p. [4] *Library of Congress Catalog Card Number:* 63–21690 | *Manufactured in the United States of America*; p. [5] dedication; p. [6] note on the William Blake drawings, notes on the maps and diagrams by C. W. Scott-Giles; remaining pagination is the same as A48a.; the Blake drawings are not paged, but are part of the collation. The text appears to be a photographic reproduction of A48a.III.

THE COMEDY | OF | DANTE ALIGHIERI | THE FLOREN-TINE | [leaf and tendril decoration] | CANTICA II | PURGATORY | (IL PURGATORIO) | [leaf and tendril decoration] | TRANS-LATED BY | DOROTHY L. SAYERS | [leaf and tendril decoration] | ILLUSTRATED WITH A SELECTION | OF WILLIAM BLAKE'S DRAWINGS | BASIC BOOKS, INC., PUBLISHERS | NEW YORK

Collation: [A–N]¹⁶ 208 leaves.

pp. [1–6] same format as volume I; pp. [7]–390 appears to be a photographic reproduction of A54a.I.; pp. [391–396] blank; the Blake drawings are not paged, but are part of the collation; as in A54a.I.: between pp. 350–351 are two unpaged leaves, part of the collation which are diagrams for the Universal 24-Hour Clock.

THE COMEDY | OF | DANTE ALIGHIERI | THE FLORENTINE | [leaf and tendril decoration] | CANTICA III | PARADISE | (IL (PARADISO) | [leaf and tendril decoration] | TRANSLATED BY | DOROTHY L. SAYERS | [leaf and tendril design] | ILLUS-TRATED WITH A SELECTION | OF WILLIAM BLAKE'S DRAWINGS | BASIC BOOKS, INC., PUBLISHERS | NEW YORK

Collation: [A–M]¹⁶ [N]⁴ [O]¹⁶ 212 leaves.

pp. [1–6] same format as volumes I and II; pp. [7]–400 appears to be a photographic reproduction of A58*a*.; pp. [401–403] reprinted from fold-outs at the end of A58*a*., but in page rather than fold-out form; pp. [404–408] blank, the Blake drawings are not paged, but are part of the collation.

21 × 13·3 cm. Bulk: Volume I 2·5/3 cm.; Volume II 2·7/3·3 cm.; Volume III 2·6/3·2 cm. White wove paper; trimmed; white wove endpapers. Bound in gray cloth; front and back blank; spine [within 8 × 3 cm. black label, in gold:] DANTE | The | Divine | Comedy | [one (two or three) leaf and tendril decorations] | HELL [PURGATORY or PARADISE] | I [II or III] | BASIC BOOKS

Price: $15 the set; number of copies not disclosed. Issued in 1963, the official date was not disclosed, nor the publication itself acknowledged, by Basic Books, Inc.

A59   THE POETRY OF SEARCH AND   1963
THE POETRY OF STATEMENT

THE POETRY OF SEARCH | AND | THE POETRY OF STATE-MENT | AND OTHER POSTHUMOUS ESSAYS ON LITERA-TURE, | RELIGION AND LANGUAGE | by | DOROTHY L. SAYERS | LONDON | VICTOR GOLLANCZ LTD | 1963

Collation: [1]¹⁶ 2–9¹⁶ [$1 signed with added – POS] 144 leaves.
p. [1] THE POETRY OF SEARCH | AND THE POETRY OF STATE-MENT; p. [2] blank; p. [3] title-page; p. [4] copyright, printer's notices; p. [5] CONTENTS; p. [6] NOTE; pp. [7]–286 text; pp. [7, 21, 45, 69, 91, 127, 155, 177, 201, 227, 243, 263] chapter headings and text pp. [20, 126, 154, 200, 226, 242, 262] blank; p. [287] list of sources; p. [288] blank.

21·2 × 13·5 cm. Bulk: 2·2/2·5 cm. Cream wove paper, trimmed; cream wove endpapers. Bound in blue cloth; front, back blank; spine [stamped in gold:] THE POETRY | OF | SEARCH | AND | THE POETRY | OF | STATE-MENT | [asterisk] | DOROTHY | L. | SAYERS | GOLLANCZ

Price: 30*s*; number of copies: 3,000. Published 29 August 1963. Dust jacket: yellow, printed in black and magenta.
Printed by The Garden City Press Ltd., Letchworth, Herts.

Contents: The Poetry of Search and the Poetry of Statement – Dante the Maker – The Beatrician Vision in Dante and Other Poets – Charles Williams: A Poet's Critic – On Translating the *Divina Commedia* – The Translation of Verse – The Lost Tools of Learning – The Teaching of Latin: A New Approach

– The Writing and Reading of Allegory – The Faust Legend and the Idea of the Devil – *Oedipus Simplex*: Freedom and Fate in Folklore and Fiction – Poetry, Language and Ambiguity.

Notes: Distributed in America by Lawrence Verry, Inc., August 1966, $6, imported from Victor Gollancz Ltd.
Consult the Index for dates of first printings or lectures.

A60   CHRISTIAN LETTERS TO A   1969
             POST-CHRISTIAN WORLD

Christian Letters | to a | Post-Christian | World | A Selection of Essays | by | DOROTHY L. SAYERS | *Selected and introduced by Roderick Jellema* | WILLIAM B. EERDMANS PUBLISHING COMPANY | GRAND RAPIDS, MICHIGAN

Collation: [A–H]¹⁶ 128 leaves.
p. [i] Christian Letters | to a | Post-Christian | World; p. [ii] blank; *inset*: Frontispiece portrait of Sayers; p. [iii] title-page; p. [iv] copyright, rights reservation, printed in the United States of America, Library of Congress number, permission to reprint selections notices; p. v CONTENTS; p. vi ACKNOWLEDGEMENTS; pp. vii–xiii INTRODUCTION; p. [xiv] blank; pp. [1]–236 text, pp. [1, 11, 47, 67, 131, 157] section headings; pp. [2, 12, 46, 48, 66, 68, 130, 132, 156, 158] blank, *inset*: between pp. 2–3 a color plate of "The Calendar of Unholy and Dead Letter Days"; pp. [237–242] blank.

21·5 × 13·7 cm. Bulk: 1·7/2·4 cm. White wove paper, trimmed; white wove endpapers. Bound in orange-yellow cloth, front and back blank; spine [top to bottom, stamped in brown:] Christian Letters To A Post-Christian World Sayers | [upright:] EERDMANS

Price: $6·95; number of copies: 2,000 cloth; (4,000 paper). Published August 1969. Dust jacket: white printed in brown with sepia photomontage in the shape of a cross.

Contents: from "The Pantheon Papers" (The Kalendar of Unholy and Dead Letter Days, The Cosmic Synthesis, The Creed of St. Euthanasia, The Polar Synthesis) – The Greatest Drama Ever Staged – Strong Meat – The Dogma Is the Drama – What Do We Believe? – Creed or Chaos? – A Vote of Thanks to Cyrus – The Dates in "The Red-Headed League" – Towards a Christian Aesthetic – Creative Mind – The Image of God – Problem Picture – Christian Morality – The Other Six Deadly Sins – Dante and Charles Williams – The Writing and Reading of Allegory – *Oedipus Simplex* – The Faust Legend and The Idea of the Devil.

A61   LORD PETER: A COLLECTION OF   1972
             ALL THE LORD PETER WIMSEY
                      STORIES

a. First edition:

LORD PETER | A COLLECTION OF ALL THE LORD PETER WIMSEY STORIES | BY DOROTHY L. SAYERS | *Compiled and with an introduction by* | JAMES SANDOE | *coda by Carolyn Heilbrun* | *codetta by E. C. Bentley* | HARPER & ROW, PUBLISHERS | *New York, Evanston, San Francisco, London*

Collation: [A–P]^{16} 240 leaves.
p. [i] LORD PETER; p. [ii] blank; p. [iii] title-page; p. [iv] copyright notice, "FIRST EDITION", Standard book number, Library of Congress number; p. [v] CONTENTS p. [vi] blank; pp. [vii–xii] INTRODUCTION; p. [xiii] LORD PETER; p. [xiv] blank; pp. 1–464 text; p. [465] blank; p. [466] (extreme right) 72 73 10 9 8 7 6 5 4 3 2 1

21·2 × 14·3 cm. Bulk: 3·4/4·0 cm. White wove paper; gold wove endpapers; trimmed. Bound in red cloth; front [lower right: stamped in gold, publisher's device]; back blank; spine [stamped in black and gold:] Dorothy L. Sayers | [gold rule] | [fat letters, top to bottom:] LORD PETER | [upright:] Harper & Row

Price: $10; number of copies not disclosed. Published January 1972. Dust jacket: white printed in red, black and gold with a small illustration of the Wimsey arms.

Contents: The Abominable History of the Man with Copper Fingers – The Entertaining Episode of the Article in Question – The Fascinating Problem of Uncle Meleager's Will – The Fantastic Horror of the Cat in the Bag – The Unprincipled Affair of the Practical Joker – The Undignified Melodrama of the Bone of Contention – The Vindictive Story of the Footsteps That Ran – The Bibulous Business of a Matter of Taste – The Learned Adventure of the Dragon's Head – The Piscatorial Farce of the Stolen Stomach – The Unsolved Puzzle of the Man with No Face – The Adventurous Exploit of the Cave of Ali Baba – The Image in the Mirror – The Incredible Elopement of Lord Peter Wimsey – The Queen's Square – The Necklace of Pearls – In the Teeth of the Evidence – Absolutely Elsewhere – Striding Folly – The Haunted Policeman – Coda: Sayers, Lord Peter and God, by Carolyn Heilbrun – Codetta: Greedy Night: A Parody, by E. C. Bentley.

Notes: "Sayers, Lord Peter and God" was first published in *The American Scholar* vol. 37, Spring 1968, pp. 324–330. "Greedy Night: A Parody" was first published in *Parody Party*, edited by Leonard Russell, London: Hutchinson, 1936, pp. 77–94; p. [76] is an illustration by Nicholas Bentley of Lord Peter and the Bishop of Glastonbury. For the printing history of the stories, see entries for each in this bibliography; consult the Index.

*b.*I. *Second edition* 1972:

[Title-page as A61*a*.]

> *Collation:* [A–Q]¹⁶ 256 leaves.
>
> pp. [i–iii] as A61*a*.; p. [iv] as A61*a*. but lacking "FIRST EDITION"; pp. [v]–430 as A61*a*.; pp. 431–453 text of "Talboys"; pp. 454–487 text as A61*a*. pp. 431–464; pp. [488–498] blank; p. [498] [lower right, bottom to top:] HB10E
>
> 21·2 × 14·3 cm. Bulk: 3·5/4·1 cm. Bound in gold cloth; front [lower right, stamped in red, publisher's device]; back blank; spine [printed in black and red: Dorothy L. Sayers | [red rule] | [fat letters, top to bottom:] LORD PETER | [upright:] Harper & Row
>
> *Price:* $12·50; number of copies not disclosed. Published 8 May 1972. Dust jacket: white printed in red, black and gold with a small illustration of the Wimsey Arms.
>
> *Notes:* This is apparently the first printing of "Talboys"; see notes to A62 regarding the publishing history of this story. The blurb inside the dust jacket and the Introduction (pp. vii–xii) are not revised to include "Talboys", the twenty-first story; the front and the back of the dust jacket announce a "never-before-published" story. The table of contents (p. v) is revised. This edition was also distributed by The Book-of-the-Month Club.

*b.*II. *Avon Books (New York) Flare paperback issue* December 1972: 487 pp.

> Text produced from A61*b.*I.
>
> *Translation:* German.

A62   TALBOYS   1972

TALBOYS | by Dorothy L. Sayers | HARPER & ROW, PUBLISH-ERS | New York [dot] Evanston [dot] San Francisco [dot] London

> *Collation:* 16 leaves staped at fold.

p. [1] [bold faced, very heavy type:] EXTRA! | [regular type:] A brand-new, long-lost Dorothy L. Sayers story | – about Lord Peter Wimsey and Harriet | and their three sons. | Just discovered! | Copyright © 1972 by Harper & Row, Publishers, Inc. | All rights reserved; p. [2] blank; p. [3] title-page; p. [4] blank; p. [5] PUBLISHER'S NOTE | All mystery fans will be delighted to learn that a new Lord Peter | Wimsey story – "Talboys," written in 1942 and never before in | print – has just been discovered by the author's heir. "Talboys" | will be included in the second edition of the recently published | collection in *Lord Peter* by Dorothy L. Sayers. Meantime, we have | rushed the story into print so that it will be available to all those | who wish to make their first edition copies of *Lord Peter* absolutely complete with every Wimsey story Dorothy L. Sayers | ever wrote.; p. [6] blank; pp. [7–29] (numbered 431–453) text; pp. [30–32] blank.

2·5 × 14·2 cm. Bulk: ·2 cm. White wove paper, trimmed. No endpapers, unbound.

Notes: This story, written in 1942 and discovered in 1961, was rejected in 1961 by three American magazines. The manuscript and the typescript are now held by the Marion E. Wade Collection (G7.77). The text of this pamphlet is numbered exactly as it appeared in the second edition of LORD PETER (A61*b*.1.). According to its publishers, the following are the circumstances of the publication of the story "Talboys": because it was not known to the publishers, it was not included in the first edition of LORD PETER (A61*a*.); it was therefore included in the second edition, which was published May 8, 1972; the pamphlet TALBOYS (A62) was "printed" after the second edition of LORD PETER (A61*b*.1.); a small number were printed in March, 1972, to give to persons who had bought the first edition and who requested the story. One must assume that the giving of the copies (its publication) occurred after the May 8, 1972, publication of the second edition of LORD PETER. The printing of both the pamphlet and the second edition would obviously precede publication; no evidence – from trade journals and the like – has been found to indicate that copies of the pamphlet were given away before the publication of the second edition of LORD PETER (A61*b*.1.). For the first English printing of "Talboys" see A32*h*.; see also A61 and A64.

A63   A MATTER OF ETERNITY   1973

a.1. *First edition:*

A MATTER | OF ETERNITY | SELECTIONS FROM THE WRITINGS OF | DOROTHY L. SAYERS | CHOSEN AND INTRODUCED BY | ROSAMOND KENT SPRAGUE | WILLIAM B. EERDMANS PUBLISHING COMPANY | GRAND RAPIDS, MICHIGAN

Collation: [A–C]¹⁶ [D]⁸ [E]¹⁶ 72 leaves.

p. [1] A MATTER | OF ETERNITY; p. [2] blank; p. [3] title-page; p. [4] copyright, rights reservation, ISBN number, printing notice, notice of British publication, copyright; [5] CONTENTS; p. [6] ACKNOWLEDGMENTS; p. [7] Five line quotation from THE EMPEROR CONSTANTINE; p. [8] blank; pp. 9–10 ABBREVIATIONS; pp. 11–14 INTRODUCTION; pp. 15–139 text, pp. [15, 21, 27, 31, 39, 47, 53, 59, 67, 71, 83, 89, 93, 97, 107, 137] section headings; pp. [26, 46, 79, 106, 136] blank; p. [140] Four line quotation from THE EMPEROR CONSTANTINE; pp. [141–144] blank.

21·2 × 12·3 cm. Bulk: 1·2/1·6 cm. White wove paper, trimmed; aqua end-papers. Bound in dark blue cloth, front and back blank; spine [stamped in gold, top to bottom:] SAYERS A MATTER OF ETERNITY EERD-MANS.

Price: $4.50; number of copies: 10,000. Published May 1973. Dust jacket: purple printed in white with magenta and gold decorations.

Notes: The blank p. [79] should have the section heading "Purgatory". This is the first book publication of the poem "For Timothy, in the Coinherence," (C195).

*a.*II. *English issue* 1973:

A MATTER | OF ETERNITY | SELECTIONS FROM THE WRITINGS OF | DOROTHY L. SAYERS | CHOSEN AND INTRODUCED BY | ROSAMOND KENT SPRAGUE | A. R. MOWBRAY & CO. LTD. | LONDON & OXFORD

Otherwise, as A63*a.*I., except as follows: spine of book and spine of dustwrapper "MOWBRAY" for "EERDMANS"; front fold of dustwrapper £1·75 for $4·50.

A64   STRIDING FOLLY   1973

Striding Folly | *including* | *three final Lord Peter Wimsey stories* | Dorothy L. Sayers | NEW ENGLISH LIBRARY | TIMES MIRROR

Collation: [1]⁸ 2–8⁸ [$1 signed] 64 leaves.

p. [1] STRIDING FOLLY; p. [2] advertisement; p. [3] title-page; p. [4] copyright, publication, conditions of sale, and publishers notice; p. [5] NOTE; p. [6] blank; p. [7] CONTENTS; p. [8] blank; pp. 9–31 INTRODUCTION; p. [32] blank; pp. 33–124 text, pp. [33, 57, 91] story title pages, pp. 34, 38, [40], 46, 49, 58, 67, 70, 92, 105, 124, full page illustrations without text, p. [90] blank; pp. [125–128] advertisements.

17·9 × 10·8 cm. Bulk: 1·0/1·1 cm. Cream wove paper; no endpapers; trimmed. Bound in illustrated paper covers.

Price: 30 pence; number of copies not disclosed. Published May 1973. Made and printed by Hunt Barnard Printing Ltd., Aylesbury, Bucks.

Contents: Striding Folly – The Haunted Policeman – Talboys.

Notes: Reprinted 1974, 1975, 1977. These stories are entered elsewhere in this bibliography; consult the Index. The introduction is by Janet Hitchman.

A65   WILKIE COLLINS: A CRITICAL AND   1977
BIOGRAPHICAL STUDY

Dorothy L. Sayers | WILKIE COLLINS | A CRITICAL AND BIOGRAPHICAL STUDY | *Edited from the Manuscript* | Humanities *Research Center* | *Austin, Texas* | *by* | E. R. Gregory | THE FRIENDS OF THE UNIVERSITY OF | TOLEDO LIBRARIES | 1977

Collation: 62 leaves, glued at spine.

p. [1] blank; p. [2] advertisement; p. [3] title-page; p. [4] copyright notices, Library of Congress data; pp. [5–6] PREFACE; pp. 7–24 INTRODUCTION; pp. 25–120 text; pp. [121–122] blank; p. [123] sketch of Sayers with a facsimile of her autograph; p. [124] DOROTHY L. SAYERS | WILKIE COLLINS | A CRITICAL AND BIOGRAPHICAL STUDY | WAS DESIGNED BY THOMAS DURNFORD | JOANNE JOYS AND SANDRA KEIL OF THE | UNIVERSITY OF TOLEDO PUBLICATIONS OFFICE | IT WAS SET IN 10 POINT SCHOOLBOOK BY | AMERICAN COMPOSITION OF TOLEDO, INC. | PRINTED IN SEPTEMBER 1977 ON 70 POUND | WARREN'S OLD STYLE BY | COMMERCIAL LITHOGRAPH, INC | OF LIMA, OHIO | AND PUBLISHED BY THE FRIENDS OF THE |UNIVERSITY OF TOLEDO LIBRARIES | IN OCTOBER 1977 IN AN | EDITION OF 1000 | NUMBERED | COPIES | THIS COPY NUMBER [handwritten in black on the copy examined:] 53

23 × 15 cm. Bulk: 1·0/1·2 cm. White wove paper; trimmed. No endpapers. Bound in white, stiff paper covers which fold inward, full page in size, front and back. The interior of the front fold has a 23 × 17·5 cm. reproduction in yellow and brown tones of a sketch of the child Collins by his father. The face of the child is visible through a 5·2 cm. cut-out circle, described below. On the fold (where usually the paste-down endpaper would be) there are printed biographical notes about Dorothy L. Sayers and E. R. Gregory. Back printed in black, right bottom corner: L1 157 877 11C; front [printed in black:] DOROTHY L. SAYERS | [5·2 cm. circle cut-out to reveal the face of the child Collins] | [bold italic:] *Wilkie Collins*; spine [printed in black, top to bottom:] DOROTHY L. SAYERS [bold italic:] *Wilkie Collins*

Price: $12·50; 1000 copies. Published September 1977.

Note: For information about Sayers' typescripts and manuscripts on Collins, see G5·2.

A66   THE WIMSEY FAMILY   1977

THE WIMSEY FAMILY | *A Fragmentary History* | *compiled from correspondence with* | DOROTHY L. SAYERS | by | C. W. SCOTT-GILES | *Fitzalan Pursuivant of Arms* | *Extraordinary* | [French rule] | LONDON | VICTOR GOLLANCZ LTD | 1977

Collation: [A–D]⁸ [E]⁴ [F]⁸ 44 leaves.
p. [1] THE WIMSEY FAMILY; p. [2] list of books by Sayers; p. [3] blank; p. [4] frontispiece; p. [5] title-page; p. [6] copyright, ISBN, and printer's notices; p. [7] CONTENTS; p. [8] blank; p. [9] ILLUSTRATIONS; p. [10] blank; p. [11] THE WIMSEY FAMILY; p. [12] blank; pp. [13]–88 text, pp. [13, 26, 31, 38, 45, 79] section title-pages with text, pp. [13], 34, 84, 85 illustrations with text, pp. [32, 36, 59], 63 full-page illustrations.

21·5 × 13·5 cm. Bulk: ·8/1·2 cm. White wove paper; gold wove endpapers illustrated in black with the Wimsey and the Vane coats of arms; trimmed. Bound in black cloth; front and back blank; spine [stamped in gold:] [top to bottom:] THE WIMSEY FAMILY C. W. SCOTT-GILES | [upright:] GOLLANCZ

Price: £2·95; number of copies not disclosed. Published 24 November 1977. Dust jacket: white printed in black, illustrated in color with the armorial bearings of the Wimsey family.

Notes: This investigation into the history of the Wimsey family, prepared by the noted expert in Heraldry, C. W. Scott-Giles, includes excerpts from Sayers' letters on the subject (dating from February 1936) published for the first time. (An earlier published account of Sayers' letters is Scott-Giles' article "On the Wimsey Heraldry", *Coat of Arms*, The Heraldry Society, vol. V, number 37, January 1959). Also published for the first time is "Songs for Voyce and Lute by Roger Wimsey". Reprinted are extracts from PAPERS RELATING TO THE FAMILY OF WIMSEY (A23) and AN ACCOUNT OF LORD MORTIMER WIMSEY (A27).

A67   EPHEMERA   1917–1949

The following list is obviously and necessarily incomplete. A great many items are presently in private collections. Sayers wrote and designed a number of cards which have not been available for examination.

A67.1   CHRISTMAS CARD–EPIPHANY HYMN   1917

Folded card; p. [1] printed in red and black, a quotation from Virgil (7 lines) and from The Bible, Luke x.24; p. [2] blank; p. [3] text, 20-line poem ("Lord Christ and have we found Thee then, / Desire of all the ages. . . . "); p. [4] blank.

A67.2   MUSTARD CLUB   1926–1930

THE | RECIPE-BOOK | OF THE | MUSTARD CLUB | *A Treasury of Delectable* | *Dishes both New and* | *Old, in the right tradition* | *of Good English Cookery,* | *edited by "Gourmet."* | *With illustrations by* | *J. Gilroy.* | [Mustard Club device and slogan] | Published for the Mustard Club by | J. & J. COLMAN LTD., Carrow Works, NORWICH

16 leaves staped at fold; enclosed in bright colored illustrated paper covers depicting officers of the Mustard Club; title of the pamphlet and "Rules of the Mustard Club" printed in black.

Notes: According to Colman's, Sayers prepared this book and a great deal of the copy for the Mustard Club advertising campaign while she was a copy-writer at S. H. Benson's. Many of the recipes in THE RECIPE-BOOK OF THE MUSTARD CLUB were concocted and "tested" by Sayers' husband, who wrote under the pseudonym "Gourmet" for the *Evening News* (London) and *The Sunday Chronicle* (London); he was also the author of *Gourmet's Book of Food and Drink*, London: John Lane, The Bodley Head, 1933. Other Mustard Club related items which have some Sayers' material are *The Adventures of the Mustard Club* and *The Secret History of the Mustard Club*, two booklets prepared by Robert Bevan, largely made up of advertising copy used in the Mustard Club campaign. *Mustard Uses Mustered*, prepared by unknown hands at Benson's for "the Baron de Beef", has material from THE RECIPE-BOOK OF THE MUSTARD CLUB as well as from advertising copy; there are also Mustard Club Menu Cards, a "Mustering the Mustard Club" card game, badges, and the like. Advertisements can be found from September 1926 to 1930 in *The Daily Mail* (London), *The Daily Sketch* (London), *The Liverpool Post* (Liverpool), and in other newspapers. Some of the original copy is held by Colman's at Carrow Works, Norwich.

A67.3   LORD, I THANK THEE

Dorothy [swash "D"] *L. Sayers* | LORD, I THANK THEE ... [ornament, in red] | *Printed at the Overbrook Press in* [swash "n"] | *Stamford*, Connecticut [swash final "t"] *January* [swash "J"] *mcmxliij*

> *Collation:* 10 leaves sewn at fold.
>
> pp. [1–4] blank; p. [5] title-page; p. [6] *Copyright, 1942, by Harper & Brothers* | *Reprinted with the permission of the publishers* | Printed in the United States of America; pp. [7–14] text with running title at top left of p. [7] printed in red: *Lord, I Thank Thee* [swash final "e"] and running title at the top of the outer margin of pp. [8–14] printed in red *Lord,* | *I Thank Thee* (swash final "e"]; p. [15] blank; p. [16] [in red:] *One Hundred Copies have been printed at* [swash "t"] | *The Overbrook Press in Stamford Connecticut January* [swash "J"] *mcmxliij*; pp. [17–20] blank.
>
> 21·5 × 14·8 cm. Bulk: ·15/·17 cm. Light blue laid paper; no endpapers; all edges trimmed. Cover made of heavy blue laid paper pasted over card. Back and spine blank; front [printed in red:] *Lord, I Thank Thee* [swash final "c"] | BY DOROTHY L. SAYERS | [ornament] | The Overbrook Press | Mcmliij

A67.4   AENEAS AT THE COURT OF DIDO   1945

[to the left:] AENEAS AT THE | COURT OF DIDO | [to the left:] BY DOROTHY L. SAYERS | CHRISTMAS, 1945

> *Collation:* 4 leaves stapled at fold.
>
> p. [1] title-page; p. [2] THE ARGUMENT; pp. [3–6] text (verse); pp. [7–8] blank.
>
> 18·4 × 12·5 cm. Bulk: ·1 cm. Cream laid paper; no endpapers; trimmed. Privately printed as a Christmas card 1945.

A67.5   THE HEART OF STONE   1946

[cover:] THE HEART OF STONE | BEING THE FOUR *CAN-ZONI* | OF THE "PIETRA" GROUP, | DONE INTO ENGLISH BY | DOROTHY L. SAYERS | FROM THE ITALIAN OF | DANTE ALIGHIERI | (1265–1321) | WOOD ENGRAVINGS BY | NORAH LAMBOURNE

> *Collation:* 8 leaves.
>
> p. [1] CHRISTMAS 1946 | [woodcut] | THE HEART OF STONE | DANTE

ALIGHIERI; p. [2] prefatory note; pp. [3–13] text; pp. [14–16] OF THE
CANZONE [three pages of text, with woodcut and printer's colophon at
the bottom of p. 16:] PRINTED FOR D. L. SAYERS | AND N. LAM-
BOURNE | BY J. H. CLARKE & CO. | WITHAM, ESSEX, MCXLV
Privately printed as a Christmas card.

A67.6   A CAT'S CHRISTMAS CAROL   1947

[to the left:] A CAT'S CHRISTMAS | CAROL | [centered:] Verses
by DOROTHY L. SAYERS | Lino-cuts by NORAH LAM-
BOURNE

Collation: 4 leaves stapled at fold.
p. [1] title-page; pp. [2–7] text, with lino-cuts 10×7·3 cm. in two colors and
black and white on each page; p. [8] blank.

21·5×13·7 cm. Bulk: ·1 cm. Cream wove paper; no endpapers or covers;
trimmed. The pages of text begin with rubrics of differing colors. Privately
printed as a Christmas card.

A67.7   COUSIN PARKER'S   [circa 1947]
              CHRISTMAS CARD

Folded card: p. [1] [photograph of a cat] | Christmas Greetings; p. [2] blank;
p. [3] printed greetings and Sayers' autograph "To Cousin Parker" and her
five cats' "signatures" in a mannered hand.

A67.8   FROM THE CATALECTS OF   [circa 1948]
              PUSSIUS CATUS I.

Folded card: p. [1] lino-cut of a cat on a brick wall; p. [2] lower left corner:
LINO CUT & VERSE BY D. L. S.; p. [3] eight lines of verse ("I often think
that men would be...."); p. [4] blank.

A67.9   FROM THE CATALECTS OF PUSSIUS   [1948]
              CATUS II.

Folded Christmas card: p. [1] photograph of Sayers and "Fatima", a pig; p. [2]
blank; p. [3] 13 lines of verse ("This is our yard and in it stands..."); p. [4]
blank.

ST. BERNARD'S HYMN | TO THE BLESSED VIRGIN | in the
Rose of Paradise | [left:] translated by | DOROTHY L. SAYERS |
from the Italian of | DANTE ALIGHIERI | CHRISTMAS 1949

Collation: folded card: p. [1] title-page; p. [2] blank; p. [3] text; p. [4] blank.
20 × 12·8 cm. Bulk: ·05 cm. Heavy, cream wove paper; no endpapers or covers;
untrimmed.
Privately issued as a Christmas card 1949; the verses are from *Paradiso* XXXIII,
1–21 (see A58).

B

CONTRIBUTIONS TO BOOKS, PAMPHLETS, AND MISCELLANEA

B1 OXFORD POETRY 1915 1915

OXFORD POETRY | 1915 | EDITED BY | G. D. H. C. AND T. W. E. | OXFORD | B. H. BLACKWELL, BROAD STREET | 1915

Collation: [π]⁴ 1–4⁸ 5⁴ [$1 signed] 40 leaves.
p. [i] OXFORD POETRY | 1915; p. [ii] printer's notice; p. [iii] title page; p. [iv] blank; pp. v–[vii] CONTENTS; p. viii acknowledgements; pp. 1–[72] text with printer's notice at the bottom of p. [72].

19·5 × 12·5 cm. Bulk: ·7 cm. White laid paper; untrimmed; no endpapers. Heavy dark blue paper covers. Back blank; front [6·1 × 4·3 cm. white label printed in blue within single rules:] Oxford Poetry | 1915 | [Gothic:] Oxford | B. H. Blackwell; spine [·3 × 6 cm. white label, printed in blue, bottom to top:] Oxford Poetry 1915. Variant binding: quarter "parchment"; boards in dark blue paper; labels as described above. Bulk: ·7/1·2 cm. White wove endpapers.

Price: 2s6d parchment, 1s paper; number of copies not recorded. Published December 1915.
Printed by Billing and Sons Ltd., Guildford.

Notes: Sayers' contribution is "Lay" (pp. 50–57). OXFORD POETRY 1914–1916, published in 1917, includes Sayers' poem "Lay" from OXFORD POETRY 1915.

B2 OXFORD POETRY 1917 1918

OXFORD POETRY | 1917 | EDITED BY | W. R. C., T. W. E., AND D. L. S. | OXFORD | B. H. BLACKWELL, BROAD STREET | 1917

Collation: [1]⁸ 2–4⁸ [$1 signed]; 32 leaves.

p. [i] title page; p. [ii] list of Oxford Poetry Series, New York agents; pp. iii–iv CONTENTS; pp. 1–[60] text with printer's notice at the bottom of p. [60].

19·5 × 12·5 cm. Bulk: ·5 cm. White wove paper; no endpapers; untrimmed. Bound in heavy dark blue papers covers. Back blank; front [6·1 × 4·3 cm. white label printed in blue within single rules:] *Oxford | Poetry | 1917 | [leaf] | OXFORD | BLACKWELL*; spine [·3 × 6 cm. white label, printed in blue, bottom to top:] [rule] *Oxford Poetry 1917* [rule]

Price: 2s6d parchment, 1s3d paper; number of copies: 1,000. Published 11 March 1918.

Printed by Billing and Sons Ltd., Guildford.

Notes: Sayers' contribution is "Fair Erembours" (pp. 52–53).

B3   OXFORD POETRY 1918   1918

OXFORD POETRY | 1918 | EDITED BY | T. W. E., E. F. A. G. AND D. L. S. | OXFORD | B. H. BLACKWELL, BROAD STREET | 1918

Collation: [1]⁸ 2–4⁸ [$1 signed] 32 leaves.

p. [i] OXFORD POETRY | 1918; p. [ii] publisher's New York agent listed; p. [iii] title-page; p. [iv] blank; pp. v–vi CONTENTS; pp. 1–[56] text with pp. [35, 56] unnumbered; pp. [57–58] advertisements.

19·4 × 12·4 cm. Bulk: ·6/·7 cm. Cream wove paper; untrimmed. Bound in dark blue paper covers; back blank; front [6·1 × 4·3 cm. white label, printed in blue:] *Oxford | Poetry | 1918 | [leaf] | OXFORD | BLACKWELL*; spine [·3 × 6 cm. white label, printed in blue, bottom to top:] [rule] *Oxford Poetry 1918* [rule]

Price: 2s6d parchment; 1s6d paper; number of copies: 2,000. Published 14 November 1918.

Printed by Billing and Sons Ltd., Guildford.

Notes: Sayers' contribution is "Pygmalion" (pp. 46–48). Page number, p. 26, type damaged; p. 27 is numbered "2" on some copies.

B4   THE NEW DECAMERON VOLUME I   1919

*a.*1. *First edition:*

THE NEW DECAMERON | VOLUME THE FIRST, CON-

TAINING | THE PROLOGUE & THE FIRST DAY | OXFORD
B. H. BLACKWELL, BROAD STREET | 1919

Collation: [A]⁴ B–P⁸ Q² [$1 signed] 118 leaves.
pp. [2] blank; p. [i] THE NEW DECAMERON; p. [ii] blank; p. [iii] title-
page; p. [iv] printer's notice; p. v CONTENTS; p. [vi] blank; p. [1] advertisement for Turpin's Tempermental Tours; pp. 2–225 text; p. [226] blank;
pp. 227–[228] BIBLIOGRAPHY with printer's notice at the bottom of p.
[228].

19·2 × 12·7 cm. Bulk: 2·8/3·3 cm. White, heavy, laid paper; untrimmed.
Slate-blue endpapers illustrated in dark blue with sketches of the travellers.
Quarter-bound in tan cloth, slate-blue cloth on boards; front and back blank;
spine [white label, printed in dark blue:] THE NEW [leaf] | DECAMERON
| [leaf] | THE PROLOGUE | AND FIRST DAY

Price: 6s; number of copies: 2,000. Published 12 June 1919.
Printed by Hazell, Watson & Viney, Ltd., London and Aylesbury.

Notes: Sayers contribution is "The Priest's Tale: The Journeyman" (pp.
25–28).

*a.*II. *American issue 1919:*

THE NEW DECAMERON | VOLUME THE FIRST, CON-
TAINING | THE PROLOGUE & THE FIRST DAY | [publisher's
device] | NEW YORK | ROBERT M. McBRIDE & CO. | 1919

Collation and pagination as B4*a.*I.; except for publisher's device and imprint
on the title-page.

19·0 × 13·0 cm. Bulk: 1·8/2·2 cm. White wove paper, untrimmed. Grey endpapers with drawings of the travellers. Bound in tan cloth; front and back
blank; spine [5·7 × 2·5 cm. label printed in black:] | [rule] | THE NEW [leaf]
| DECAMERON | [leaf with tendril] | THE PROLOGUE | AND FIRST
DAY | [rule]

Price: $1·60; number of copies not known. Published October 1919.

Notes: Sayers' contribution is "The Priest's Tale: The Journeyman" (pp. 25–
28). The text and endpapers produced from B4*a.*I.

B5   OXFORD POETRY 1919   1919

OXFORD POETRY | 1919 | EDITED BY | T. W. E., D. L. S.,
AND S. S. | OXFORD | B. H. BLACKWELL, BROAD STREET
| 1920

Collation: [1]^8 2–4^8 5^2 [$1 signed] 34 leaves.

p. [i] OXFORD POETRY | 1919; p. [ii] list of Oxford Poetry series; p. [iii] title-page; p. [iv] acknowledgements; pp. v–vi CONTENTS; pp. 1–[62] text with printer's notice at the bottom of p. [62].

19·5 × 12·5 cm. Bulk: ·6 cm. White wove paper; no endpapers; untrimmed. Bound in heavy, dark blue paper covers. Back blank; front [6·1 × 4·2 cm. white label, printed in aqua within single rules:] OXFORD | POETRY | 1919 | [leaf] | OXFORD | BLACKWELL; spine [·3 × 6 cm. white label, printed in aqua, bottom to top:] OXFORD POETRY [leaf] 1919

Price: 3s parchment; 1s6d paper; number of copies: 2,000. Published 24 December 1919.
Printed by Billing and Sons Ltd., Guildford.

Notes: Sayers' contributions are "For Phaon" (p. 50), "Sympathy" (p. 51), "Vials Full of Odours" (p. 52). Erratum slip tipped in between pp. 6–7. Some labels printed in grey. "Vials Full of Odours" was reprinted as "The Bean Flower," set to music by E. J. Moeran, published by J. & W. Chester Ltd., London, 1924. OXFORD POETRY 1917–1919, published in 1920, contains the poems by Sayers published in the 1917, 1918, and 1919 volumes.

B6   THE NEW DECAMERON VOLUME II   1920

a.1. First edition:

THE NEW DECAMERON | VOLUME THE SECOND, CON-
TAINING | THE SECOND DAY | OXFORD | BASIL BLACK-
WELL | 1920

Collation: [A]^4 B–M^8 N^4 [$1 signed] 96 leaves.
pp. [2] blank; p. [i] THE NEW DECAMERON; p. [ii] blank; p. [iii] title-page, p. [iv] printer's notice; pp. v–vi CONTENTS; pp. [1]–183 text; p. [184] PRESS OPINIONS OF THE "FIRST DAY".

19·2 × 12·7 cm. Bulk: 2·2/2·6 cm. White, heavy, laid paper; untrimmed. Slate-blue endpapers illustrated in dark blue with sketches of the travellers. Quarter bound in tan cloth, slate-blue cloth on boards; front and back blank; spine [white label, printed in dark blue:] THE NEW [leaf] | DECAMERON | [leaf] | THE SECOND DAY

Price: 6s; number of copies not known. Published May 1920.
Printed by Hazell, Watson & Viney Ltd., London and Aylesbury.

Notes: Sayers' contribution is "The Priest's Second Tale: The Master-Thief" (pp. 76–81). Volumes III–VI do not contain contributions by Sayers.

THE NEW DECAMERON | VOLUME THE SECOND, CON-
TAINING | THE SECOND DAY | [publisher's device] | NEW
YORK | ROBERT M. McBRIDE & CO. | 1920

Collation: [A]$^{4(\pm 1)}$ B–M^8 N^4 [$1 signed] 96 leaves.
p. [i] THE NEW DECAMERON; p. [ii] blank; p. [iii] title-page; p. [iv]
blank; pp. v–vi CONTENTS; pp. [1]–183 text; p. [184] PRESS OPINIONS
OF THE "FIRST DAY"; pp. [185–186] blank.

19·0 × 13·0 cm. Bulk: 2·0/2·4 cm. White wove paper, untrimmed. Grey endpapers with drawings of the travellers. Bound in tan cloth; front and back
blank; spine [5·6 × 2·7 cm. white label printed in brown:] [rule] | THE NEW
[leaf] | DECAMERON | [leaf with tendril] | THE SECOND DAY | [rule]

Price: $1·90; number of copies not known. Published November 1920. Dust
jacket: light orange printed in green.

Notes: Sayers' contribution is "The Priest's Second Tale: The Master-Thief"
(pp. 76–81). The text and endpapers produced from B6*a*.I.

B7   MY BEST DETECTIVE STORY   1931

MY BEST | DETECTIVE STORY | [star] | AN ANTHOLOGY
OF STORIES | CHOSEN BY | THEIR OWN AUTHORS |
LONDON | FABER & FABER LIMITED | 24 RUSSELL
SQUARE

Collation: [A]^{16} B–P^{16} Q^6 [$1 signed] 246 leaves.
p. [1] MY BEST DETECTIVE STORY; p. [2] blank; p. [3] title-page; p. [4]
publication, publisher's, printer's notices, rights reservation; p. [5] PUB-
LISHER'S NOTE; p. [6] blank; p. [7] CONTENTS; p. [8] blank; pp. 9–491
text; p. [492] blank.

19 × 12 cm. Bulk: 2·7/3·3 cm. White wove paper; white wove endpapers;
trimmed; top edge red. Bound in black smooth cloth; front and back blank;
spine [stamped in gold:] [triple rule] | MY BEST | DETECTIVE | STORY
| *BERTRAM ATKEY* | *H. C. BAILEY* | *J. J. BELL* | *J. D. BERESFORD*
| *ERNEST BRAMAH* | *THOMAS BURKE* | *G. K. CHESTERTON* |
AGATHA CHRISTIE | *FREEMAN WILLS CROFTS* | *JOHN FERGU-
SON* | *J. S. FLETCHER* | *GILBERT FRANKAU* | *R. AUSTIN FREE-
MAN* | *IAN HAY* | *FATHER RONALD KNOX* | *Mrs. BELLOC LOWN-
DES* | *G. R. MALLOCH* | *E. PHILLIPS OPPENHEIM* | *"SAPPER"* |
DOROTHY L. SAYERS | *H. DE VERE STACPOOLE* | *H. A. VACHELL*

| FABER & FABER | [triple rule]; variant binding: top edge white; spine stamped in red.

Price: 7s6d; number of copies not known. Published September 1931. Printed by Latimer Trend & Co. Ltd., Plymouth.

Notes: Sayers' contribution is "The Inspiration of Mr. Budd" (pp. 41–55), which appeared later in IN THE TEETH OF THE EVIDENCE. (A32).

B8 THE MERCURY BOOK OF VERSE 1931

THE MERCURY | BOOK OF VERSE | Being a Selection of Poems published | in *The London Mercury*, 1919–1930 | WITH AN INTRODUCTION BY | SIR HENRY NEWBOLT | MACMIL-LAN AND CO., LIMITED | ST. MARTIN'S STREET, LONDON | 1931

Collation: [A]⁸ B–S⁸ T⁶ [$1 signed] 150 leaves.
p. [i] THE MERCURY | BOOK OF VERSE; p. [ii] list of Macmillan agents; p. [iii] title-page; p. [iv] "ACKNOWLEDGEMENT," copyright and printer's notices; pp. v–vi INTRODUCTION; pp. vii–xv CONTENTS; p. [xvi] blank; pp. 1–282 text; p. [283] text and printer's notice; p. [284] blank.

19·8 × 13·0 cm. Bulk: 2·0/2·5 cm. White wove paper; trimmed; top edge red; white wove endpapers. Bound in red cloth; back blank; front [center, stamped in gold:] [publisher's device]; spine [stamped in gold:] THE | MERCURY | BOOK OF | VERSE | [solid circle] | With an | Introduction by | SIR HENRY | NEWBOLT | MACMILLAN

Price: 7s6d; number of copies not known. Published May 1931.

Notes: Sayers' contribution "The Poem" (p. 227) which was first published in *The London Mercury* October 1921 (C32), was also printed in *Younger Poets of Today* selected by J. C. Squire, London: Martin Secker, 1932.

B9 MANY MYSTERIES 1933

MANY | MYSTERIES | Selected by | E. PHILLIPS OPPENHEIM | 1933 | RICH & COWAN, LIMITED | MAIDEN LANE, STRAND | LONDON

Collation: [π]⁴ 1–29¹⁶ 30⁴ [$1, 5 signed] 472 leaves.
p. [i] MANY MYSTERIES; p. [ii] claim regarding fictitiousness; p. [iii]

title-page; p. [iv] publication and printer's notices; pp. v–vi FOREWORD; pp. vii–viii CONTENTS; pp. [1]–935 text, pp. [1, 35, 67, 103, 149, 167, 191, 225, 273, 345, 373, 397, 423, 455, 483, 509, 543, 581, 619, 655, 691, 703, 737, 765, 795, 827, 857, 895] story title-pages, pp. [2, 36, 68, 102, 104, 148, 150, 166, 168, 190, 192, 226, 274, 346, 374, 396, 398, 424, 454, 456, 484, 508, 510, 542, 544, 582, 618, 620, 654, 656, 690, 692, 702, 704, 738, 764, 766, 796, 828, 858, 894, 896] blank; p. [936] blank.

18·2 × 12 cm. Bulk: 3·2/3·5 cm. Cream wove paper; trimmed; cream wove endpapers. Bound in magenta cloth; front and back blank; spine [stamped in aqua:] MANY | MYSTERIES | SELECTED BY | E. PHILLIPS | OPPENHEIM | RICH & COWAN

Price: 7s6d; number of copies not known. Published May 1933. Made and printed by Hazell, Watson and Viney, Ltd., London and Aylesbury.

Notes: Sayers' contribution "The Man Who Knew How" (pp. 737–763) was simultaneously printed in HANGMAN'S HOLIDAY (A18).

B10   MY BEST STORY SECOND SERIES   1933

MY BEST STORY | *SECOND SERIES* | [two stars] | AN ANTHOLOGY OF STORIES | CHOSEN BY | THEIR OWN AUTHORS | LONDON | FABER & FABER LIMITED | 24 RUSSELL SQUARE

Collation: [A]¹⁶ B–P¹⁶ Q¹² [$1 signed, Q3 signed Q★] 252 leaves.
p. [1] MY BEST STORY | *SECOND SERIES*; p. [2] blank; p. [3] title-page; p. [4] publication, publisher's and printer's notices; p. 7 CONTENTS: p. [8] blank; pp. 9–502 text; pp. [503–504] blank.

18·5 × 12·2 cm. Bulk: 2·7/3 cm. Cream wove paper; trimmed; cream wove endpapers. Bound in magenta cloth; front and back blank; spine [stamped yellow:] MY BEST | STORY | second series | E. F. BENSON | STELLA BENSON | G. A. BIRMINGHAM | A. BLACKWOOD | ERNEST BRAMAH | A. E. COPPARD | CLEMENCE DANE | WALTER DE LA MARE | LORD DUNSANY | JOHN GALSWORTHY | DAVID GARNETT | IAN HAY | ROBERT HICHENS | W. W. JACOBS | MARGARET KENNEDY | ERIC LINKLATER | W. B. MAXWELL | LEONARD MERRICK | GEOFFREY MOSS | J. B. PRIESTLEY | DOROTHY SAYERS | G. B. STERN | HENRY WILLIAMSON | FABER AND | FABER

Price: 7s6d; number of copies not known. Published June 1933.
Printed by Latimer Trend & Co., Plymouth.

141

Notes: Sayers' contribution, "The Fountain Plays" (pp. 455–470), was to have appeared first in this anthology and then in HAMGMAN'S HOLIDAY (A18), but publication delays reversed the order by one month.

B11 MY BEST THRILLER 1933

MY BEST THRILLER | [star] | AN ANTHOLOGY OF STORIES | CHOSEN BY | THEIR OWN AUTHORS | LONDON | FABER & FABER LIMITED | 24 RUSSELL SQUARE

Collation: [A]^{16} B–P^{16} Q^8 [$1 signed] 248 leaves.
p. [1] MY BEST THRILLER; p. [2] list of similar anthologies; p. [3] title-page; p. [4] publication notice, publisher's and printer's notices; rights reservation; p. [5] PUBLISHER'S NOTE; p. [6] blank; pp. 7–8 CONTENTS; pp. 9–492 text; pp. [493–496] blank.

19 × 12·2 cm. Bulk: 3·4/3·7 cm. White wove paper; white wove endpapers; trimmed. Bound in black cloth; front and back blank; spine [stamped in gold:] [triple rule] | MY | BEST | THRILLER | F. Britten Austin | Francis Beeding | J. D. Beresford | Victor Bridges | Thomas Burke | Agatha Christie | J. J. Farjeon | Bruce Graeme | Sydney Horler | F. Tennyson Jesse | G. R. Mallock | A. E. W. Mason | Elinor Mordaunt | E. Phillips Oppenheim | Baroness Orczy | Max Pemberton | J. B. Priestly | Sax Rohmer | 'Sapper' | Dorothy L. Sayers | Andrew Soutar | J. C. Squire | H. de V. Stacpoole | H. A. Vachell | David Whitelaw | Valentine Williams | FABER AND | FABER | [triple rule]

Price: 7s6d; number of copies not known. Published September 1933.
Printed by Latimer Trend & Co., Plymouth.

Notes: Sayers' contribution is "The Cyprian Cat" (pp. 366–380), which later appeared in IN THE TEETH OF THE EVIDENCE (A32).

B12 BAKER-STREET STUDIES 1934

BAKER-STREET | STUDIES | *Edited by H. W. Bell* | [rule] | DOROTHY L. SAYERS | HELEN SIMPSON | VERNON RENDALL | VINCENT STARRETT | RONALD A. KNOX | A. G. MACDONELL | S. C. ROBERTS | H. W. BELL | [rule] | CONSTABLE & CO LTD. | 1934

Collation: [A]^4 b^1 B–P^8 [$1, 2 signed] 117 leaves.
p. [i] BAKER-STREET STUDIES; p. [ii] advertisement, *Sherlock Holmes*

and Doctor Watson by H. W. Bell including a comment by Sayers; p. [iii] title-page; p. [iv] publisher's notices, printer's notice; p. v CONTENTS; p. [vi] blank; pp. vii–ix INTRODUCTORY NOTE; p. x EXPLANATION; pp. 1–223 text with pp. 1, 35, 63, 85, 131, 159, 177, 201 section headings; pp. [2, 36, 62, 64, 86, 132, 160, 176, 178, 200, 202] blank; p. [224] blank.

18·8 × 12·4 cm. Bulk: 2·6/3·0 cm. White wove paper; white wove endpapers; trimmed; top edge green. Bound in brown cloth; front and back blank; spine [stamped in gold:] BAKER | STREET | STUDIES | [rule] | edited by | H. W. Bell | [rule] | Constable

Price: 7s6d; number of copies not known. Published 26 July 1934.

Notes: Sayers' contribution is "Holmes' College Career" (pp. 1–34), which was later published in UNPOPULAR OPINIONS (A43).

B13   NINE O'CLOCK STORIES   1934

NINE O'CLOCK | STORIES | By | FOURTEEN AUTHORS | LONDON | G. BELL & SONS LTD | 1934

Collation: [A]⁸ B–P⁸ [$1 signed] 120 leaves.
p. [1] NINE O'CLOCK STORIES; p. [2] blank; p. [3] title-page; p. [4] printer's notice; p. [5] CONTENTS; p. [6] blank; p. [7] *Most of the stories in this book | were broadcast by the B.B.C.*; p. [8] blank; pp. [9]–240 text with pp. [9, 25, 41, 57, 69, 81, 101, 119, 137, 151, 171, 187, 205, 221] story title pages; pp. [10, 24, 26, 42, 56, 58, 70, 80, 82, 100, 102, 120, 136, 138, 152, 172, 186, 188, 204, 206, 220, 222] blank.

19 × 12·2 cm. Bulk: 2·0/2·5 cm. White wove paper; trimmed; white wove endpapers. Bound in yellow cloth; front and back blank; spine [stamped in black:] Nine | o'Clock | Stories | [clock design] | by | Fourteen | Authors | BELL

Price: 6s; number of copies not known. Published October 1934.
Printed by The Camelot Press Ltd., London and Southampton.

Notes: Sayers' contribution "Dilemma" (pp. 187–203) was broadcast 6 April 1934 on BBC (E9). It was later published in IN THE TEETH OF THE EVI-DENCE (A32).

B14   BEST CRIME STORIES   1934

BEST | CRIME STORIES | [star] | LONDON | FABER & FABER LIMITED | 24 RUSSELL SQUARE

Collation: [A]¹⁶ B–P¹⁶ 240 leaves.

p. [1] BEST CRIME STORIES; p. [2] list of similar anthologies; p. [3] title-page; p. [4] publication, publisher's, and printer's notices, rights reservation; pp. 5–6 CONTENTS with PUBLISHER'S NOTE on p. 6; pp. 7–480 text.

18·6 × 12·4 cm. Bulk: 3·0/3·5 cm. White wove paper; trimmed; white wove endpapers. Bound in black cloth; front and back blank; spine [stamped in yellow:] Best | Crime | Stories | [solid circle] | H. C. Bailey | Oliver Baldwin | H. Bousfield | Clive Burnley | Leslie Charteris | Agatha Christie | Hylton Cleaver | W. C. Wilson | Vincent Cornier | W. A. Darlington | H. de V. Stacpoole | Van Harrison | E. P. Oppenheim | Stephen Phillips | D. L. Sayers | David Sharp | Margery Sharp | T. Topham | Edgar Wallace | Faber | and Faber

Price: 7s6d; number of copies not known. Published October 1934. Dust jacket: dark blue printed in orange and illustrated in green, purple, and yellow by James E. McConnell.
Printed by Latimer Trend and Co., Plymouth.

Notes: Sayers' contribution is "Absolutely Elsewhere" (pp. 385–404), which later appeared in IN THE TEETH OF THE EVIDENCE (A32).

B15   GREAT UNSOLVED CRIMES   [1935]

a. First edition:

GREAT UNSOLVED CRIMES | [French rule] | *Contributors* | A. J. ALAN | ANTHONY ARMSTRONG | MARTIN ARM-STRONG | J. D. BERESFORD | ANTHONY BERKELEY | EX-CHIEF INSPECTOR BERRETT | GERALD BULLETT | MARGARET COLE | EX-SUPERINTENDENT CHARLES COOPER | EX-SUPERINTENDENT CORNISH | FREEMAN WILLS CROFTS | A. J. CRONIN | DR. HAROLD DEARDEN | E. M. DELAFIELD | J. JEFFERSON FARJEON | J. S. FLETCHER | R. AUSTIN FREEMAN | VAL GIELGUD | EX-CHIEF IN-SPECTOR WILLIAM GOUGH | LEONARD R. GRIBBLE | FRANCIS D. GRIERSON | 72 | *Illustrations* | HUTCHINSON & CO. (*Publishers*) *Ltd.* | [French rule] | London
[Second title-page:] GREAT UNSOLVED CRIMES | [French rule] | *Contributors* | (*cont.*) PERCY HOSKINS | FRANCIS ILES | F. TENNYSON JESSE | MILWARD KENNEDY | MRS. BELLOC LOWNDES | ANTONY MARSDEN | HON. H.

FLETCHER MOULTON | HELENA NORMANTON | EX-SUPERINTENDENT JOHN PROTHERO | C. E. BECHHOFER ROBERTS | EX-SUPERINTENDENT PERCY SAVAGE | DOROTHY L. SAYERS | EDWARD SHANKS | HELEN SIMPSON | G. B. STERN | L. A. G. STRONG | SIR BASIL THOMSON | RUSSELL THORNDIKE | HENRY WADE | H. RUSSELL WAKEFIELD | CLENNEL WILKINSON

Collation: [A]⁸ B–Y⁸ [$1 signed] 176 leaves.
p. [1] GREAT UNSOLVED CRIMES | [French rule]; p. [2] title-page; p. [3] second title-page; p. [4] printer's notice; pp. 5–7 CONTENTS; pp. 8–10 ILLUSTRATIONS; pp.11–351 text, *inset*: 32 illustrations; p. [352] blank; 48 pages of advertisements inserted.

18·4×12 cm. Bulk: 4·1/4·4 cm. White wove paper; white wove endpapers; trimmed. Bound in black cloth; front [stamped in yellow:] GREAT UN-SOLVED | CRIMES; spine [stamped in yellow:] GREAT | UNSOLVED | CRIMES | HUTCHINSON. Variant binding: Bulk: 3·5/3·9. White wove paper; white wove endpapers. Bound in red-brown cloth: back blank; front [stamped in black:] GREAT UNSOLVED | CRIMES; spine [stamped in black:] GREAT | UNSOLVED | CRIMES | HUTCHINSON

Price: 8s6d; number of copies not known. Published 12 April 1935. Dust jacket printed in red and black.
Printed at the Mayflower Press, Plymouth, by William Brendon & Son Ltd.

Notes: Sayers' contribution is "The Murder of Julia Wallace" (pp. 111–122), which first appeared in *The Evening Standard* (C55) and which with added detail was later published in THE ANATOMY OF MURDER (B18). The variant binding has 16 rather than 48 pages of advertisements inserted.

b. Hutchinson Pocket Library Edition No. 10 1938: 252 pp.

B16   WRITING FOR THE PRESS   1935

WRITING FOR | THE PRESS | By | LEONARD RUSSELL | A. & C. BLACK, LTD. | 4, 5 & 6 Soho Square, London, W. I. | 1935

Collation: [A]⁸ B–K⁸ [$1 signed] 80 leaves.
p. [i] WRITING FOR THE PRESS; p. [ii] list of books in Writers' and Artists' Library; p. [iii] title-page; p. [iv] printer's notice; p. [v] dedication; p. [vi] blank; pp. vii–x CONTENTS; pp. [1]–150 text, with pp. [1, 105] section headings, pp. [2, 106] blank.

18·5 × 12·4 cm. Bulk: 2·0/2·4 cm. White wove paper; white wove endpapers; trimmed. Bound in green cloth; back blank; front [top, stamped in black:] [Writers' and Artists' Library device]; spine [stamped in black:] WRITING | FOR THE | PRESS | [leaf] | LEONARD | RUSSELL | A. & C. BLACK; variant binding: light blue stamped in red.

Price: 3s6d; number of copies not known. Published 6 September 1935.

Notes: Sayers' contribution is "The King's English" (pp. 88–104), which was first published in Nash's *Pall Mall Magazine*, 1935 (C56). It was published without the "twelve treasons" in UNPOPULAR OPINIONS (A43) as "The English Language." †Issued in America by Macmillan (New York), 1935.

B17   SIX AGAINST THE YARD   1936

a. First edition:

[rule] | SIX AGAINST THE YARD | [rule] | *In Which* | Margery Allingham | Anthony Berkeley | Freeman Wills Crofts | Father Ronald Knox | Dorothy L. Sayers | Russell Thorndike | *Commit the Crime of Murder which* | Ex-Superintendent | Cornish, C. I. D. | *is called upon to solve* | [rule] | SELWYN & BLOUNT, PATERNOSTER HOUSE, | PATERNOSTER ROW – LONDON, E. C. 4 | [rule]

Collation: [A]⁸ B–S⁸ [$1 signed] 144 leaves.
p. [1] blurb for *Six Against the Yard*; p. [2] blank; p. [3] title-page; p. [4] printer's notice; p. [5] CONTENTS; p. [6] blank; pp. 7–288 text; *inset:* 32 page Selwyn and Blount 1936 Spring list.

18·5 × 13 cm. Bulk: 3/3·5 cm. White wove paper; white wove endpapers; trimmed. Bound in salmon colored cloth; front and back blank; spine [stamped in black:] SIX | AGAINST | THE YARD | [solid square] | Margery | AL-LINGHAM | Anthony | BERKELEY | Freeman Wills | CROFTS | Ronald | KNOX | Dorothy L. | SAYERS | Russell | THORNDIKE | *Versus* | Ex-Supt. | CORNISH | of the | C.I.D. | [solid square] | SELWYN & BLOUNT

Price: 7s6d; number of copies not known. Published June 1936.

Notes: Sayers' contribution is "Blood Sacrifice" (pp. 197–233), which was first published in *The London Daily Mail* (C63) and later appeared in IN THE TEETH OF THE EVIDENCE (A32).

†*b*.1. *First American edition* 1936: SIX AGAINST SCOTLAND YARD. New York: Doubleday, Doran, vi, 302 pp.; $2.

Printed at the Country Life Press, Garden City, New York.

b.11. *Sun Dial (Garden City) issue* 1937:

[outline letters:] SIX AGAINST | SCOTLAND | YARD | *In which* | MARGERY ALLINGHAM | ANTHONY BERKELEY | FREEMAN WILLS CROFTS | FATHER RONALD KNOX | DOROTHY L. SAYERS | RUSSELL THORNDIKE | *Commit the Crime of Murder Which* | EX-SUPERINTENDENT CORNISH, C.I.D. | *Is called Upon to Solve* | [publisher's device] | [rule] | THE SUN DIAL PRESS, INC. | Garden City New York

Collation: [A–R]⁸ [S]¹² [T]⁸ 156 leaves.
pp. [2] blank; p. [3] blurb; p. [4] blank; p. [i] Six Against Scotland Yard; p. [ii] blank; p. [iii] title-page; p. [iv] printer's, publisher's, copyright, and rights reservation notices; pp. v–vi *Contents*; pp. [1]–302 text with pp. [1, 41, 51, 89, 103, 145, 155, 195, 205, 243, 251, 289] story title-pages and pp. [2, 42, 52, 90, 102, 104, 144, 146, 156, 196, 204, 206, 244, 252, 288, 290] blank.

19 × 13 cm. Bulk: 2·7/3·2 cm. White wove paper; buff wove endpapers, untrimmed; top edge red. Bound in red cloth; back and front blank; spine [stamped in black:] SIX | AGAINST | [top to bottom:] SCOTLAND YARD | [upright:] [illustration of Scotland Yard] | [publisher's device, with letters in red:] SUN DIAL | MYSTERIES

Price: 69 cents; number of copies not known. Published 1937.
Printed at the Country Life Press, Garden City, New York.

Notes: No copy of the Doubleday Doran edition (B17.*b*.1) was available for examination. It was standard practice, however, for Sun Dial to issue books from Doubleday, Doran plates; in this case, both have the same number of pages and both were printed at the Country Life Press.

B18   THE ANATOMY OF MURDER   •   1936

a.1. *First edition:*

THE ANATOMY OF | MURDER | *Famous Crimes Critically Considered by* | *members of the Detection Club* | HELEN SIMPSON JOHN RHODE | MARGARET COLE E. R. PUNSHON |

DOROTHY L. SAYERS FRANCIS ILES | FREEMAN WILLIS CROFTS | [star] | [publisher's device] | JOHN LANE THE BODLEY HEAD | BURY STREET W C 1 | LONDON

Collation: [A]⁸ B–X⁸ Y⁴ [$1 signed] 172 leaves.
p. [i] THE ANATOMY OF | MURDER; p. [ii] blank; p. [iii] title-page; p. [iv] publication and printer's notices; p. v. FOREWORD; p. [vi] blank; p. vii CONTENTS; p. [viii] blank; pp. [1]–[336] text, pp. [1, 41, 87, 117, 155, 213, 303] section title pages, pp. [2, 42, 88, 118, 154, 156, 212, 214, 304] blank; p. [336] unnumbered with text, other pages numbered.

21·5 × 13·6 cm. Bulk: 3·6/4·0. White laid paper; white wove endpapers; trimmed; top edge black. Bound in bright yellow cloth; front and back blank; spine [stamped in black:] THE | ANATOMY | OF | MURDER | Famous crimes | critically | considered by | HELEN SIMPSON | MARGARET COLE | DOROTHY L. SAYERS | JOHN RHODE | E. R. PUNSHON | FRANCIS ILES | FREEMAN WILLS | CROFTS | members of the | Detective Club | [publisher's device] | THE BODLEY | HEAD; variant binding: top edge white, bound in black cloth; front and back blank; spine [stamped in red:] THE | ANATOMY | OF | MURDER | by | HELEN SIMPSON | MARGARET COLE | DOROTHY L. SAYERS | JOHN RHODE | E. R. PUNSHON | FRANCIS ILES | FREEMAN WILLS | CROFTS | THE BODLEY | HEAD

Price: 8s6d; number of copies not disclosed. Published November 1936.
Printed by Sherratt & Hughes, The Saint Ann's Press Timperley Cheshire.

Notes: Sayers' contribution is "The Murder of Julia Wallace" (pp. 157–211). P. 194 "neccesary" for "necessary". This version examines the case in greater detail than the essays in The Evening Standard (C55) and in GREAT UNSOLVED CRIMES (B15).

a.II. American issue 1937:

THE ANATOMY OF | MURDER | *Famous crimes critically considered by* | *members of the Detection Club* | HELEN SIMPSON JOHN RHODE | MARGARET COLE E. R. PUNSHON | DOROTHY L. SAYERS FRANCIS ILES | FREEMAN WILLS CROFTS | NEW YORK | THE MACMILLAN COMPANY | 1937

Collation: [A–K]¹⁶ [L]⁸ [M]⁴ 172 leaves.
Pagination as B18a.I. (pp. [i–ii] have not been seen in rebound copies), except p. [iv] copyright, rights reservation, "First printing," printer's notice.

20·2 × 13·2 cm. Bulk: 3·0/3·5 cm. White wove paper; original endpapers not seen; trimmed. Original binding not seen.

Price: $2·50; number of copies not known. Published 13 July 1937.
Printed in the United States of America by the Polygraphic Company of America, New York.

Notes: Sayers' contribution is "The Murder of Julia Wallace" (pp. 157–211); p. 194 "neccesary" for "necessary". This issue appears to be a reproduction of B18*a*.1; punctuation of quotations follows British custom. This version of "The Murder of Julia Wallace" was reprinted in *The Portable Murder Book*, edited by Joseph Henry Jackson, Viking, 1945, and in *Trial and Terror*, edited by Joan Kahn, Houghton Mifflin, 1973.

B19   TITLES TO FAME   1937

TITLES TO FAME | *Edited by* | DENYS KILHAM ROBERTS | THOMAS NELSON & SONS LIMITED | LONDON EDIN-BURGH PARIS MELBOURNE | TORONTO AND NEW YORK

Collation: [1]⁴ 2–31⁴ 32⁶ [$1 signed; second leaf of 32 signed 32*a*] 130 leaves. pp. [i–ii] blank; p. [iii] TITLES TO FAME; p. [iv] blank; p. [v] title-page; p. [vi] rights reservation, publisher's and publication notices; p. vii CONTENTS; p. [viii] blank; p. ix ILLUSTRATIONS; p. [x] blank; p. xi TITLES TO FAME; p. [xii] blank; pp. xiii–xviii FOREWORD; pp. 1–231 text, pp. 1, 21, 51, 73, 97, 119, 139, 167, 189, 209, being section headings and pp. [2, 22, 52, 72, 74, 96, 98, 118, 120, 140, 166, 168, 188, 190, 208, 210] being blank; p. [232] blank; pp. 233–242 NOTES ON THE CONTRIBUTORS, with printer's notice at the bottom of p. 242.

20 × 13·8 cm. Bulk: 3·2/3·7 cm. White wove paper; white wove endpapers; trimmed; top edge green. Bound in blue cloth, front and back blank; spine [stamped in gold:] TITLES | TO | FAME | COLLECTED | BY | D. KIL-HAM | ROBERTS | *A. J. Cronin* | *E. M. Delafield* | *Margaret Irwin* | *Margaret Kennedy* | *R. H. Mottram* | *Ernest Raymond* | *E. Arnot Robertson* | *Dorothy L. Sayers* | *H. M. Tomlinson* | *Hugh Walpole* | NELSON

Price: 8s6d; number of copies not known. Published 8 November 1937.

Notes: Sayers' contribution is an essay, "Gaudy Night" (pp. 73–95). There are tipped in photographs of the authors, including one of Sayers between pp. 78–79. "Gaudy Night" was reprinted in shortened form in America in *The Art of the Mystery Story*, edited by Howard Haycraft, New York: Simon and Schuster, 1946, which also includes a reprint of the Introduction to GREAT SHORT STORIES OF DETECTION, MYSTERY AND HORROR (A7).

[a frame 1·2 cm. wide at top and sides, 2·4 cm. wide at bottom, consisting of thin double rules within and without a design of white leaves and berries, around a 10×6·2 cm. white rectangle:] *The* [swash "T"] *Laurel and Gold Series* | MORE TALES | OF MYSTERY | AND ADVENTURE | *Chosen by* | JOHN R. CROSSLAND | *Collins Clear-Type Press*

> *Collation:* [A]¹⁶ B–F¹⁶ [$1 signed] 96 leaves.
> p. [1] THE LAUREL AND GOLD SERIES | *General Editor: John R. Crossland* | VOLUME 78; p. [2] within a frame identical to that of the title-page, 6 line quotation from Shakespeare; p. [3] title-page; p. [4] publication and printer's notices; p. 5 CONTENTS: p. [6] blank; pp. 7–191 text; p. 192 *ACKNOWLEDGEMENTS.*

> 15·4×10 cm. Bulk: 1·0/1·4 cm. White wove paper; white wove endpapers; trimmed. Bound in green cloth; back blank; front [stamped in gold:] [series device]; spine [stamped in gold:] [rule] | [decoration] | [within single rules, top to bottom:] MORE MYSTERY & ADVENTURE | [decoration] | [upright:] 78 | COLLINS | [rule]

> *Price:* 1s2d; number of copies not known. Published January 1939.
> Printed by Collins Clear-Type Press, Cathedral Street, Glasgow.

> *Notes:* Sayers' contribution is "Bitter Almonds" (pp. 172–191), later published in IN THE TEETH OF THE EVIDENCE (A32).

B21 DETECTION MEDLEY [1939]

DETECTION MEDLEY | *Edited by* | JOHN RHODE | [rule] | [in left column:] A. A. MILNE | MARGERY ALLINGHAM | H. C. BAILEY | E. C. BENTLEY | NICHOLAS BLAKE | J. DICKSON CARR | G. K. CHESTERTON | AGATHA CHRISTIE | G. D. H. AND M. COLE | J. J. CONNINGTON | FREEMAN WILLS CROFTS | CARTER DICKSON | [in right column:] EDGAR JEPSON AND | ROBERT EUSTACE | R. AUSTIN FREEMAN | ANTHONY GILBERT | LORD GORELL | IANTHE JERROLD | MILWARD KENNEDY | E. C. R. LORAC | ARTHUR MORRISON | THE BARONESS ORCZY | E. R. PUNSHON | DOROTHY L. SAYERS | HENRY WADE | HUGH WALPOLE | [rule] | HUTCHINSON & CO. (*Publishers*) LTD.

Collation: [A]⁸ B–I⁸ I⁸ [repeated] L–U⁸ X–Z⁸ 2A–2K⁸ [$1 signed] 264 leaves.
p. [1] *Detection Medley*; p. [2] blank; p. [3] title-page; p. [4] printer's notice;
pp. 5–6 CONTENTS; pp. 7–9 FOREWORD; [10] blank; pp. 11–13 IN-
TRODUCTION; p. [14] blank; pp. 15–528 text; *inset*: 52 page catalogue of
Hutchinson books.

18·5 × 13 cm. Bulk: 4·2/4·4 cm. White laid paper; white wove endpapers;
trimmed. Bound in black cloth; back blank; front [stamped in gold, diagonally
across lower right corner:] *Hutchinson*; spine [stamped in gold:] DETECTION
| MEDLEY | Edited by | John Rhode | [dot] | Introduction by | A. A. Milne
| HUTCHINSON

Price: 8s6d; number of copies not known. Published 7 November 1939.
Dust jacket: printed in green, black, and red listing authors and short stories.

Notes: Sayers' contributions are "Striding Folly" (pp. 445–458) and "The
Haunted Policeman" (pp. 459–481). These stories were first printed in *The
Strand* (C58, C83). In copies examined, pp. 129–144, signature I, is repeated;
pp. 145–160, signature K, which includes most of the story "Too Clever By
Half" by G. D. H. and M. Cole, is missing. "Striding Folly" and "The Haunted
Policeman" were printed in America in *Line-Up*, edited by C.J.C. Street (John
Rhode), New York: Dodd, Mead, 1940, pp. 287–302, 303–327, and in *The
Avon Book of Modern Crime Stories*, edited by John Rhode, New York: Avon,
1942, pp. 277–292, 293–318. These two American books do not contain several
of the stories published in *Detection Medley*. "Striding Folly" and "The Haunted
Policeman" also appear, along with "Talboys," in LORD PETER (A61)
and in STRIDING FOLLY (A64).

B22   THE CHURCH LOOKS AHEAD   1941

THE CHURCH LOOKS | AHEAD | Broadcast Talks | by | J. H.
OLDHAM | MARUICE B. RECKITT | PHILIP MAIRET |
DOROTHY L. SAYERS | M. C. D'ARCY, S. J. | V. A. DEMANT
| T. S. ELIOT | *with a preface by* | E. L. MASCALL | FABER AND
FABER LTD | 24 Russell Square | London

Collation: [A]⁸ B–H⁸ [$1 signed] 64 leaves.
p. [1] THE CHURCH LOOKS AHEAD; p. [2] blank; p. [3] title-page; p. [4]
publication notice, publisher's notice, printer's notice, rights reservation; p. 5
CONTENTS; p. [6] ACKNOWLEDGEMENTS; pp. 7–16 INTRODUC-
TION; pp. 17–117 text; p. [118] blank; pp. 119–122 APPENDIX; pp. [123–
128] blank.

19·0 × 12·4 cm. Bulk: ·8/1·0 cm. White wove paper; white wove endpapers;
trimmed. Bound in light blue cloth; front and back blank; spine [stamped in
black, top to bottom:] THE CHURCH LOOKS AHEAD – Broadcast Talks
| [upright:] FABER

Price: 3s6d; number of copies not known. Published November 1941.

Notes: Sayers' contribution is "The Religions Behind the Nation" (pp. 67–78); see E20.

B23   MALVERN, 1941: THE LIFE OF   1942
THE CHURCH AND THE ORDER OF
SOCIETY

MALVERN, 1941 | THE | LIFE OF THE CHURCH | AND THE | ORDER OF SOCIETY | BEING THE PROCEEDINGS OF | THE ARCHBISHOP OF YORK'S CONFERENCE | LONG-MANS, GREEN AND CO. | LONDON: NEW YORK: TORONTO

Collation: [A]⁸ B–P⁸ Q⁶ [$1 signed] 126 leaves.
p. [i] MALVERN, 1941: | THE LIFE OF THE CHURCH AND THE | ORDER OF SOCIETY; p. [ii] blank; p. [iii] title-page; p. [iv] publisher's notice, publication notice, code number, printer's notice; pp. v–vi CONTENTS; pp. vii–viii INTRODUCTION; pp. ix–xiii DOCUMENT A; pp. xiv–xv DOCUMENT B; p. [xvi] blank; pp. 1–225 text, pp. [16, 18, 36, 38, 54, 56, 80, 118, 120, 150, 152, 164, 180, 182, 198, 200, 216] blank, pp. [17, 37, 55, 79, 117, 119, 151, 163, 181, 199] section headings, pp. 19, 39, 57, 81, 121, 153, 165, 183, 201 title pages with text; p. [226] blank; [227] LIST OF MEMBERS; p. [228] blank; pp. 229–235 list of members; p. [226] blank.

21·6 × 13·7 cm. Bulk: 1·6/1·8 cm. White wove paper, trimmed; white wove endpapers. Bound in blue cloth, front and back blank; spine [stamped in black:] MALVERN | 1941 | [rule] | The Life of the | Church and the | Order of Society | LONGMANS

Price: 10s6d; number of copies not known. Published January 1942. Dust jacket: buff, printed in red.
Made and printed by the Kemp Hall Press Ltd., Oxford.

Notes: Sayers' contribution is "The Church's Responsibility" (pp. 57–78).

B24   THE BEST POEMS OF 1941   1942

The | BEST POEMS | of 1941 | Selected by | THOMAS MOULT | LONDON | Jonathan Cape Limited | TORONTO

Collation: [A]⁸ B–H⁸ [$1 signed] 64 leaves.
p. [1] THE BEST POEMS OF 1941; p. [2] illustration; p. [3] title-page; p. [4]

publication, publisher's and printer's notices; p. [5] dedication; p. [6] blank; pp. 7–12 *Contents*; pp. 13–14 *Introduction*; p. [15] THE BEST POEMS OF 1941; p. [16] blank; pp. 17–128 text.

18·5 × 12·7 cm. Bulk: ·8/1·2 cm. Cream wove paper; cream wove endpapers with red decoration; trimmed. Bound in yellow cloth; back blank; front [stamped in red:] [decoration]; spine [4·4 × 1 cm. white paper label, printed in black:] *The* | BEST | POEMS | *of* | 1941

Price: 6s; number of copies not known. Published 2 January 1942. Dust jacket: white printed in black and red.

Notes: Sayers' contribution is "The English War" (pp. 38–40), first published in the *Times Literary Supplement* (C130). This poem was also published in *The Terrible Rain: The War Poets 1939–1945*, selected by Brian Gardner, London: Methuen, 1966, pp. 45–47.

B25   WHAT IS CHRISTIAN EDUCATION?   1942

WHAT IS CHRISTIAN | EDUCATION? | *A PIECE OF GROUP THINKING* | RECORDED BY | MARJORIE REEVES AND JOHN DREWETT | WITH A FOREWORD BY | DOROTHY L. SAYERS | LONDON | THE SHELDON PRESS | NOR-THUMBERLAND AVENUE, W.C.2 | NEW YORK: THE MACMILLAN COMPANY

Collation: [A]⁸ B–H⁸ [$1 signed] 64 leaves.
pp. [4] blank; p. [i] [left:] *The Christian News-Letter Books, No. 13* | [rule] | [center:] WHAT IS CHRISTIAN | EDUCATION? | *General Editor:* | ALEC R. VIDLER, WARDEN OF ST DEINIOL'S LIBRARY, HAWARDEN; p. [ii] GENERAL PREFACE; p. [iii] title-page; p. [iv] list of Christian News-Letter Books, publication notice, "MADE IN GREAT BRITAIN"; pp. v–vi CONTENTS; pp. vii–xii FOREWORD; pp. xiii–xvi EDITOR'S FOREWORD; pp. 1–102 text; pp. 103–105 BIBLIOGRAPHY; p. [106] PRINTED AND BOUND IN GREAT BRITAIN BY | RICHARD CLAY AND COMPANY, LTD., | BUNGAY, SUFFOLK; pp. [107–108] blank.

18·2 × 12 cm. Bulk: 1·4/1·5 cm. Cream wove paper; no endpapers. Aqua and white paper covers; back [white, printed in aqua:] Sheldon Press; front [5 aqua rules of varying sizes, white letters on largest rule:] CHRISTIAN NEWS-LETTER BOOKS | [printed in aqua on white center, left:] WHAT IS | CHRISTIAN | EDUCATION? | [in aqua, right:] MARJORIE REEVES | AND | JOHN DREWETT | [8 aqua rules of varying sizes]; spine [5 aqua rules continued from front] | [bottom to top in aqua:] WHAT IS CHRISTIAN EDUCATION? | [8 aqua rules continued from front]

Price: 1s6d; number of copies not known. Published March 1942.

Notes: Sayers' contribution is the Foreword (pp. vii–xii).

B26   A CHRISTIAN BASIS FOR THE   1942
              POST-WAR WORLD

A CHRISTIAN BASIS | FOR THE | POST-WAR WORLD | A Commentary on the Ten Peace Points | by | A. E. BAKER KENNETH INGRAM | MARGARET BONDFIELD A. D. LINDSAY | SIDNEY DARK DOROTHY L. SAYERS | LETITIA FAIRFIELD R. R. STOKES | JOHN A. HUGHES BARBARA WARD | THE ARCHBISHOP OF CANTERBURY | With a Preface by | THE BISHOP OF CARLISLE | Edited by A. E. BAKER | STUDENT CHRISTIAN MOVEMENT PRESS | 56 BLOOMSBURY STREET, LONDON, W.C.1.

Collation: [A]⁸ B–G⁸ H⁴ [$1 signed] 60 leaves.
p. [1] title-page; p. [2] publication notice, Canadian agent's notice, War economy notice, printer's notice; p. [3] CONTENTS; p. [4] blank; pp. [5]–6 THE CONTRIBUTORS; pp. [7]–8 PREFACE; pp. [9]–11 INTRODUCTION; p. [12] blank; pp. 13–16 THE TEN PEACE POINTS; pp. 17–107 TEXT; pp. 108–112 EPILOGUE; pp. 113–120 QUESTIONS FOR DISCUSSION

18·4 × 12·0 cm. Bulk: 1·2 cm. White wove paper; no endpapers; trimmed. Tan paper wraps; back blank; front [printed in brown:] A CHRISTIAN BASIS | FOR THE POST-WAR WORLD | *A Commentary on* | *the Ten Peace Points* | BY | A. E. BAKER KENNETH INGRAM | MARGARET BONDFIELD A. D. LINDSAY | SIDNEY DARK DOROTHY SAYERS | LETITIA FAIRFIELD R. R. STOKES | JOHN A. HUGHES BARBARA WARD | THE ARCHBISHOP OF CANTERBURY; spine: [printed in brown, bottom to top:] [upright:] 2/6 net | A CHRISTIAN BASIS FOR THE POST-WAR WORLD S. C. M.

Price: 2s6d; number of copies not known. Published May 1942.

Notes: Sayers' contribution is "Vocation in Work" (pp. 88–103), from an address, "Work and Vocation," given at Brighton on 8 March 1941 (F22). Reprinted as "A Plea for Vocation in Work" in *Bulletins from Britain*, 19 August 1942, pp. 7–10 (C143).

[flush left:] LONDON | [flush right:] CALLING | EDITED BY |
Storm Jameson | [publisher's device] | HARPER & BROTHERS
[dot] *PUBLISHERS* | New York and London | 1942

Collation: [A–X]⁸ 168 leaves.

p. [i] *London Calling*; p. [ii] title and list of authors; p. [iii] title-page; p. [iv]
copyright, printing, rights reservation and edition notices; pp. v–vi *Contents*;
p. [vii] *London Calling*; p. [viii] blank; pp. 1–308 text; pp. 309–322 biographical
notes; p. [323] designer's, manufacturers, and publisher's notices; pp. [324–
328] blank.

20·6 × 13·8 cm. Bulk: 2·7/3·2 cm. White wove paper; top edges trimmed;
white wove endpapers. Bound in red-brown cloth; back blank; front lower
right, blind stamped: [publisher's device]; spine [grey rectangle enclosing
red-brown rectangle with single gold rules and lettered in gold:] London |
Calling | [stamped in gold on the grey:] Edited by | STORM JAMESON
| [in grey:] HARPER

Price: $2·50, number of copies: 2,000. Published 13 November 1942. Dust
jacket: white printed in black, green and tan.

Notes: Sayers' contribution is "Lord, I Thank Thee –" (pp. 293–298). It was
also printed in *Britain*, November 1942, pp. 37–41 (C144) and in 1943 by
The Overbrook Press, Stamford, Connecticut (A67·3).

B28   QUEEN MARY'S BOOK FOR INDIA   1943

Queen Mary's | *Book* | FOR INDIA | [Emblem] | WITH A FORE-
WORD BY | THE RIGHT HON. L. S. AMERY M. P. | GEORGE
G. HARRAP & CO. LTD. | LONDON TORONTO BOMBAY
SIDNEY

Collation: [A]⁸ B–E⁸ F¹² [$1 signed, F₃ signed F₂] 52 leaves.

p. [1] *Queen Mary's Book* | *for India*; [2] blank; p. [3] title-page; p. [4] publication,
copyright, rights reservation, war economy and printer's notices; p. [5] MES-
SAGE FROM QUEEN MARY; p. 6 ACKNOWLEDGEMENTS; pp. 7–8
FOREWORD; pp. 9–10 CONTENTS; p. 11 ILLUSTRATIONS; p. [12]
blank; pp. 13–[103] text; pp. [40–41] map; p. [104] blank.

19·7 × 13·4 cm. Bulk: 1·0/1·2 cm. White wove paper, trimmed; white wove
endpapers. Bound in dark blue cloth; front and back blank; spine [stamped
in gold, top to bottom:] [asterisk] QUEEN MARY'S BOOK *for* INDIA
[asterisk]

Price: 7s6d; number of copies not known. Published July 1943.

Notes: Frontispiece (photograph of Queen Mary) and five pages of photographs inset. Sayers' contribution is "Dr. Watson's Christian Name" (pp. 78–82), which was later printed in UNPOPULAR OPINIONS (A43). The first American publication of "Dr. Watson's Christian Name" is in *Profile by Gaslight*, edited by Edgar W. Smith, New York: Simon and Schuster, 1944.

B29 FIVE GREAT SUBJECTS 1943

FIVE | GREAT SUBJECTS | *Broadcast Talks* | by | W. A. L. ELMSLIE | Principal of Westminster College, formerly | Fellow of Christ's College, Cambridge | with a Foreword by | DOROTHY L. SAYERS | STUDENT CHRISTIAN MOVEMENT PRESS LTD. | 56 Bloomsbury Street, London, W.C.1

Collation: 20 leaves, stapled at fold.
p. [1] title-page; p. [2] publication notice, Canadian distribution notice and printer's notice; pp. 3–4 PREFACE; p. 5 CONTENTS; pp. 6–8 FORE-WORD; pp. 9–40 text.

18·2 × 12·4 cm. Bulk: ·4 cm. White wove paper; trimmed. No endpapers. Cream paper wraps; back and spine blank; front [in black and red:] FIVE GREAT | SUBJECTS | Broadcast Talks | by | W. A. L. Elmslie | Foreword by | Dorothy L. Sayers | STUDENT CHRISTIAN MOVEMENT PRESS LTD. | *One shilling and sixpence net*

Price: 1s6d; number of copies not known. Published August 1943.

Notes: Sayers' contribution is the Foreword (pp. 6–8).

B30 THE MOONSTONE 1944

a.1. First edition:

THE MOONSTONE | [decoration] | WILKIE COLLINS | LON-DON: J. M. DENT & SONS LTD. | NEW YORK: E. P. DUTTON & CO. INC.

Collation: [A]¹⁶ B–O¹⁶ [$1 signed] 224 leaves.
p. [i] Everyman, I will go with thee, and be thy guide, | In thy most need to go by thy side. | [French rule] | EVERYMAN'S LIBRARY | EDITED BY ERNEST RHYS | No. 979 | FICTION | THE MOONSTONE | BY WILKIE COLLINS | WITH AN INTRODUCTION | BY DOROTHY L. SAYERS;

p. [ii] biographical note; p. [iii] title-page; p. [iv] rights reservation, press, decorations and publisher's notices, publication notice, economy standard notice; pp. v–xi INTRODUCTION; p. [xii] blank; p. xiii BIBLIOGRA-PHICAL NOTE; p. xiv blank; pp. xv–xvi AUTHOR'S PREFACES; pp. xvii–xviii CONTENTS; pp. 1–430 text.

16·9 × 10·6 cm. Bulk: 1·8/2·0 White (thin) wove paper; white and light orange decorated endpapers; trimmed; top edge red. Bound in red cloth; back blank; front [blind stamp of publisher's device]; spine [stamped in gold:] THE | MOON- | STONE | WILKIE | COLLINS | EVERYMANS | LIBRARY

Price: 3s; number of copies not disclosed. Published October 1944. Made at the Chaucer Press, Bungay, and decorated by Eric Ravilous.

Notes: Sayers' contribution is the Introduction (pp. v–xi). In some copies, p. 22, the second 2 is smaller. Issued in America by E. P. Dutton.

†a.II. *J. M. Dent (London) re-issue* June 1957. 430 pp.

†a.III. *J. M. Dent (London) paperback issue* September 1967. 430 pp.

B31   A TIME IS BORN   1945

A TIME IS BORN | GARET GARRETT | *With a Foreword by* | DOROTHY L. SAYERS | BASIL BLACKWELL | OXFORD | 1945

Collation: [A]⁸ B–I⁸ [$1 signed] 72 leaves.
p. [i] title-page; p. [ii] printer's notice; p. [iii] *It has happened many times before | that a time was born and | died. If this one lives | it will be an Age.* p. [iv] blank; pp. v–ix INTRODUCTION; p. [x] blank; p. xi CONTENTS; p. [xii] blank; pp. [1]–131 text; p. [132] blank.

21·4 × 13·8 cm. Bulk: ·8/1·3 cm. White wove paper; trimmed; white wove endpapers. Bound in red cloth; front and back blank; spine [stamped in gold:] A | Time | is | Born | GARET | GARRETT | BLACKWELL

Price: 7s6d; number of copies: 1,000. Published March 1945. Dust jacket: cream printed in red.
Printed by A. R. Mowbray & Co. Ltd., London and Oxford.

Notes: Sayer's contribution is the Introduction (pp. v–ix).

a.i. First trade edition:

[within triple rules:] THE | POET'S | CAT | *An Anthology compiled by* | MONA GOODEN | *With a Frontispiece engraved by* | STEPHEN GOODEN | [publisher's device] | LONDON | GEORGE G. HARRAP CO. LTD. | SYDNEY TORONTO BOMBAY STOCKHOLM

Collation: [A]⁸ B–F⁸ G¹⁰ [$1 signed; G₁ and G₂ signed] 58 leaves.

p. [1] THE POET'S CAT; p. [2] blank; *inset:* frontispiece [plate of a cat with books and a bust] p. [3] title-page; p. [4] dedication, publication, publisher's, copyright, war economy standard and printer's notices; pp. 5–6 ACKNOW-LEDGEMENTS; pp. 7–11 CONTENTS; p. [12] blank; p. 13–21 INTRO-DUCTION; p. [22] blank; pp. 23–113 text; p. [114] blank; pp. 115–[116] INDEX OF AUTHORS.

20 × 13·3 cm. Bulk: ·6/·9 cm. White wove paper, trimmed; white wove end-papers. Red cloth binding; front and back blank; spine [stamped in gold:] THE | POET'S | CAT | [head of a cat with six whiskers] | MONA | GOODEN | HARRAP; variant binding: blue leather; front and back blank; spine [stamped in gold:] THE | POET'S | CAT | [head of a cat with six whiskers] | MONA | GOODEN; slip case [brown with white label:] [within a border of diamond designs:] THE POET'S CAT | [rule] | *An Anthology compiled by* | MONA GOODEN

Price: 7s6d; number of copies: 5,300. Published 12 March 1947.

Printed by R. & R. Clarke, Edinburgh; composed in Fournier type. Dust jacket: pink printed in white and black; front decorated with leaves and stars; back has publisher's device.

Notes: Sayers' contribution is "War Cat" (pp. 95–98); it was first published in *Time and Tide* 4 December 1943 (C148).

a.ii. Limited issue:

[within a sepia rectangle 20 × 12·4 cm.:] THE POET'S CAT | AN ANTHOLOGY | Compiled by Mona [swash M] Gooden [swash G] | [illustration of a cat with books and a bust] | LONDON | GEORGE G. HARRAP & Co Ltd | 1946 [swash 9 and 6]

Collation: [A]⁴ B–P⁴ [$1 signed] 60 leaves.

p. [1] THE POET'S CAT; p. [2] limited edition statement and number, author and illustrator's signatures, dedication, publication, publisher's, copyright and printer's notices; p. [3] title-page; p. [4] blank; pp. 5–[116] as B31a.ii.; p. [117]

FINIS [illustration of a cat in 17th century garb with flag "FINIS"]; p. [118] blank.

23·6×15 cm. Bulk: 1·1/1·6 cm. Heavy white wove paper, untrimmed, top edge gilt; white wove endpapers. Bound in quarter black calf and white cloth; front and back blank; spine [stamped in gold:] [fleur de lis upright] | [top to bottom:] THE POET'S CAT | [fleur de lis upside down]

Price: 15s; number of copies: 116. Published 12 March 1947.
Composed in Fournier type, printed by R. & R. Clarke, Edinburgh.

Notes: Sayers' contribution is "War Cat" (pp. 95–98).

B33   ESSAYS PRESENTED TO   1947
                    CHARLES WILLIAMS

a.i. First edition:

Essays presented to | CHARLES | WILLIAMS | [chain rule] | *Contributors* | DOROTHY SAYERS | J. R. R. TOLKIEN | C. S. LEWIS | A. O. BARFIELD | GERVASE MATHEW | W. H. LEWIS | [chain rule] | GEOFFERY CUMBERLEGE | OXFORD UNIVERSITY PRESS | *London New York Toronto* | 1947

Collation: [A]⁸ B–I⁸ K¹⁰ [$1 signed] 82 leaves.
p. [i] *Essays presented to* | CHARLES WILLIAMS; p. [ii] blank; p. [iii] title-page; p. [iv] publisher's notice "PRINTED IN GREAT BRITAIN"; pp. [v]–xiv PREFACE; p. [xv] CONTENTS; p. [xvi] blank; pp. [1]–145 text, with pp. [1, 38, 90, 106, 128, 136] title-pages with text; p. [146] printer's notice; pp. [147–148] blank.

21·5×13·8 cm. Bulk: 1·4/1·6 cm. Cream wove paper, trimmed. Cream wove endpapers. Bound in blue cloth; front and back blank; spine [stamped in gold:] [fleur de lis design, upright] | [rule] | ESSAYS | *presented* | *to* | Charles | Williams | [rule] | [fleur de lis design, downward] | OXFORD

Price: 12s6d; number of copies not known. Published December 1947.
Printed at the Oxford University Press by Charles Batey. Dust jacket: buff printed in blue and black.

Notes: Sayers' contribution is "' ... And Telling You a Story': A Note on *The Divine Comedy*" (pp. 1–37). Frontispiece photograph of Charles Williams.

a.ii. Eerdmans (Grand Rapids Michigan) issue 1966: 145 pp.

Produced from B33.*a.i.*

a.III. *Books for Libraries (Freeport, New York) issue* 1972: 145 pp.

Produced from B33.*a.i.*

B34   OUR CULTURE   1948

OUR CULTURE: | ITS CHRISTIAN ROOTS AND PRESENT
CRISIS | *Edward Alleyn Lectures* 1944 | *Edited by* | V. A. Demant,
D. Litt. | *Canon and Chancellor of St. Paul's* | LONDON | SOCIETY
FOR PROMOTING | CHRISTIAN KNOWLEDGE | NOR-
THUMBERLAND AVENUE, W.C.2.

> *Collation:* [A]⁸ B–G⁸ H⁶ [$1 signed] 62 leaves.
> p. [i] OUR CULTURE: | ITS CHRISTIAN ROOTS AND PRESENT
> CRISIS; p. [2] blank; p. [iii] title-page; p. [iv] *First published* 1947 | MADE
> IN GREAT BRITAIN; pp. v–vi PREFACE; p. vii CONTENTS; p. [viii]
> blank; pp. 1–113 text; p. [114] printer's notice; pp. [115–116] blank.
>
> 18·3 × 12 cm. Bulk: ·9/1·1 cm. White wove paper; white wove endpapers;
> trimmed; top edge blue. Bound in blue cloth; front and back blank; spine
> [stamped in gold:] OUR | CULTURE | S.P.C.K.
>
> *Price:* 5s; number of copies not known. Published January 1948.
>
> *Notes:* Sayers' contribution "Towards a Christian Aesthetic" (pp. 50–69),
> first printed in UNPOPULAR OPINIONS (A43), was to have been printed
> first in OUR CULTURE, but publication was delayed until January 1948.

B35   A SHORT HISTORY OF WESTERN   1950
                   PHILOSOPHY IN THE MIDDLE AGES

A SHORT HISTORY | OF WESTERN PHILOSOPHY | IN THE
MIDDLE AGES | by | S. J. CURTIS, M.A., Ph.D. | *Senior Lecturer
in Education, and Honorary* | *Lecturer in Mediaeval Philosophy, the
Univer-* | *sity of Leeds* | MACDONALD & CO., (Publishers) LTD. |
LONDON

> *Collation:* [A]¹⁶ B–I¹⁶ [$1 signed] 144 leaves.
> p. [i] A SHORT HISTORY OF WESTERN PHILOSOPHY | IN THE
> MIDDLE AGES; p. [ii] blank; p. [iii] title-page; p. [iv] publication, printer's
> notices; p. v CONTENTS; pp. vi–viii FOREWORD; pp. ix–x AUTHOR'S
> PREFACE; pp. 11–12 INTRODUCTION; pp. 13–278 text; *inset:* APPEN-
> DIX I CHRONOLOGICAL CHART; p. 279 APPENDIX II; p. 280 [blank];
> pp. 281–286 INDEX; pp. [287–288] blank.

22 × 13·8 cm. Bulk: 1·7/2·2 cm. White wove paper, trimmed; cream wove endpapers. Bound in blue cloth; front and back blank; spine [stamped in gold:] A | SHORT | HISTORY | OF | WESTERN | PHILOSOPHY | IN THE | MIDDLE | AGES | S. J. CURTIS | MACDONALD

Price: 15s; number of copies not known. Published February 1950. Printed by Purnell and Sons Ltd.

Notes: Sayers' contribution is the Foreword (pp. vi–viii). †Issued in America by the Newman Press, 1950, price $3·50.

B36   MONDAY TO FRIDAY IS NOT ENOUGH   1951

Monday to Friday Is not Enough | Frederick M. Meek | *Minister of Old South Church in Boston* | [publisher's device] | NEW YORK | Oxford University Press | 1951

Collation: [A–H]¹⁶ 128 leaves.
p. [i] Monday to Friday Is not Enough; p. [ii] blank; p. [iii] title-page; p. [iv] COPYRIGHT 1951 BY OXFORD UNIVERSITY PRESS, INC. | PRINTED IN THE UNITED STATES OF AMERICA: p. [v] dedication; p. [vi] blank; pp. vii–viii Preface; p. ix Contents; p. x Sermons for Special Days; pp. xi–xii Foreword; p. [1] Monday to Friday Is not Enough; p. [2] blank; pp. 3–238 text; pp. 239–240 References; pp. [241–244] blank.

20·5 × 13·5 cm. Bulk: 1·7/2·2 cm. White wove paper; white wove endpapers; trimmed. Bound in light green cloth; front and back blank; spine [stamped in green:] MEEK | [decorated rule] | [top to bottom:] Monday to Friday Is not Enough | [decorated rule] | [upright:] OXFORD

Price: $3; number of copies not known. Published 13 September 1951.

Notes: Sayers' contribution is "A Letter Addressed to 'Average People'" (pp. 170–171), originally published in *City Temple Pulpit and Church Tidings* (C159). This book was distributed in England by Oxford University Press at 18s.

B37   JAMES I   1951

JAMES I. | BY | CHARLES WILLIAMS | [publisher's device] | *London* | [short rule] | ARTHUR BARKER LTD.

Collation: [A]⁸ B–S⁸ T¹⁰ U⁸ [$1 signed, T5 signed T plus star] 162 leaves.
p. [i] JAMES I.; p. [ii] list of works by Charles Williams; p. [iii] title-page; p. [iv] publication and printer's notices; p. [v] PREFACE; p. [vi] blank; p. [vii] CONTENTS; p. [viii] blank; pp. ix–xiii INTRODUCTION; p. [xiv]

blank; pp. 1–300 text, pp. [185, 297] unnumbered chapter headings with text; pp. 301–302 CHRONOLOGY; pp. 303–304 SHORT BIBLIOGRAPHY; pp. 305–310 INDEX.

21·5 × 14·0 cm. Bulk: 2·2/2·9 cm. White wove paper; white wove endpapers; trimmed. Bound in red cloth; front and back blank; spine [stamped in gold on black rectangle within single gold rules:] JAMES | I | [small gold crown] | CHARLES | WILLIAMS | [stamped in black:] [publisher's device] | [stamped in gold on black rectangle within single gold rules:] ARTHUR | BARKER

Price: 10s6d; number of copies not known. Published September 1951. Dust jacket: black and white with a portrait of James I on the front.

Notes: Sayers' contribution is the Introduction (pp. ix–xiii), based on a review for *Time and Tide* (D122). Frontispiece, plate of James I, tipped in. P. 9 signed "2" bottom left.

B38   THE SURPRISE   1952

a.I. First edition:

THE SURPRISE | BY | G. K. CHESTERTON | *With a Preface by* | DOROTHY L. SAYERS | SHEED AND WARD | LONDON AND NEW YORK

Collation: [1]⁸ 2–4⁸ [$1 signed] 32 leaves.
p. [1] [top, right] THE SURPRISE; p. [2] blank; p. [3] title-page; p. [4] publication, copyright and printer's notices; pp. 5–9 PREFACE; p. [10] CHARACTERS, production note; pp. 11–63 text; p. [64] blank.

18·5 × 12·2 cm. Bulk: ·5/1·0 cm. White wove paper; trimmed. White wove endpapers. Bound in green cloth; back and spine blank; front [stamped in black:] THE SURPRISE | *A Play* | G. K. CHESTERTON

Price: 5s; number of copies: 3,000. Published 15 October 1952. Dust jacket: white printed in green.

Notes: Sayer's contribution is the Preface (pp. 5–9)

a.II. American issue 1953:

The Surprise | BY G. K. CHESTERTON | WITH A PREFACE BY | Dorothy L. Sayers | SHEED & WARD | [double rule] | NEW YORK [dot] 1953

Collation: [A–D]⁸ 32 leaves.
p. [1] [center:] The Surprise; p. [2] blank; p. [3] title-page, p. [4] copyright,

Library of Congress card number, rights reservation, "MANUFACTURED IN | THE UNITED STATES OF AMERICA"; pp. 3–[64] exactly as B37a.1.

19· × 12·5 cm. Bulk: ·5/1·0 cm. White wove paper; trimmed; top edge green. White wove endpapers. Bound in white boards with a black and green wavy stripe design; back and spine blank; front [white label 7 × 4·7 cm., printed in green:] [within single rules:] [decoration] | The Surprise | *A PLAY* | *by* | G. K. CHESTERTON | *With a Preface by* | Dorothy L. Sayers | [decoration]

Price: $1·50; number of copies: 5,000. Published 11 March 1953.

Notes: Sayers' contribution is the Preface (pp. 5–9).

B39   S. RICHARD OF CHICHESTER   1953

S. RICHARD OF | CHICHESTER | BY | CAROLINE M. DUNCAN-JONES | INTRODUCTION BY | DOROTHY SAYERS | LONDON | THE FAITH PRESS, LTD. | 7 TUFTON STREET, WESTMINSTER, S.W.1 | MOREHOUSE-GORHAM CO., NEW YORK, U.S.A.

Collation: [A]⁸ B–C⁸ [$1 signed] 24 leaves.
p. [i] [extreme right:] S. RICHARD OF | CHICHESTER; p. [ii] blank; p. [iii] title-page; p. [iv] printer's notice; pp. v–vii INTRODUCTION; p. [viii] notice of acknowledgements; pp. 1–39 text, p. 4 an illustration; p. [40] a prayer ascribed to S. Richard [7 lines], printer's notice.

18.2 × 12 cm. Bulk: ·7 cm. White wove paper; trimmed; no endpapers. Blue paper covers; front [printed in dark blue:] [extreme left:] S. RICHARD | OF | CHICHESTER | [centre:] Caroline M. Duncan-Jones; spine and back blank.

Price: 2s6d; number of copies not known. Published January 13, 1953. Printed by the Faith Press Ltd., Leighton Buzzard.

Notes: Sayers' contribution is the Introduction (pp. v–vii). Plates: frontispiece of S. Richard; facing p. 8, S. Richard's altar and statue at Chichester Cathedral; facing p. 24, statue of S. Richard at Droitwich Spa; facing p. 32, fresco of S. Richard at Norwich Cathedral.

B40   ASKING THEM QUESTIONS – THIRD SERIES   1953

Asking them Questions | *Third Series* | 'They found Him . . . sitting in the | midst of the doctors, both hearing | them, and asking them questions.' | LUKE ii. 46 | *Edited by* | RONALD SELBY WRIGHT |

Minister at the Canongate, Edinburgh | *Geoffrey Cumberlege* | OXFORD
UNIVERSITY PRESS | *London New York Toronto* | 1950

Collation: [π]² [A]⁸ B–M⁸ N¹⁰ [$1 signed; N2 signed] 108 leaves.

pp. [2] blank; p. [i] *Asking them Questions* | *Third Series*; p. [ii] blank; p. [iii]
title-page; p. [iv] press and publisher's notices "PRINTED IN GREAT
BRITAIN"; p. [v] DEDICATION; p. [vi] blank; pp. [vii]–xii PREFACE;
pp. [xiii]–xiv NOTE; pp. [xv]–xviii LIST OF CONTRIBUTORS; pp.
[1]–188 text with pp. [1, 7, 12, 16, 23, 32, 38, 48, 54, 63, 70, 75, 83, 87, 91, 98,
104, 109, 115, 123, 127, 137, 143, 150, 155, 162, 168, 175, 181] unnumbered
essay title-pages with text; pp. [189]–194 SUBJECT INDEX AND GLOS-
SARY; p. [195] printer's colophon; p. [196] blank.

18·5 × 12·2 cm. Bulk: 1·6/2·2 cm. White wove paper; white wove endpapers;
trimmed. Bound in blue cloth; front and back blank; spine [stamped in gold:]
[rule] | *Asking* | *them* | *Questions* | [three asterisks] | OXFORD | [rule]

Price: 8s6d; number of copies: 5,000. Published 21 May 1953. Dust jacket:
buff printed in blue and black.

Notes: Sayers' contribution is: "Is there a Definite Evil Power that attacks
People in the Same Way that there is a Good Power that influences People?"
(pp. 127–136). Reprinted October 1954 (5,000 copies); August 1960 (2,000
copies); May 1963 (2,000 copies); February 1967 (2,000 copies).

B41   ST. ANNE'S HOUSE   1953

St. Anne's House | The First Decade, 1943–1953 | "Christianity can
only become the living truth for | successive generations, if thinkers
constantly arise in it | who, in the spirit of Jesus, make belief in him
capable | of intellectual apprehension in the thought-forms of the |
world-view proper to their time." | *Albert Schweitzer* | 57 DEAN
STREET | LONDON, W. 1 | Telephone: GERrard 5006

Collation: Six leaves stapled at fold.

p. [1] title-page; p. [2] blank; pp. 3–12 text with division titles: p. 3 INTRO-
DUCTION, p. 6 ST. ANNE'S HOUSE: ITS MISSION AND METHOD,
p. 11 TO SUM UP.

21·4 × 14·1 cm. Bulk: 1·2/1·5 cm. Cream wove paper; cream wove card covers;
front [orange, printed in black:] Saint Anne's | House | An | Experimental |
Centre | The First Decade: 1943–1953 | *Price* 1s.6d.; spine blank; back [list
of officers of the Centre] | [short rule] | [account of damage done to St. Anne's,

notice of services and hours of chapel opening] | [rule] | Claridge, Lewis & Jordan Ltd., 68–70 Wardour Street, London, W. I. GER. 7242/0795. Inside front cover FOREWORD [full page concerning the experiment at St. Anne's signed:] DOROTHY L. SAYERS

Price: 1s6d; number of copies not known. Published 1953.

Notes: Sayers' contribution is the Foreword, inside front cover.

B42 THE GREAT MYSTERY OF LIFE 1957
HEREAFTER

The Great Mystery | of | Life Hereafter | By | Dorothy Sayers | Bertrand Russell | Sir Basil Henriques | The Abbot of Downside | Air Chief Marshal Lord Dowding | Bishop J. W. C. Wand | H. H. the Aga Khan | Lieut. – Col. Robert E. Key | Christmas Humphreys | W. E. Sangster | Arabinda Basu | E. N. da C. Andrade | LONDON | HODDER & STOUGHTON

Collation: [A]^{16} B–D^{16} [$1 signed] 64 leaves.
p. [1] THE GREAT MYSTERY OF | LIFE HEREAFTER; p. [2] blank; [3] title-page; p. [4] FIRST PRINTED [dot] 1957 | printer's notice; p. 5 CONTENTS; p. [6] blank; pp. 7–8 INTRODUCTION; pp. [9]–126 text, pp. [9, 19, 29, 39, 49, 59, 69, 77, 87, 97, 107, 117] section headings, pp. [10, 20, 28, 30, 38, 40, 48, 50, 60, 68, 70, 76, 78, 88, 96, 98, 106, 108, 118] blank; pp. 11, 21, 31, 41, 51, 61, 71, 79, 89, 99, 109, 119 being chapter headings with text; pp. [127–128] blank.

17·8 × 11·0 cm. Bulk: 1·0/1·1 White wove paper; no endpapers; trimmed. Bound in stiff paper covers; front [background of soft reds, yellows, greens:] [black horizontal tube printed in white:] The Great Mystery | of Life Hereafter | [printed in black with one dot to left of each name:] DOROTHY SAYERS | BERTRAND RUSSELL | SIR BASIL HENRIQUES | THE ABBOT OF DOWNSIDE | AIR CHIEF MARSHAL LORD DOWDING | BISHOP J. W. C. WAND | H. H. THE AGA KHAN | LIEUT. COL. ROBERT E. KEY | CHRISTMAS HUMPHREYS | W. E. SANGSTER | ARABINDA BASU | E. N. da C. ANDRADE | [stylized "2/- NET"] [publisher's device]; back [black and white, printing on white:] [publisher's device in yellow and black] | [blurb printed in black] | C302; spine [black, top to bottom, letters in white:] THE GREAT MYSTERY OF LIFE HEREAFTER | [black and white, upright:] [publisher's device]

Price: 2s; number of copies not known. Published 18 July 1957.

Notes: Sayers' contribution is "Christian Belief about Heaven and Hell"

(pp. 9–18), which is her own title for *The Times* article "My Belief about Heaven and Hell" (C190).

B43   ADVENTURE IN SEARCH OF A CREED   1957

ADVENTURE | IN SEARCH OF | A CREED | [decoration] | F. C. HAPPOLD | FABER AND FABER LTD | 24 Russell Square | London

Collation: [A]⁸ B–N⁸ O⁶ [$1 signed] 110 leaves.

pp. [1–2] blank; p. [3] Adventure in Search of a Creed; p. [4] a list of works by Happold; p. [5] title-page; p. [6] publication, publisher's, and printer's notices; p. [7] dedication; p. [8] blank; p. 9 CONTENTS; p. [10] blank; pp. 11–12 PREFACE; pp. 13–208 text; pp. 209–216 BIBLIOGRAPHY; pp. 217–219 INDEX; p. [220] blank.

20 × 13·3 cm. Bulk: 1·7 × 2·0 cm. White wove paper; white wove endpapers; trimmed. Bound in maroon cloth; front and back blank; spine [stamped in gold:] Adventure | in Search | of | a Creed | [star] | F. C. | Happold | Faber

Price: 15s; number of copies not known. Published 25 October 1957.

Notes: Sayers' contribution is "The Creed of St. Euthanasia" (p. 15), reprinted from *Punch* (C179).

B44   ETON MICROCOSM   1964

ETON | MICROCOSM | *edited by* | ANTHONY CHEETHAM | AND | DEREK PARFIT | *Illustrations by* | EDWARD PAGRAM | SIDGWICK AND JACKSON | LONDON | 1964

Collation: [A]⁴ B–N⁸ [$1 signed] 100 leaves.

p. [1] ETON MICROCOSM | [ornament] p. [2] blank; *inset:* frontispiece, tipped in photograph; p. [3] title-page; p. [4] copyright, dedication, "AC-KNOWLEDGEMENTS" and printer's notice; p. 5–6 CONTENTS; p. 7 INTRODUCTION; p. [8] blank; pp. [9]–191 text with pp. [9, 29, 67, 105, 129, 143, 185] section headings; pp. [10, 28, 30, 66, 68, 104, 106, 128, 130, 144, 184] blank and pp. [15, 17, 19, 21, 48, 52, 64, 73, 79, 83, 86, 110, 147, 155, 186] full page black and white illustrations; p. [192] blank; p. [193] section heading for GLOSSARY; p. [194] blank; pp. 195–197 glossary; p. 198 GOOD-BYE; pp. [199–200] blank.

24·7 × 18·7 cm. Bulk: 1·4/1·8 cm. White wove paper; black and white decorated endpapers; trimmed. Bound in black cloth; back blank; front [stamped in

blue:] [six diagonal stripes]; spine [stamped in blue, top to bottom:] ETON
MICROCOSM *Edited by* CHEETHAM & PARFIT

Price: 42s; number of copies not known. Published 29 October 1964. Dust
jacket: lavender, illustrated in black and white.

Notes: Sayers' contribution is "Schools for Heroes" (pp. 152–156), on why
Lord Peter Wimsey went to Eton and why the details of his days there are
not chronicled. "Schools for Heroes" was first published in *The Etonian Review*
(C50).

B45   MISCELLANEA   1931–1975

B45.1   SLEUTHS   1931

First biographical notice for Lord Peter Wimsey. *Sleuths: Twenty-Three
Great Detectives of Fiction and Their Best Stories.* Ed. by Kenneth Macgowan.
New York: Harcourt, Brace and Company, 1931, p. 462; followed by "The
Entertaining Episode of the Article in Question", pp. 463–474. See A3e.1.
for notes on other biographical notices of Wimsey.

B45.2   THE CAMBRIDGE BIBLIOGRAPHY   1940
               OF ENGLISH LITERATURE

"William Wilkie Collins (1824–1898)." *The Cambridge Bibliography of English
Literature.* Ed. F. W. Bateson. Cambridge: University Press, 1940. III (1800–
1900), 480–482. Sayers entered in this CBEL bibliography her own study of
Collins, described as being "in preparation." The Collins bibliography in
CBEL and the introduction to the J. M. Dent edition of Collins' *The Moonstone*
(B30) are the only works on Collins published by Sayers in her lifetime. Alexan-
der Woolcott, in the foreword to the 1937 Modern Library edition of *The
Moonstone and The Woman in White*, had been rightly "oppressed by a doubt"
that Sayers would "ever get around to finishing" the promised study of Collins.
The incomplete study – in typescript and manuscript – is now held by the
Humanities Research Center of the University of Texas at Austin; it has been
edited by E. R. Gregory and published by The Friends of the University of
Toledo Library (A65).

B45.3   THE REVOLT AGAINST REASON   1951

Excerpt of a letter from Sayers. Sir Arnold Lunn. *The Revolt Against Reason.* New York: Sheed and Ward, 1951, p. 256.

B45.4   THE MYSTERY WRITER'S HANDBOOK   1956

Michael Gilbert. "Technicalese." *The Mystery Writer's Handbook.* Ed. Herbert Brean. New York: Harper, 1956, 64–65. A three-paragraph quotation from a letter to Gilbert on the subject of lacing a story with acquired technical knowledge (i.e., change-ringing in THE NINE TAILORS).

B45.5   THE SHERLOCK HOLMES SCRAPBOOK   1973

"Conan Doyle: Crusader". *The Sherlock Holmes Scrapbook.* Ed. Peter Haining. London: New English Library, 1973, p. 55. This article, first published thus in book form, is a shortened version of Sayers' review of *The Life of Sir Arthur Conan Doyle* by John Dickson Carr (D119).

B45.6   C. S. LEWIS: A BIOGRAPHY   1974

Excerpts of letters from Sayers to C. S. Lewis. Roger Lancelyn Green and Walter Hooper. *C. S. Lewis: A Biography.* London: Collins, 1974. From a letter dated 21 December 1953 about *Out of the Silent Planet* (p. 165); from a letter dated 3 December 1945 about *That Hideous Strength* (pp. 178–179); from a letter dated 13 May 1943 on miracles (p. 226). See also "Charles Williams" (C133) and "Christianity Regained" (D123).

B45.7.   SUCH A STRANGE LADY   1975

Excerpts of letters from Sayers. Janet Hitchman. *Such A Strange Lady.* London: New English Library, 1975, pp. 73–74; 87; 94–95; 97–98; 100–101; 106; 108; 128–129; 135–136; 144–145; 147–152; 159–160; 167–169; 179–184; 189; 191; 193. There are numerous quotations from Sayers' works as well as very brief quotations attributed to Sayers throughout this biography.

C

CONTRIBUTIONS TO NEWSPAPERS
AND PERIODICALS

1909

C1   The Kindergarten Plays. *Godolphin Gazette*, Summer Term 1909.

Review of "Cock Robin and Jenny Wrenn" and "King Arthur" performed by the Godolphin Kindergarten 29 May 1909.

C2   *L'Avare* au County Hall. *Godolphin Gazette*, Autumn Term 1909.

Review, in French, of *L'Avare* performed by the M. Roubaud troup of actors at Salisbury, 13 October 1909.

1910

C3   The Death of the Sun. *Godolphin Gazette*, Spring Term 1910.

Poem "from the French of Le conte de Lisle".

C4   To Sir Ernest Shackleton and His Brave Companions. *Godolphin Gazette*, Autumn Term 1910.

Poem. This issue was edited by Sayers.

C5   Captivo Ignoto. *Godolphin Gazette*, Autumn Term, 1910.

Poem.

1911

C6   Ode. *Godolphin Gazette*, Summer Term, 1911.

Poem "from the French of P. Ronsard".

C7   Duke Hilary. *Godolphin Gazette*, Summer Term, 1911.

Poem.

C8 Labiche et Molière au "Picturedome", le 28 Octobre, 1911. *Godolphin Gazette*, Autumn Term, 1911.

Review, in French, of *La Poudre aux Yeux* by Labiche and *Les Précieuses Ridicules* by Molière, performed by the M. Roubaud troup of actors.

1915

C9 To a Leader of Men. *Oxford Magazine*, vol. XXXIII, no. 10, 5 February 1915, p. 174.

Poem.

C10 Mirth. *The Fritillary*, no. 64, March 1915, p. 5.

Poem.

C11 Hymn in Contemplation of Death. *Oxford Magazine*, vol. XXXIV, no. 3, 5 November, 1915, p. 37.

Poem.

C12 Matter of Brittany. *The Fritillary*, no. 66, December 1915, p. 42.

Poem.

1916

C13 To Members of the Bach Choir on Active Service. *Oxford Magazine*, vol. XXXIV, no. 12, 18 February 1916, p. 194.

Poem.

C14 Epitaph for a Young Musician. *Oxford Magazine*, vol. XXXIV, no. 13, 25 February 1916, p. 212.

Poem.

C15 Ballade. *The Fritillary*, no. 67, March 1916, pp. 60–61.

Poem.

C16 Icarus. *Oxford Magazine*, vol. XXXIV, no. 17, 5 May 1916, p. 286.

Poem.

C17 Thomas Angulo's "Death". *The Saturday Westminster Gazette*, 20 May 1916, p. 9.

Poem written under the pseudonym "H. P. Rallentando".

1917

C18 Who Calls the Tune? *The Blue Moon*, vol. 1, no. 1, published for the Mutual Admiration Society.

Story.

1918

C19 Rex Doloris. *The New Witness*, vol. XI, no. 286, 26 April 1918, p. 591.

Poem.

C20 Letter to the editor on CATHOLIC TALES AND CHRISTIAN SONGS. *The New Witness*, vol. XIII, no. 320, 20 December 1918, p. 156.

In reply to a review of her book Sayers wrote: "As regards the person of our Lord, I believe 'in unum Dominum Jesum Christum, Filium Dei unigenitum, consubstantialem Patri . . . qui homo factus est.' And that He is 'perfectus Deus, perfectus homo, ex anima rationali et humana carne subsistens.' I understand these words, without quibble or mental reservation, in the sense in which they have always been understood by the Catholic Church, and in no other."

1919

C21 Great Tom. *Oxford Journal Illustrated*, 15 January 1919, p. 4.

Poem.

C22 Vials Full of Odours. *The Oxford Chronicle*, no. 4370, 30 May 1919, p. 13, column b.

Poem.

C23 Eros in Academe. *The Oxford Outlook*, vol. 1, no. 2, June 1919, pp. 110–116.

Essay.

C24 A Sonnet in the Elizabethan Manner. *The Oxford Chronicle*, no. 4371, 6 June 1919, p. 13, column g.

Poem.

C25 Sleeplessness. *The Oxford Chronicle*, no. 4395, 21 November 1919, p. II University Pages, column d.

Poem.

C26 A Song of the Web. *The Oxford Chronicle*, no. 4396, 28 November 1919, p. II University Pages, column c.

Poem.

C27 Cares of State. *The Oxford Chronicle*, no. 4397, 5 December 1919, p. II University Pages, column d.

Poem.

1920

C28 The Sentimental Shepherdess. *The Oxford Chronicle*, no. 4410, 5 March 1920, p. II University Pages, column b.

Poem.

C29 Lord William's Lover. *The Oxford Chronicle*, no. 4118, 30 April 1920, p. II University Pages, column d.

Poem.

C30 The Tristan of Thomas – A Verse Translation Part I. *Modern Languages*, vol. 1, no. 5, June 1920, pp. 142–147. Part II. *Modern Languages*, vol. 1, no. 6, August 1920, pp. 180–182.

1921

C31 Obsequies for Music. *The London Mercury*, vol. III, no. 15, January 1921, pp. 249–253.

Poem.

C32 The Poem. *The London Mercury*, vol. IV, no. 24, October 1921, p. 577.

Poem.

1925

C33 The Problem of Uncle Meleager's Will. *Pearson's*, vol. 60, July 1925, pp. 27–35.

C34 The Article in Question. *Pearson's*, vol. 60, October 1925, pp. 355–361.

C35 Beyond the Reach of the Law. *Pearson's*, vol. 61, February 1926, pp. 121–127.

Variant title for "The Unprincipled Affair of the Practical Joker".

C36 The Inspiration of Mr. Budd. *Pearson's*, vol. 61, March 1926, pp. 227–235.

C37 The Learned Adventure of the Dragon's Head. *Pearson's*, vol. 61, June 1926, pp. 557–566.

C38 Wilkie Collins. *The Times Literary Supplement* 21 June 1928, p. 468.

A letter asking for communications regarding letters, manuscripts, papers relating to Wilkie Collins for a proposed critical and biographical study; a similar letter was sent to *The New York Times Book Review*, 3 November 1929.

C39 Wilkie Collins. *The Hornsey Journal* 29 March 1929, p. 16.

Letter to the editor on Collins' school at Highbury.

C40 A Sport of Noble Minds. *The Saturday Review of Literature*, vol. VI, no. 2, 3 August 1929, pp. 22–23.

Essay from the Introduction to GREAT SHORT STORIES OF DE-TECTION, MYSTERY AND HORROR, a bit shortened. Printed in England in *Life And Letters Today*, vol. IV, no. 20, January 1930, pp. 41–54.

C41 Behind the Screen – III. *The Listener*, vol. IV, no. 77, 2 July 1930, pp. 28–30.

Sayers' contribution to a six-part serial written for the BBC by six members of the Detection Club.

C42 The Crime Club. *The Times Literary Supplement*, 25 September 1930, p. 758.

A letter, signed by Sayers and eight other members of the Detection Club, criticizing the advertising practices of W. Collins Sons and Co. Ltd.

C43 The Present Status of the Mystery Story. *The London Mercury*, vol. XXIII, no. 133, November 1930, pp. 47–52; and in *The Author*, Spring, 1931.

1931

C44 The Scoop – I. Over The Wire. *The Listener*, vol. V, 14 January 1931, pp. 70–71.

A twelve-part serial written by Sayers and five other Detection Club members.

C45 Week by Week. *The Listener*, vol. V, 11 February 1931, p. 23.

Reply to a query on the planning of detective serials such as "Behind the Screen" and "The Scoop."

C46 The Scoop – XII. The Final Scoop. *The Listener*, vol. V, 8 April 1931, pp. 600–601.

1932

C47 Trials and Sorrows of the Mystery Writer. *The Listener*, vol. VII, 6 January 1932, p. 26.

C48 The Man Who Knew How. *Harper's Bazaar* (London), February 1932, pp. 22–23, 72–73.

C49 The Milk-Bottles. *Nash's Pall Mall*, vol. 89, no. 470, July 1932, pp. 38–41, 90–91.

1933

C50 Schools for Heroes. *The Etonian Review*, July 1933, pp. 25–27.
Essay.

C51 Suspicion. *Mystery League Magazine*, vol. 1, no. 1, October 1933, pp. 102–109.

1934

C52 Impossible Alibi. *Mystery*, vol. 9, no. 1, January 1934, pp. 19–21, 104, 106, 108.

Variant title for "Absolutely Elsewhere", see below.

Absolutely Elsewhere. *The Strand*, vol. 87, no. 12, February 1934, pp. 185–196.

C53 An Arrow o'er the House. *The Strand*, vol. 87, no. 32, May 1934, pp. 496–502.

C54 The Dates in "The Red-Headed League." *The Colophon, A Book-Collector's Quarterly*, part 17, no. 10, June 1934. (8 pp.)

C55 The Mysterious Telephone Call: The Murder of Julia Wallace. *The Evening Standard*, No. 34386, 6 November 1934, pp. 26–27.

1935

C56 The King's English. *Nash's Pall Mall*, May 1935, pp. 16–17, 88–90.

C57 What Is Right with Oxford? *Oxford*, vol. 2, no. 1, Summer 1935, pp. 34–41.

Essay from a speech given at the Somerville College Gaudy, 1934.

C58 Striding Folly. *The Strand*, vol. 89, no. 43, July 1935, pp. 687–695. Reprinted "slightly abridged by permission of the author" in *The Sunday Graphic and Sunday News*, no. 1107, 21 June 1936, pp. 22–34.

C59 Emile Gaboriau 1835–1873: The Detective Novelist's Dilemma. *The Times Literary Supplement*, no. 1761, 2 November 1935, pp. 677–678.

Unsigned but written by Sayers according to agents' records.

C60 An Apology for Lord Peter. *Book Society Newsletter*, November 1935.

See "How I Came to Invent the Character of Lord Peter" (C65). This issue of the *Book Society Newsletter* accompanied the Society's copies of GAUDY NIGHT (A21).

C61 If You Had to Live in a Play or a Novel Which One Would You Choose? *The Strand*, December 1935, pp. 158–161.

Sayers and others reply to the question placed in the title; a photograph of Sayers appears on p. 159.

C62   Aristotle on Detective Fiction. *English: The Magazine of the English Association*, vol. 1, no. 1, 1936, pp. 23–35.

C63   Blood Sacrifice. *The London Daily Mail*, 23 April p. 21; 24 April p. 22; 25 April p. 20; 28 April p. 22; 29 April p. 22.

Sayers' contribution to the serial publication of SIX AGAINST THE YARD (B17).

C64   P.S. from Lord Peter Wimsey. *The London Daily Mail*, 30 April 1936 p. 18.

On "Blood Sacrifice."

C65   How I Came to Invent the Character of Lord Peter. *Harcourt Brace News* (N.Y.) vol. 1, 15 July 1936, pp. 1–2.

Written in 1935, this article was published to promote the sales of Harcourt's edition of GAUDY NIGHT (A21).

C66   Have Everything Ready. *Sunday Dispatch*, no. 7030, 26 July 1936, p. 2.

How to make a murder police proof, included in the "Almost in Confidence" column by the Marquess of Donegall.

C67   Detective Cavalcade. *The Evening Standard* No. 34921, 29 July 1936, p. 7.

On detective stories. Sayers edited this series of "Great Detective Stories" for *The Evening Standard* with a brief introduction:

No. 34921   29 July 1936, A Case of Identity by Sir Arthur Conan Doyle, pp. 22–23, 26.

No. 34922   30 July 1936, The Invisible Man by G. K. Chesterton, pp. 22–23, 26.

No. 34923   31 July 1936, East Wind by Freeman Wills Crofts, pp. 22–23, 26.

(Sayers also provided some of the clues for the Detective Cavalcade Competition.)

No. 34924   1 August 1936, The Hanover Court Murder by Sir Basil Thomson, pp. 20–22.

No. 34925   3 August 1936, The Stealer of Marble by Edgar Wallace, pp. 16–17, 20.

No. 34926   4 August 1936, Mystery of Hunter's Lodge by Agatha Christie, pp. 16–17.

No. 34927   5 August 1936, The Nail and the Requiem by C. Daly King, pp. 18–19, 22.

No. 34928   6 August 1936, The Missing Undergraduate by Henry Wade, pp. 18–19, 22.

No. 34929   7 August 1936, Clever Cockatoo by E. C. Bentley, pp. 16–17, 19.

No. 34930   8 August 1936, The Tremarn Case by Baroness Orczy, pp. 18–19, 22.

No. 34931   10 August 1936, The Elusive Bullet by John Rhode, pp. 16–17, 19.

No. 34932   11 August 1936, Sower of Pestilence by R. Austin Freeman, pp. 18–19, 22.

No. 34933   12 August 1936, The Learned Adventure of the Dragon's Head by Dorothy L. Sayers, pp. 18–19, 22.

No. 34934   13 August 1936, The Wrong Problem by John Dickson Carr, pp. 22–23, 26.

No. 34935   14 August 1936, The Cyprian Bees by Anthony Wynne, pp. 18–19, 22.

No. 34936   15 August 1936, Gentlemen and Players by E. W. Hornung, pp. 20–22.

No. 34937   17 August 1936, The Case of the Hundred Cats by Gladys Mitchell, pp. 16–17.

No. 34938   18 August 1936, A Drop Too Much by Christopher Bush, pp. 16–17.

No. 34939   19 August 1936, A Question of Coincidence by G. D. H. and M. Cole, pp. 18–19, 22.

No. 34940   20 August 1936, Policeman's Cape by David Frome, pp. 18–19.

No. 34941   21 August 1936, Diamond Cut Diamond by F. Britten Austin, pp. 18–19, 22–23.

No. 34942   22 August 1936, The Ghost at Massingham Mansions by Ernest Bramah, pp. 20–22, 24.

No. 34943   24 August 1936, The Wrong Hand by Melville Davison Post, pp. 16–17.

No. 34944   25 August 1936, The Borderline Case by Margery Allingham, pp. 18, 23.

No. 34945   26 August 1936, A Study in the Obvious by E. R. Punshon, p. 18, 22.

No. 34946   27 August 1936, Lord Chizelrigg's Missing Fortune by Robert Barr, pp. 22–24.

No. 34947   28 August 1936, White Butterfly by Anthony Berkeley, pp. 24–25.

No. 34948   29 August 1936, Seven Black Cats by Ellery Queen, pp. 20–22.

No. 34949   31 August 1936, Locked In by E. Charles Vivian, pp. 16–17.

No. 34950   1 September 1936, Before Insulin by J. J. Connington, pp. 22–23.

C68   A New Association. *The Times*, 15 September 1936, 15e.
A letter to the editor in Latin signed "Sc. D."

C69   Dirt Cheap. *Pearson's*, vol. 82, October 1936, pp. 310–318.

C70   Lord Peter Wimsey to Take the Stage. Interview in *The Evening Standard*, no. 35006, 5 November 1936, p. 9.
On the forthcoming production of *Busman's Honeymoon*.

Circa 1936–1937

C71   Doing A Man's Job. *Eve's Journal*, late 1936–1937.
Copies of this journal were unobtainable; those at the British Library were destroyed by bombing in the war.

C72 The Late Provost's Ghost Stories. *The Eton College Chronicle* 4 February 1937 p. 300.

A letter from Lord Charles Wimsey dated 1654 is included.

C73 Would You Like To Be 21 Again? I Wouldn't. *The Daily Express*, no. 11461, 9 February 1937, p. 10.

C74 Chekhov at the Westminster. *The New Statesman and Nation*, vol. XIII, no. 314, 27 February 1937, p. 324.

Letter to the Editor about a production of *Uncle Vanya*.

C75 The Fen Floods: Fiction and Fact. *The Spectator*, no. 5675, 2 April 1937, pp. 611–612.

C76 Ink of Poppies. *The Spectator*, no. 5681, 14 May 1937, pp. 897–898.

On bad writing.

C77 The Riddle of the Poisoned Nurse. (Part I of *Night of Secrets*; prologue by John Chancellor.) *The Sunday Chronicle*, 23 May 1937, pp. 6–7.

The first publication of DOUBLE DEATH (A29) as a six-part serial by Sayers and five other Detection Club members.

C78 Plain English. *Nash's Pall Mall*, July 1937, pp. 86–88.

C79 Doodles. *Evening Standard*, no. 35275, 18 September 1937, p. 19.

Sayers submitted a page of rabbits "rescued from the glory hole" to the *Evening Standard's* "Royal Academy For Doodlers."

C80 The Psychology of Advertising. *The Spectator*, no. 5708, 19 November 1937, pp. 896–898.

Letter to the Editor in reply to a letter on The Psychology of Advertising. *The Spectator*, no. 5711, 10 December 1937, p. 1056.

C81 The Wimsey Chin. *The Times*, 4 December 1937, p. 15 Column e.

Letter to the Editor, signed "Matthew Wimsey *p.p.* Dorothy L. Sayers".

C82 Pointers. *Evening Standard*, 20 January 1938, p. 20.

A puzzle, with the solution.

C83 Haunted Policeman. *Harper's Bazaar* (New York), vol. 73, February 1938, pp. 62–63, 130–135.

First published in England in *The Strand*, vol. XCIV, no. 25, March 1938, pp. 482–494.

C84 The Dogma Is the Drama. *St. Martin's Review*, no. 566, Literary Supplement, April 1938, pp. 167–170.

C85 The Greatest Drama Ever Staged. *The Sunday Times*, no. 5999, 3 April 1938, p. 20.

C86 The Triumph of Easter. *The Sunday Times*, no. 6001, 17 April 1938, p. 10.

C87 Detective Stories for the Screen: Some Advice to Producers. *Sight And Sound*, vol. 7. no. 26, Summer 1938, pp. 49–50.

C88 Writing a Local Play. *The Farmer's Weekly*, 26 August 1938, pp. 42–43.

C89 *Troilus and Cressida* at the Westminster. *The Times*, 24 September 1938, p. 11 column d.

Letter to the Editor.

C90 Tight Rope. *The Daily Express*, no. 12005, 10 November 1938, p. 5, columns e, f, g.

Advertisement for Horlick's; does *not* feature Lord Peter Wimsey.

C91 Major Road Ahead. *Radio Times*, vol. 61, no. 789, 11 November 1938, p. 67.

Advertisement for Horlick's featuring a hero named "Peter," who is *not* Lord Peter Wimsey.

C92 Whither Wimsey? *The Times*, no. 48160, 24 November 1938, p. 15 column e.

In reply to a letter to *The Times* 21 November 1938 criticizing Sayers' advertisements for Horlick's; Sayers says that "the advertisers refused to make use of the elegant copy I prepared for them and rewrote it according to their own notion of what was fitting. This is what invariably happens to copy-writers." Sayers goes on to say that the advertisements were written to finance the provincial tour of *The Zeal of Thy House.*

C93 Et Laudavit Dominus. *The Times,* no. 48165, 30 November 1938, p. 15, column e.

Letter to the Editor in reply to a letter (26 November 1938 p. 13, e.) which presumed to correct Sayers' Latin.

C94 Nativity Play. *Radio Times,* vol. 61, no. 795, 23 December 1938, p. 13.

Introduces *He That Should Come* broadcast 25 December 1938.

1939

C95 Letter to the Editor on Reviewing Detective Fiction. *Evening Standard, no.* 35678, 7 January 1939, p. 15.

Reviewers must not give away the clues; in response to Howard Spring's review of *Hercule Poirot's Christmas* by Agatha Christie. Reprinted in *Publisher's Weekly* 135, 15 April 1939, p. 1427 and *The Saturday Review of Literature* 25, 19 December 1942, p. 13.

C96 Adam and Eve – A Carol. *The Church Times,* vol. CXXI, no. 3974, 24 March 1939, p. 328.

Poem set to music from *He That Should Come.*

C97 The Food of the Full-Grown. *The Sunday Times,* no. 6052, 9 April 1939, p. 12.

Essay.

C98 Other People's Great Detectives. *Illustrated,* no. 9, vol. 1, 29 April 1939, pp. 18–19.

Those Sayers thinks will "pass the test of time" are Wilkie Collins' Sergeant Cuff, Conan Doyle's Sherlock Holmes, G. K. Chesterton's Father Brown; those "great" in their own time who influenced the development of Detective Fiction include E. C. Bentley's Philip Trent, H. C. Bailey's Mr. Fortune, and Gladys Mitchell's Mrs. Bradley.

C99 Letter to the Editor. *The Times,* 6 September 1939, p. 4f.

Sayers and Helen Simpson urge keeping churches open in time of war even if theatres are closed.

C100 What Do We Believe? *The Sunday Times,* no. 6074, 10 September 1939, p. 8.

C101 How to Enjoy the Dark Nights. *The Star* (London), 14 September 1939, p. 2.

On the blackout.

C102 Wimsey Papers. *The Spectator*, no. 5812, 17 November 1939, pp. 672–674.

War-time letters and documents exchanged among members of the Wimsey family and their friends.

C103 Bitter Almonds. *The Sunday Graphic*, 19 November 1939, pp. 20–21.

C104 Wimsey Papers – II. *The Spectator*, no. 5813, 24 November 1939, pp. 736–737.

C105 The Secret of the Mystery Professor. *The Sunday Graphic*, 26 November 1939, pp. 22–23.

Variant title for "The Professor's Manuscript."

C106 Prevention Is Better than Cure. *St. Martin's Review*, no. 586, December 1939, pp. 546–548.

Essay.

C107 Wimsey Papers – III. *The Spectator*, no. 5814, 1 December 1939, pp. 770–771.

C108 Wimsey Papers – IV. *The Spectator*, no. 5815, 8 December 1939, pp. 809–810.

C109 Wimsey Papers – V. *The Spectator*, no. 5816, 15 December 1939, pp. 859–860.

C110 Is This He That Should Come? *The Christian Newsletter*, no. 8, 20 December 1939, The Supplement (4 pp.).

C111 Wimsey Papers – VI. *The Spectator*, no. 5817, 22 December 1939, pp. 894–895.

C112 Wimsey Papers – VII. *The Spectator*, no. 5818, 29 December 1939, pp. 925–926.

1939–1940

C113 The Alternatives Before Society. *The Spectator*, no. 5815, 8

December 1939, p. 820; no. 5817, 22 December 1939, p. 904; no. 5819, 5 January 1940, p. 19.

Letters on theology.

1940

C114 Wimsey Papers – VIII. *The Spectator*, no. 5819, 5 January 1940, pp. 8–9.

C115 Wimsey Papers – IX. *The Spectator*, no. 5820, 12 January 1940, pp. 38–39.

C116 Wimsey Papers – X. *The Spectator*, no. 5821, 19 January 1940, pp. 70–71.

C117 Wimsey Papers – XI. *The Spectator*, no. 5822, 26 January 1940, pp. 104–105.

The papers were to continue on an irregular basis, but no more appeared.

C118 Divine Comedy. *The Guardian* (London) no. 4919, 15 March 1940, p. 128.

On producing Christian drama.

C119 The Feast of St. Verb. *The Sunday Times*, no. 6102, 24 March 1940, p. 8.

On Reason and Christianity, including the observation that Eastern Orthodox Christians dedicate churches to Holy Wisdom, The Holy Word, etc. Letter to the Editor on "The Feast of St. Verb." *The Sunday Times* no. 6103, 31 March 1940, p. 8. About a church in Lower Kingswood, Surrey, The Church of the Wisdom of God; said to be the only one in Europe so named which has Byzantine decorations brought from Asia Minor.

C120 The Contempt of Learning in 20th Century England. *The Fortnightly*, Vol. CXLVII, New Series no. 880, April 1940, pp. 373–382.

C121 The War as a Crusade. *The Guardian*, no. 4927, 10 May 1940, p. 225.

Excerpt from lecture *Creed or Chaos?*

C122 A Vote of Thanks to Cyrus. *St. Martin's Review*, no. 591, May 1940, pp. 228–230.

C123 Notes on the Way. *Time And Tide*, vol. 21, no. 24, 15 June 1940, pp. 633–634; vol. 21, no. 25, 22 June 1940, pp. 657–658.
On the war.

C124 For Albert Late King of the Belgians. *Life And Letters Today*, vol. 26, no. 35, July 1940, p. 36.
Poem.

C125 Dogma or Doctrine. *The Spectator*, no. 5847, 19 July 1940, p. 62.
Letter to the Editor in response to criticism of *Creed or Chaos?*

C126 Vox Populi. *The Spectator*, no. 5849, 2 August 1940, p. 117.
On a war-time campaign to curb careless talk.

C127 Pot *Versus* Kettle. *Time and Tide*, vol. 21, no. 32, 10 August 1940, pp. 826, 828.
Letter to the editor in reply to criticism of "Pot Versus Kettle," *Time and Tide*, vol. 21, no. 35, 31 August 1940, p. 884.

C128 Devil, Who Made Thee? *World Review*, August 1940, pp. 35–39.

C129 Letter to the Editor. *The Times*, 24 August 1940, p. 5e.
In support of appeals such as the Spitfire and Red Cross funds.

C130 The English War. *The Times Literary Supplement*, no. 2014, 7 September 1940, p. 445.
Poem.

C131 Letter to the Editor on Mr. Winston Churchill. *Time and Tide*, vol. 21, no. 43, 26 October 1940, p. 1044.

1941

C132 Helen Simpson. *The Fortnightly*, New Series vol. 149, no. 889, January 1941, pp. 54–59.
Eulogy.

C133 The Church in the New Age. *World Review*, March 1941, pp. 11–15; reprinted in America as: The Church in War's Aftermath. *The Living Age*. (Boston) 360: July 1941, pp. 441–445.

C134 Forgiveness and the Enemy. *The Fortnightly*, New Series, vol. 149, no. 892, April 1941, pp. 379–383.

C135 The Snob Offensive. *Woman's Journal*, June 1941, pp. 16–17, 68. A version of THE MYSTERIOUS ENGLISH (A36, F20).

C136 How Free Is the Press? *World Review*, June 1941, pp. 19–24.

C137 Night Bombing – A Discussion. *The Fortnightly*, vol. 149, June 1941, pp. 555–563.

Sayers responds to the Bishop of Chichester on p. 559.

C138 Religious Education. *The Times*, 26 August 1941, p. 5, column e.

Letter to the Editor.

C139 The Human-Not-Quite-Human. *Christendom: A Journal of Christian Sociology*, vol. XI, no. 43, September 1941, pp. 156–162.

C140 The Insured Life. *Homes and Gardens*, vol. 23, no. 5, October 1941, pp. 10–11, 58.

C141 Introducing Children to the Bible. *Housewife*, vol. 3, no. 11, November 1941, pp. 81–83, 146.

1942

C142 Work – Taskmaster or Liberator? *Homes and Gardens*, vol. 24, no. 1, June 1942, pp. 16–17, 62.

Reprinted in UNPOPULAR OPINIONS (A43) as "Living to Work".

C143 A Plea For Vocation in Work. *Bulletins from Britain* (New York) 103:19, August 1942, pp. 7–10.

See B26; variant title: "Vocation in Work".

C144 Lord I Thank Thee –. *Britain*, vol. 1, no. 1, November 1942, pp. 37–41.

Poem.

C145 Words I Am Weary Of. *Strand*. vol. CV, no. 629, May 1943, pp. 20–21.

C146 Aerial Reconnaissance. *The Fortnightly*, New Series, vol. 154, no. 922, October 1943, pp. 268–270.

Poem.

C147 They Tried To Be Good! *World Review*, November 1943, pp. 30–34.

C148 War Cat. *Time and Tide*, vol. 24, no. 49, 4 December 1943, p. 994.

Poem.

C149 Peculiar People. *Woman's Journal*, February 1944, pp. 10–11, 84–85.

Variant title: The Gulf Stream and the Channel.

C150 Target Area. *The Fortnightly*, New Series, vol. 155, no. 927, March 1944, pp. 181–184.

Poem. Also in *The Atlantic Monthly*, March 1944, pp. 48–50.

C151 Tolerance and Criticism. *John O'London's Weekly*, vol. LI, no. 1230, 7 April 1944, p. 16.

Letter to the editor on literary criticism.

C152 When 2 = 3. *John O'London's Weekly*, vol. LI, no. 1233, 19 May 1944, p. 77.

In reply to a query about the letter "Tolerance and Criticism."

C153 Frankenstein. *John O'London's Weekly*, vol. LI, no. 1233, 19 May 1944, p. 78.

Sayers offers this correction: "Frankenstein was not the name of the monster, but of the poor mutt who made the monster."

C154 The Map. *Good Housekeeping*, vol. XLVI, no. 1, July 1944, p. 1.

Poem.

C155 The Other Six Deadly Sins. *Woman's Journal*, October 1944, pp. 20–21, 86.

1945

C156 The Cenotaph Line. *St. Martin's Review*, no. 647, January 1945, pp. 10–12.

C157 The Execution of God. *Radio Times*, vol. 87, no. 1121, 23 March 1945, p. 3.

On THE MAN BORN TO BE KING.

1946

C158 Mission to London. *Daily Sketch*, 5 March 1946 p. 2.

Letter to the editor on "The Christian Mission": services, lectures, and discussions during Lent 1946.

C159 A Letter Addressed to "Average People". *The City Temple Tidings*, vol. xxiv, no. 284, July 1946, pp. 165–166.

On learning about Christianity.

C160 The Faust Legend and the Idea of the Devil. *Publications of the English Goethe Society*, New Series, vol. XV, 1946, pp. 1–20.

1947

C161 The Lost Tools of Learning. *The Hibbert Journal*, vol. XLVI, no. 1, October 1947, pp. 1–13.

C162 Problems of Religious Broadcasting: A Letter from Miss Dorothy L. Sayers. *The BBC Quarterly*, vol. 2, no. 1, April 1947, pp. 29–31.

Christian programmes should lead "to a practical increase of belief in God or of Charity to one's neighbor"; they should not be solely entertainment.

C163 "Problems of Religious Broadcasting: A Further Letter from Miss Sayers." *The BBC Quarterly*, vol. 2, no. 2, July 1947, p. 104.

In reply to a letter from Mr. Kenneth Grayson: "the fight is about the Faith, and . . . I am fighting (*a*) those critics of his department, without the Church, who demand that it should broadcast propaganda for anti-Christian religions; (*b*) those critics of his department, within the Church, who would like to reduce its teaching to an endless emotional orgy with no nasty dogma about it; (*c*) the enemies of Christianity, who and wheresoever."

C164 You Are "The Treasury". *Tory Challenge*, vol. I, no. I, July 1947, pp. 3–4.

1949

C165 Love Was Dante's Salvation. *Everybody's Weekly*, 19 November 1949, p. 25.

1950

C166 Socialism Means Tyranny. *Evening Standard*, no. 39123, 17 February 1950, p. 11.

C167 The Enduring Significance of Dante. *The Listener*, vol. XLIV, no. 1121, 20 July 1950, pp. 87–89.

1951

C168 The Way to Learn to Enjoy the Best in Books. *John O'London's Weekly*, vol. LX, no. 1408, 30 March 1951, p. 168.
Very brief comments.

1952

C169 Types of Christian Drama: With Some Notes on Production. *The New Outlook for Faith and Society*, vol. I, no. 3, New Year 1952, pp. 104–112.
From a lecture at St. Anne's House, Soho, *Church and Theatre* (F27): Part I appears here, Part II was to appear in the Spring issue. The entire article appears in three parts in *The Episcopal Churchnews* (C181).

C170 Constantine – Christ's Emperor. *Everybody's Weekly*, 16 February 1952, pp. 15, 20.

C171 Pussydise Lost. *Everybody's Weekly*, 7 June 1952, p. 22.
Poem.

C172 Ignorance and Dissatisfaction. *Latin Teaching: The Journal* *of the Association for the Reform of Latin Teaching*, vol. XXXVIII, no. 3, October 1952, pp. 69–92.

"The Teaching of Latin: A New Approach" is the variant title.

C173 Projects At School. *The Times*, 26 November 1952, p. 9e.

Letter to the Editor.

C174 Binyon's Dante. *Times Literary Supplement*, 27 March 1953 p. 205.

Letter to the editor.

C175 St. Anne's Church, Soho. *The Times*, 8 August 1953, p. 9a.

Letter to the Editor by Sayers, Church Warden, and Rev. P. McLaughlin, Rector.

C176 Pantheon Papers: The Cosmic Synthesis. *Punch*, vol. 226, 2 November 1953, pp. 17–19.

Includes: Correspondence between Didymus Pantheon, Professor of Comparative Irreligion in Mansoul University, and Sayers; "The Calendar", St. Lukewarm of Laodicea, Martyr", "SS. Ursa and Ursalina", "St. Simian Stylites", "St. Supercilia", "For an Evening Service".

C177 These Stones Cry Out. *Everybody's Weekly*, 26 December 1953, pp. 6–7.

An appeal for the restoration of Westminster Abbey.

1954

C178 More Pantheon Papers; Kalendar Showing the moveable feasts together with unholy and dead-letter days for the season of Cacophony. *Punch*, vol. 226, 6 January 1954, p. 60.

C179 More Pantheon Papers: The Cosmic Synthesis. *Punch*, vol. 226, 13 January 1954, p. 84.

Includes correspondence from "practising members of the Polar Cult"; "Spiritual Weapons for Polar Rearmament", "Creed of St. Euthanasia".

C180 The Polar Synthesis: A Sermon for Cacophony – Tide. *Punch*, vol. 226, 20 January 1954, p. 124.

Final Pantheon Papers include: Sermon; collect for the third Sunday in Cacophony.

C181 Sacred Plays. *The Episcopal Churchnews*. vol. 120, nos. 1–3, 9, 23 January and 6 February 1955, pp. 20–22, 35; pp. 24–25, 34; pp. 24, 31–33. The first part was published in *The New Outlook for Faith*; from the lecture "Church and Theatre" (F27).

C182 *Oedipus Simplex:* Freedom and Fate in Folk-lore and Fiction. *Royal Institution of Great Britain: Proceedings of the Society*, 36, No. 162, 1955.

C183 Charles Williams. *The Times*, 14 May 1955, p. 9e.

Letter to the Editor by Sayers and C. S. Lewis.

C184 Chronicles of Narnia. *The Spectator*, 22 July 1955, p. 123.

Letter to the editor on C. S. Lewis' books.

C185 Children of Cain. *Everybody's Weekly*, 10 December 1955, pp. 16–17, 38, 43.

Bible story.

C186 Daniel! Are You Alive? *Everybody's Weekly*, 17 December 1955, pp. 16–17, 42–43.

Bible story.

C187 The Two Mothers. *Everybody's Weekly*, 24 December, 1955, pp. 14–15, 38.

Bible story.

C188 The Bad Penny. *Everybody's Weekly*, 31 December 1955, pp. 14–15, 35.

Bible story.

C189 Playwrights Are Not Evangelists. *World Theatre*, vol. V, no. 1, Winter 1955–1956, pp. 61–66.

C190 My Belief About Heaven and Hell. *The Sunday Times*, no. 6973, 6 January 1957, p. 8.

Sayers' title for this article is "Christian Belief About Heaven and Hell."

1958

C191 The Beatrician Vision in Dante and Other Poets. *Nottingham Mediaeval Studies*, vol. II, 1958, pp. 3–23.

C192 On Translating the *Divina Commedia*. *Nottingham Mediaeval Studies*, vol. II, 1958, pp. 38–66.

C193 The Art of Translating Dante. *Nottingham Mediaeval Studies*, vol. IX, 1965, pp. 15–31.

C194 The "Terrible" Ode. *Nottingham Mediaeval Studies*, vol. IX, 1965, pp. 42–43.

1973

C195 For Timothy, in the Coinherence. *The Listener*, vol. 89, no. 2294, 15 March 1973, p. 337.

Poem.

D

BOOK REVIEWS

1933

D1 Detective Stories of the Week: The Whole Scale of Toughness. *The Sunday Times*, no. 5750, 25 June 1933, p. 9.

Review of *Inquest* by Henrietta Clandon, *The Body in the Silo* by Ronald A. Knox, *Death in Darkness* by Charles Barry, *Crime de Luxe* by Elizabeth Gill.

D2 Detective Stories of the Week: An American Nut Worth Cracking. *The Sunday Times*, no. 5751, 2 July, 1933, p. 9.

Review of *The American Gun Mystery* by Ellery Queen, *Death in Fancy Dress* by Anthony Gilbert, *Murder Rehearsal* by Roger East.

D3 Tipsters of Crime Stories: Selections to Follow. *The Sunday Times*, no. 5752, 9 July 1933, p. 9.

Review of *Murder in the Square* by Johnston Smith, *The Monkhurst Murder* by Francis D. Grierson, *Mystery on the Center Court* by Hilda Willett, *The Pepper Pot Problem* by Olive Cecil, *The Return of Arsène Lupin* by Maurice Leblanc, *The White Glove* by William Le Quex.

D4 A Formula for the Crime Book: Murders and Humor. *The Sunday Times*, no. 5753, 16 July 1933, p. 9.

Review of *Sleep No More* by Florence Ryerson and Colin Clements, *The White Cockatoo* by Mignon G. Eberhart, *The Mantle of Ishmael* by J. S. Fletcher, *The Almost Perfect Murder* by Hulbert Footner.

D5 A Sleuth Who Was Too Clever: The Case of Berkeley *v.* Sheringham. *The Sunday Times*, no. 5754, 23 July 1933, p. 7.

Review of *Jumping Jenny* by Anthony Berkeley, *The Bank Vault Mystery* by Louis F. Booth, *The Murders at the Manor* by Clive Ryland, *The Roof* by David Whitelaw.

D6 Shackles on Crime Stories: No Chance for a New Sherlock Holmes? *The Sunday Times*, no. 5755, 30 July 1933, p. 7.

Review of *Policeman's Lot* by Henry Wade, *Follow the Blue Car* by R. A. J. Walling, *Murder Comes Home* by Nellise Child.

D7 Crime Puzzlers for Holiday Makers: Mysteries That May Have Been Missed. *The Sunday Times*, no. 5756, 6 August 1933.

Review of some less-well known authors who merit attention. *The Square Mark* by Grace M. White and H. L. Deakin, *The Murder in the Laboratory* by T. L. Davidson, *The Inconsistent Villains* by N. A. Temple-Ellis, *The Secret of Bogey House* by Herbert Adams, *Murder in the Moor* by Thomas Kindon, *The Public School Murder* by R. C. Woodthorpe, *The Mummy Case* by Dermot Morrah, *Murder by Latitude* by Rufus King, E. R. Punshon's books, such as *Proof Counter-Proof* or *The Cottage Mystery*.

D8 Old Style and New in Thrillers: A Change from Crossword Crimes. *The Sunday Times*, no. 5757, 13 August 1933, p. 7.

Review of *Murder of the Only Witness* by J. S. Fletcher, *Death Whispers* by Joseph B. Carr, *The Haunted Light* by Evadne Price.

D9 A Crime Writer of Distinction: Salute to Mr. Punshon. *The Sunday Times*, no. 5758, 20 August 1933, p. 7.

Review of *Information Received* by E. R. Punshon, *Cross Marks the Spot* by James Ronald, *The Mystery of the Villa Aurelia* by Burton C. Stevenson.

D10 Crime Plot That Has Had Its Day: When the Dead Speak. *The Sunday Times*, no. 5759, 27 August 1933, p. 7.

Review of *The Case of the Three Strange Faces* by Christopher Bush, *The Second Case of Mr. Paul Savoy* by Jackson Gregory, *The Jade Hat-Pin* by Maurice G. Kiddy.

D11 One of the Few Real Detectives: Re-Enter Hercule Poirot. *The Sunday Times*, no. 5760, 3 September 1933, p. 7.

Review of *Lord Edgware Dies* by Agatha Christie, *Dead Man's Heath* by Jefferson Farjeon, *Hot Ice* by Robert J. Casey.

D12 Lost Heirs and Missing Wills. *The Sunday Times*, no. 5761, 10 September 1933, p. 7.

Review of *John Brand's Will* by Herbert Adams.

D13 America Without Slang: An Old Farce Re-Written. *The Sunday Times*, no. 5762, 17 September 1933, p. 7.

Review of *Murder Is Easy* by Armstrong Livingston, *Death on the Oxford Road* by E. C. R. Lorac, *The Affair at Aliquid* by G. D. H. and M. Cole.

D14 Mystery Out of the Ordinary. *The Sunday Times*, no. 5763, 24 September 1933, p. 7.

Review of *The Mad Hatter Mystery* by John Dickson Carr, *Behind the Headlines* by William Sutherland.

D15 Grand Manner in Crime Stories: Recapturing the Art of Victorians. *The Sunday Times*, no. 5764, 1 October 1933, p. 7.

Review of *The Album* by Mary Roberts Rinehart, *Aldringham's Last Chance* by Arthur J. Reese and *The Clueless Trail* by Percy Walsh.

D16 An Idea from the Lawyers: The Criminal's Best Defense. *The Sunday Times*, no. 5765, 8 October 1933, p. 7.

Review of *The Musical Comedy Crime* by Anthony Gilbert, *Night in Glengyle* by John Ferguson, *The Clock Ticks On* by Valentine Williams.

D17 Crime Confusion: Titles That Have Been Done to Death. *The Sunday Times*, no. 5766, 15 October 1933, p. 7.

Review of *Girl in the Dark* by E. Charles Vivian, *Raffles After Dark* by Barry Perowne, *A Killer at Scotland Yard* by G. Davison.

D18 Detective Stories: Another First-Class "Thorndyke". *The Sunday Times*, no. 5767, 22 October 1933, p. 7.

Review of *Dr. Thorndyke Intervenes* by R. Austin Freeman, *The Manuscript Murder* by Lewis Robinson, *Death Fugue* by Paul McGuire.

D19 The Criminals' Viewpoint: True Tragic Quality. *The Sunday Times*, no. 5768, 29 October 1933, p. 7.

Review of *Portrait of a Murderer* by Anne Meredith, *Week-End Murder* by Nicholas Brady, *The Eel-Pie Mystery* by David Frome, *Mr. Clerihew, Wine Merchant* by H. Warner Allen.

D20 Flesh and Blood in Crime Stories: Problem Not Yet Solved. *The Sunday Times*, no. 5769, 5 November 1933, p. 9.

Review of *Mist on the Saltings* by Henry Wade, *Death of a Home Secretary* by Alan Thomas, *Hearken to the Evidence* by H. Russell Wakefield, *The Broken Vase Mystery* by Mary Plum.

D21 "Mystery" Test for Connoisseurs: Identify the Author. *The Sunday Times*, no. 5770, 12 November, 1933, p. 7.

Review of *The Empty House* by Francis D. Grierson, *The Circle of Death* by Charles J. Dutton, *The Belfry Murder* by Moray Dalton.

D22 Murder on Board Ship: Enjoyable Yarns. *The Sunday Times*, no. 5771, 19 November 1933, p. 9.

Review of *S. S. Murder* by Q. Patrick, *The Judson Murder Case* by A. B. Leonard, *The Ressurection Murder Case* by S. Hart Page, *Murder at the Club* by Luke Allan.

D23 New Detective Stories: Mr. Fortune Again. *The Sunday Times*, no. 5772, 26 November 1933, p. 9.

Review of *Mr. Fortune Wonders* by H. C. Bailey, *Epilogue* by Bruce Graeme, *House-Party Murder* by Colin Ward.

D24 Conundrums of Crime: Off the Well-Worn Track. *The Sunday Times*, no. 5773, 3 December 1933, p. 9.

Review of *The Cotfold Conundrums* by Douglas G. Browne, *Drury Lane's Last Case* by Barnaby Ross, *The Case of the Gold Coins* by Anthony Wynne, *The Real Detective* by George Dilnot.

D25 Two Styles of Crime Story: American and English. *The Sunday Times*, no. 5774, 10 December 1933, p. 9.

Review of *The Siamese Twin Mystery* by Ellery Queen, *Death at the Cross-Roads* by Miles Burton, *The Silent Bell* by Elaine Hamilton.

D26 Originality in Crime: Turning to Serious Issues. *The Sunday Times*, no. 5775, 17 December 1933, p. 9.

Review of *The Wrong Murder Mystery* by Charles Barry, *The Kidnapper* by Sir Basil Thomson, *Murder Among Friends* by "Simon", *Death's Treasure Hunt* by William C. Harvey.

D27 What To Do with Our Villains: Crime Writers' Big Problem. *The Sunday Times*, no. 5776, 24 December 1933, p. 5.

Review of *The Clue of the Dead Goldfish* by Victor MacClure, *Murder up the Glen* by Colin Campbell, *Gathering Storm* by F. A. M. Webster.

D28 Grim and Gay Crime Stories: Death of an Ancient Mariner. *The Sunday Times*, no. 5777, 31 December 1933, p. 7.

Review of *End of an Ancient Mariner* by G. D. H. and M. Cole, *Old Man Mystery* by J. Jefferson Farjeon, *Watch the Wall* by Laurence W. Meynell *The Snapshot Mystery* by Ben Bolt.

D29 Train Drama in a Snowstorm: Crime on Classical Lines. *The Sunday Times*, no. 5778, 7 January 1934, p. 9.

Review of *Murder on the Orient Express* by Agatha Christie, *The Robthorne Mystery* by John Rhode, *Marriage and Murder* by David Sharp, *The Ellery Queen Omnibus*.

D30 A Fleet Street Comedy: Crime in a Newspaper Office. *The Sunday Times*, no. 5779, 14 January 1934, p. 7.

Review of *A Dagger in Fleet Street* by R. C. Woodthorpe, *The One Sane Man* by Francis Beeding, *The Campden Ruby Murder* by Adam Bliss.

D31 Another Mystery Monster: Dragon in a Bathing Pool. *The Sunday Times*, no. 5780, 21 January 1934, p. 9.

Review of *The Dragon Murder Case* by S. S. Van Dine, *Shadow on the House* by E. Charles Vivian, *Shortly Before Midnight* by Elizabeth Nisot.

D32 Detective Stories and a Thriller: Crime, Colour and Humor. *The Sunday Times*, no. 5781, 28 January 1934, p. 7.

Review of *Candidate for Lillies* by Roger East, *The Murder at the Flower Show* by Mark Beckett, *Disappearance* by Joan Cowdroy, *The Gallows of Chance* by E. Phillips Oppenheim.

D33 The Development in the Crime Novel: "Obelists En Route". *The Sunday Times*, no. 5782, 4 February 1934, p. 9.

Review of *Obelists En Route* by C. Daly King, *Death at Broadcasting House* by Val Gielgud and Holt Marvell, *The Crime of Peter Ropner* by Harold Heslop.

D34 Three Horrid Households: Mass Poisoners Who Made a Mistake. *The Sunday Times*, no. 5783, 11 February 1934, p. 9.

Review of *Family Matters* by Anthony Rolls, *The Cautley Conundrum* by A. Fielding, *Death by Misadventure* by Barbara Malim.

D35 Three Types of Crime: Poisons and Thrills. *The Sunday Times*, no. 5784, 18 February 1934, p. 7.

Review of *The Poison Duel* by Peter Dingwall, *Murder at Bayside* by Raymond Robins, *The Grinning Avenger* by Edgar Jepson.

D36 Detective Authors' Troubles: A New Wills Crofts Experiment. *The Sunday Times*, no. 5785, 25 February 1934, p. 9.

Review of *12.30 from Croydon* by Freeman Wills Crofts, *The Windmill*

Mystery by J. Jefferson Farjeon, *The Baddington Horror* by Walter S. Masterman.

D37 Past Present and Future Crimes: A University Puzzle of 1937. *The Sunday Times*, no. 5786, 4 March 1934, p. 9.

Review of *The Mystery of Vaucluse* by J. H. Wallis, *Ebenezar Investigates* by Nicholas Brady, *Creaking Gallows* by T. Arthur Plummer, *The Charabanc Mystery* by Miles Burton.

D38 Criminological Doubt: Mysteries That Leave the Disquiet Behind. *The Sunday Times*, no. 5787, 11 March 1934, p. 9.

Review of *Insoluble* by Francis Everton, *The Case of the 100% Alibis* by Christopher Bush, *Murder on the Blackboard* by Stuart Palmer.

D39 Adventure and Detection: From Bayswater to Trinidad. *The Sunday Times*, no. 5788, 18 March 1934, p. 9.

Review of *Death of a Ghost* by Margery Allingham, *Murder in Trinidad* by John W. Vandercook, *The Chinese Jar Mystery* by John Stephen Strange.

D40 Style in Crime Stories: Why Good Writing Pays. *The Sunday Times*, no. 5789, 25 March 1934, p. 9.

Review of *Death Among the Sun Bathers* by E. R. Punshon, *The Eight of Swords* by John Dickson Carr, *That's Your Man, Inspector* by David Frome.

D41 Crime Methods in Contrast: A Light Comedy Triumph. *The Sunday Times*, no. 5790, 1 April 1934, p. 9.

Review of *The Unfinished Clue* by Georgette Heyer, *Smash and Grab* by Clifton Robbins, *Death at the Opera* by Gladys Mitchell.

D42 Crime Without Romance: Study of an Ignoble Knight. *The Sunday Times*, no. 5791, 8 April 1934, p. 9.

Review of *Corpse in Cold Storage* by Milward Kennedy, *The Time Table Murder* by Roger Denbie, *Murder from Three Angles* by Vernon Loder, *Murder Day by Day* by Irvin S. Cobb.

D43 Skeleton in the Crime Cupboard: Every Author's Plot. *The Sunday Times*, no. 5792, 15 April 1934, p. 9.

Review of *Copper at Sea* by Gerard Fairlie, *Author in Distress* by Cecil M. Wills, *Big Ben Strikes Eleven* by David Magarshack.

D44 Murder in the Hebrides: Crime in a Castle. *The Sunday Times*, no. 5793, 22 April 1934, p. 9.

Review of *The Portcullis Room* by Valentine Williams, *The Case of the*

Sulky Girl by Erle Stanley Gardner, *Murder Runs in the Family* by Hulbert Footner.

D45 Murder Among the Doctors: Behind the Scenes in a Queer Hospital. *The Sunday Times*, no. 5794, 29 April 1934, p. 9.

Review of *The Hospital Murders* by Means Davis, *Death in the Fog* by Mignon G. Eberhart, *Strange Witness* by Beryl Symons, *A Shot in the Night* by Ben Bolt.

D46 Accident, Suicide or Murder?: Mr. Fortune Again. *The Sunday Times*, no. 5795, 6 May 1934, p. 9.

Review of *Shadow on the Wall* by H. C. Bailey, *Stark Naked* by Lawrence R. Bourne, *Inspector Higgins Sees It Through* by Cecil Freeman Gregg.

D47 Crime with Cross-References: Father Knox's Puzzle. *The Sunday Times*, no. 5796, 13 May 1934, p. 9.

Review of *Still Dead* by Ronald A. Knox, *A Career for the Gentleman* by David Farrer, *Death in the Quarry* by G. D. H. and M. Cole.

D48 Spate of Mystery Stories: Too Kind to Hasty Writing. *The Sunday Times*, no. 5797, 20 May 1934, p. 9.

Review of *An Old Lady Dies* by Anthony Gilbert, *Artifex Intervenes* by Richard Keverne, *An International Affair* by Bruce Graeme, *Murder of the Only Witness* by J. S. Fletcher.

D49 A Cross-Word Mystery: Puzzle Gives Key to the Plot. *The Sunday Times*, no. 5798, 27 May 1934.

Review of *The Cross-Word Mystery* by E. R. Punshon, *Death in the Dove-Cot* by Q. Patrick, *Murder Underground* by M. Doriel Hay, *Murder Mask* by Garstin Begbie.

D50 Whispers About a Murder: Humane and Inhumane Studies. *The Sunday Times*, no. 5799, 3 June 1934, p. 9.

Review of *Whispering Tongues* by Laurence Kirk, *Panic Party* by Anthony Berkeley, *The Bravo of London* by Ernest Bramah.

D51 Nazi Officials and a Crime: Political Setting of a Queer Story. *The Sunday Times*, no. 5800, 10 June 1934, p. 9.

Review of *The Talking Sparrow Murders* by Darwin L. Teilhet, *Poison for One* by John Rhode, *Richardson Scores Again!* by Sir Basil Thomson, *Ten Minute Alibi* by Anthony Armstrong and Herbert Shaw.

D52 One of the Best Crime Novels of the Year. *The Sunday Times*, no. 5801, 17 June 1934, p. 9.

Review of *There's Death in the Churchyard* by William Gore, *The Blank Cheque* by Richard Blake Brown, *The Horn* by Brian Flynn.

D53 Good Writing and Sound Plots: The Whole Scale of Crime. *The Sunday Times*, no. 5802, 24 June 1934, p. 9.

Review of *Journey Downstairs* by R. Philmore, *The Knife* by Herbert Adams, *Death Rides the Air Line* by William Sutherland.

D54 Criminals Who Are Too Ingenious. *The Sunday Times*, no. 5803, 1 July 1934, p. 9.

Rivews of *The Chinese Orange Mystery* by Ellery Queen, *The Berg Case* by John Bentley, *The Fleetwood Mansions Mystery* by Maurice B. Dix.

D55 Authenticity of Famous First Editions. *The Sunday Times*, no. 5803, 1 July 1934, p. 11.

Review of *An Enquiry into the Nature of Certain Nineteenth Century Pamphlets* by John Carter and Graham Pollard, one of the most famous works of detection in bibliography.

D56 Amusing Detective Adventures – Wits and Eccentrics. *The Sunday Times*, no. 5804, 8 July 1934, p. 9.

Review of *The Perfect Albi*, by C. St. John Sprigg, *Death of a Banker* by Anthony Wynne, *The King's Elm Mystery* by John Goodwin.

D57 Pretty Sinister – If You Have Ears Prepare to Shed Them Now. *The Sunday Times*, no. 5805, 15 July 1934, p. 9.

Review of *The Mystery of the Cape Cod Players* by P. A. Taylor, *Sinister Inn* by J. Jefferson Farjeon, *Sinister Quest* by T. C. H. Jacobs, and *Sinister House* by Gerald Verner.

D58 "Who" and "How" in Detective Stories. *The Sunday Times*, no. 5806, 22 July 1934, p. 9.

Review of *Desire to Kill* by Alice Campbell, *The Charge is Murder* by J. M. Spender and *Burn, Witch, Burn!* by A. Merritt.

D59 Murder of a Chief Constable: Watching the Police at Work. *The Sunday Times*, no. 5807, 29 July 1934, p. 9.

Review of *Constable, Guard Thyself!* by Henry Wade, *Silence of a Purple Shirt* by R. C. Woodthorpe, *Death in Goblin Waters* by Margaret Peterson, *Death on the Swim* by "Simon".

D60 Motives for Crime: "Respectability" as a Root Cause. *The Sunday Times*, no. 5808, 5 August 1934, p. 6.

Review of *Further Evidence* by Alan Block, *Frozen Death* by Anthony Weymouth and *Poison in Kensington* by Charles Kingston.

D61 What a Thriller Should Be. *The Sunday Times*, no. 5809, 12 August 1934, p. 7.

Review of *The Travelling Skull* by Harry Stephen Keeler, *Calling All Cars* by Henry Holt, *Death by the Mistletoe* by Angus Mac Vicar, *The Ince Murder Case* by E. J. Pond.

D62 Surprises for the Law-Breaker – And the Reader. *The Sunday Times*, no. 5810, 19 August 1934, p. 7.

Review of *Murder on the Cliff* by Clive Ryland, *Eight to Nine* by R. A. J. Walling, *The Case of the Lucky Leap* by Erle Stanley Gardner, *The Bowstring Murders* by Carter Dickson.

D63 Mr. Freeman Wills Crofts' Double Mystery. *The Sunday Times*, no. 5811, 26 August 1934, p. 7.

Review of *Mystery on Southampton Water* by Freeman Wills Crofts and *The Cadaver of Gideon Wyck* by Alexander Laing.

D64 The "Twins" Theme Once More: And a Nightmare Cruise. *The Sunday Times*, no. 5812, 2 September 1934.

Review of *The Life He Stole* by Sefton Kyle, *The Murder of Sigurd Sharon* by Harriett Ashbrook, and *Murder Cruise* by Michael Keyes.

D65 Three Good Crime Novels: Discord in a Mad and Bad Family. *The Sunday Times*, no. 5813, 9 September 1934, p. 8.

Review of *The Murder of My Aunt* by Richard Hull, *Why Didn't They Ask Evans?* by Agatha Christie, and *The Case of the Dead Shepherd* by Christopher Bush.

D66 The Whole Scale of Villainy. *The Sunday Times*, no. 5814, 16 September 1934, p. 8.

Review of *Five to Five* by D. Erskine Muir, *Death at the Pelican* by Cecil M. Wills, *Murder at Lancaster Gate* by Francis D. Grierson.

D67 Murder in Fancy Dress: Complicated Crime. *The Sunday Times*, no. 5815, 23 September 1934, p. 9.

Review of *Murder in Public* by John Crozier, *Masks Off at Midnight* by Valentine Williams, *Fancy Dress Ball* by J. Jefferson Farjeon.

D68 Accident, Suicide, or Murder?: Mr. J. J. Connington's Puzzle. *The Sunday Times*, no. 5816, 30 September 1934, p. 9.

Review of *The Ha-Ha Case* by J. J. Connington, *Three Went In* By N. A. Temple Ellis, and *Murder on the Moors* by Colin Campbell.

D69 Crippen as Tragic Figure: Fine Story Based on Real Life. *The Sunday Times*, no. 5817, 7 October 1934, p. 9.

Review of *Henbane* by Catherine Meadows, *Arsenic in Richmond* by David Frome, *The Divorce Court Murder* by Milton Propper.

D70 Christmas Eve Crime: and a Familiar "Death Trap". *The Sunday Times*, no. 5818, 14 October 1934, p. 11.

Review of *Crime at Christmas* by C. H. B. Kitchin, *The Grouse Moor Mystery* by John Ferguson, and *When the Wicked Man* by J. F. W. Hannay.

D71 "Straight" Stories and Crooked People. *The Sunday Times*, no. 5819, 21 October 1934, p. 9.

Review of *Skin and Bone* by Edwin Greenwood, *The Crooked Lane* by Frances Noyes Hart, *Inspector Richardson C.I.D.* by Sir Basil Thomson and *Death on the Set* by Victor MacClure.

D72 Crippen's Wife. *The Sunday Times*, no. 5819, 21 October 1934, p. 16.

Letter to the Editor regarding her review of Catherine Meadows' *Henbane* and the problems in writting fiction based on fact.

D73 Dr. Thorndyke Comes Again: Fine Entertainment. *The Sunday Times*, no. 5820, 28 October 1934, p. 9.

Review of *For the Defence: Dr. Thorndyke* by R. Austin Freeman, *Death Cruises South* by Roger Denbie, *Death Strikes from the Rear* by Antony Marsden and *Scarweather* by Anthony Rolls.

D74 The Professional Sleuth: Scotland Yard in Fiction. *The Sunday Times*, no. 5821, 4 November 1934, p. 9.

Review of *Mystery Villa* by E. R. Punshon, *The Execution of Diamond Deutsch* by Cecil Freeman Gregg, *Scotland Yard Takes a Holiday* by Luke Allan.

D75 An Extravaganza of Crime: Clues and Hilarity. *The Sunday Times*, no. 5822, 11 November 1934, p. 9.

Review of *The Blind Barber* by John Dickson Carr, *Shot at Dawn* by John Rhode, *Murder of My Patient* by Mignon G. Eberhart.

D76 Re-Enter Philo Vance: More Irritating than Ever. *The Sunday Times*, no. 5823, 18 November 1934, p. 7.

Review of *The Casino Murder Case* by S. S. Van Dine, *The Man in Button Boots* by Anthony Gilbert, *The Jury Disagree* by George Goodchild and C. E. Bechhofer Roberts.

D77 Thrills Without Frills: Complications at an Aero Club. *The Sunday Times*, no. 5824, 25 November 1934.

Review of *Death of an Airman* by C. St. John Sprigg, *Give Me Death* by Isabel Briggs Myers, *Pattern in Black and Red* by Cora Jarrett.

D78 Pity the Poor Crime Writer: Errors To Be Avoided. *The Sunday Times*, no. 5825, 2 December 1934.

Review of *The Secret of Matchams* by Nigel Barnsby, *Quick Curtain* by Alan Melville, *After the Execution* by Theodore Hyde.

D79 Sins of the Crime Writers: Murder of the King's English. *The Sunday Times*, no. 5826, 9 December 1934, p. 9.

Review of *Daylight Murder* by Paul McGuire, *The Paper Chase* by A. Fielding, *The Case of the Purple Calf* by Brian Flynn, *The One-Minute Murder* by John G. Brandon.

D80 Inside Story of a Murder: An Imaginary Diary. *The Sunday Times*, no. 5827, 16 December 1934, p. 7.

Review of *The Diary of a Murderer* by Virginia and Frank Vernon after Tristan Bernard, *The Diamond Ransom Murders* by Nellise Child.

D81 Detective Novel Problems: Are "Serious" Stories Wanted? *The Sunday Times*, no. 5828, 23 December 1934, p. 5.

Review of *The Murder Market* by Charles Rushton, *The Five Suspects* by R. A. J. Walling.

D82 A Resolution for the New Year: and a Glance Back. *The Sunday Times*, no. 5829, 30 December 1934, p. 6.

Review of *The Crime at the Quay Inn* by Eric Aldhouse, *He Laughed at Murder* by Richard Keverne, *First Came a Murder* by John Creasy.

1935

D83 Mrs. Christie at Her Best: Reality and Crime. *The Sunday Times*, no. 5830, 6 January 1935, p. 9.

Review of *Three Act Tragedy* by Agatha Christie, *Big Business Murder* by G. D. H. and M. Cole, *The Toll-House Murder* by Anthony Wynne.

D84 Two Detective Stories: Good Plots Well Told. *The Sunday Times*, no. 5831, 13 January 1935, p. 10.

Review of *Death in a Little Town* by R. C. Woodthrope, *Seventeen Cards* by E. Charles Vivian.

D85 Scotland Yard at War: And Sacco-Vanzetti Theories. *The Sunday Times*, no. 5831, 13 January 1935, p. 11.

Review of *Cornish of the Yard: His Reminiscences and Cases* by Ex-Superintendent G. W. Cornish and of *The Untried Case: Sacco and Vanzetti and the Morelli Gang*.

D86 Irregular but Likeable: Perry Mason Again. *The Sunday Times*, no. 5832, 20 January 1935, p.

Review of *The Case of the Howling Dog* by Erle Stanley Gardner, *The Strange Boarders of Palace Crescent* by E. Phillips Oppenheim, *Murder in Make-up* by Charles Ashton.

D87 Gloom and Gaiety in Contrast: Studies in Morbid Psychology. *The Sunday Times*, no. 5833, 27 January 1935, p. 10.

Review of *The Trial of Linda Stuart* by Mary D. Bickel, *Death Cuts a Caper* by David Magarshack, *Frame-Up* by Collin Brooks.

D88 Mystery and Beauty in Stories of Crime. *The Sunday Times*, no. 5834, 3 February 1935.

Review of *The Organ Speaks* by E. C. R. Lorac, *The Puzzle of the Silver Persian* by Stuart Palmer, *The Man with Bated Breath* by Joseph B. Carr.

D89 Convincing Crime Stories. *The Sunday Times*, no. 5835, 10 February 1935.

Review of *The "Looking-Glass" Murders* by Douglas G. Browne, *Death Follows a Formula* by Newton Gayle, *Death Joins the Party* by J. V. Turner.

D90 Drama in an Air Liner: Criminals and Cranks. *The Sunday Times*, no. 5836, 17 February 1935.

Review of *Obelists Fly High* by C. Daly King, *The Corpse in the Car* by John Rhode, *The Chamois Murder* by Cecil M. Wills.

D91 Two Crime Stories Based on Real Cases. *The Sunday Times*, no. 5837, 24 February 1935, p. 7.

Review of *Skin for Skin* by Winifred Duke, *After the Fact* by Alan Brock, *The Body in the Bunker* by Herbert Adams.

D92 The Adventures of a Highbrow Detective. *The Sunday Times*, no. 5838, 3 March 1935, p. 9.

Review of *The Adventures of Ellery Queen* by Ellery Queen, *Behind the Evidence* by Leonard Blackledge, *Naked Murder* by Firth Erskin.

D93 Trouble in Turl Street: Crime Among the Dons. *The Sunday Times*, no. 5839, 10 March 1935, p. 9.

Review of *The Body in the Turl* by David Frome, *A Question of Proof* by Nicholas Blake, *The Purple Claw* by Holloway Horn.

D94 The Week's Worst English. *The Sunday Times*, no. 5839, p. 14.

Letter to the editor in reply to "six agitated correspondents" on idiom and grammar.

D95 Crime Stories in Contrast: Horror and Quiet Argument. *The Sunday Times*, no. 5840, 17 March 1935, p. 9.

Review of *The Plague Court Murders* by Carter Dickson, *The Devereux Court Mystery* by Miles Burton, *The Chinese Fish* by Jean Bommart.

D96 The Week's Worst English. *The Sunday Times*, no. 5840, 17 March 1935, p. 11.

Letter to the editor in response to letters.

D97 A Thriller of Quality: Night Spent Among Wax Works. *The Sunday Times*, no. 5841, 24 March 1935, p. 9.

Review of *Wax* by Ethel Lina White, *The Perjured Alibi* by Walter S. Masterman, *The Strange Case of the Antlered Man* by Edwy Searles Brooks.

D98 Restrained and Fantastic: Contrasted Methods in Crime Stories. *The Sunday Times*, no. 5842, 31 March 1935, p. 9.

Review of *Poison in the Parish* by Milward Kennedy, *Death-Watch* by John Dickson Carr, *Fer-de-Lance* by Rex Stout.

D99 Salute to Mr. G. K. Chesterton: More Father Brown Stories. *The Sunday Times*, no. 5843, 7 April 1935, p. 9.

Review of *The Scandal of Father Brown* by G. K. Chesterton, *The Spanish Cape Mystery* by Ellery Queen, *Red Lilac* by Lord Gorell.

D100 Detective and Physician: Re-Enter Mr. Fortune. *The Sunday Times*, no. 5844, 14 April 1935, p. 9.

Review of *Mr. Fortune Objects* by H. C. Bailey, *The Dear Old Gentleman* by George Goodchild and Bechhofer Roberts, *The New Made Grave* by Hulbert Footner.

D101 Pleasant People in a Crime Novel. *The Sunday Times*, no. 5845, 21 April 1935, p. 7.

Review of *Death in the Stocks* by Geogette Heyer, *The Ginger Cat Mystery* by Robin Forsythe.

D102 Rich and Dainty Fare: Melodrama with a Difference. *The Sunday Times*, no. 5846, 28 April 1935, p. 9.

Review of *Pins and Needles* by Edwin Greenwood, *Rope by Arrangement* by Henrietta Clandon, *Murder Without Weapon* by Means Davis.

D103 The Grammarian's Funeral. *The Sunday Times*, no. 5847, 5 May 1935, p. 9.

Review of *The Grammarian's Funeral* by Edward Acheson, *Darker Grows the Valley* by Q. Patrick, *The Eleventh Hour* by J. S. Fletcher.

D104 Murder Among the Doctors: And Two Ingenious Problems. *The Sunday Times*, no. 5848, 12 May 1935, p. 9.

Review of *The Doctors Are Doubtful* by Anthony Weymouth, *Crime at Guildford* by Freeman Wills Crofts, *Between Murders* by Sherry King.

D105 A Crime Story: With a Dash of Ginger. *The Sunday Times*, no. 5849, 19 May 1935, p. 9.

Review of *The Clue of the Forgotten Murder* by Carleton Kendral, *Twenty-Five Sanitary Inspectors* by Roger East, *The Ten Black Pearls* by Cecil Freeman Gregg.

D106 Puppets or People in Stories of Crime? *The Sunday Times*, no. 5850, 26 May 1935, p. 9.

Review of *Death of a Beauty Queen* by E. R. Punshon, *Dr. Tancred Begins* by G. D. H. and M. Cole.

D107 Straightforward and Sound: Variety in Three Stories. *The Sunday Times*, no. 5851, 2 June 1935, p. 9.

Review of *Three Witnesses* by Sydney Fowler, *The Green Tunnel* by Cecil Champain Lowis, *The Gaol Gates Are Open* by David Hume.

D108 Hendon Police College in a Novel. *The Sunday Times*, no. 5852, 9 June 1935, p. 7.

Review of *Hendon's First Case* by John Rhode, *Wheels in the Forest* by John Newton Chance, *Death Treads . . .* by Cecil M. Wills.

D109 Three Stories of Crime: Disappointments and Compensations. *The Sunday Times*, no. 5853, 16 June 1935, p. 9.

Review of *Casual Slaughters* by James Quince, *The Mystery of the Cape Cod Tavern* by Phoebe Attwood Taylor, *Death as an Extra* by Val Gielgud and Holt Marvel.

D110 Crime Writers Go Abroad: Ruritania, Germany and France. *The Sunday Times*, no. 5854, 23 June 1935, p.

Review of *Death of a Queen* by C. St. John Sprigg, *The Death-Riders* by Cornelius Cofyn, *The Spy Paramount* by E. Phillips Oppenheim, *Richardson Goes Abroad* by Sir Basil Thomson, *Motive for Murder* by Aceituna and Joy Griffin.

D111 Crime Writers at the Turning Point. *The Sunday Times*, no. 5859, 28 July 1935, p. 7.

Review of *The White Priory Murders* by Carter Dickson, *Thanks to Murder* by Joseph Krumgold, *Keep Away from Water* by Alice Campbell.

D112 Lively Reading in Three Stories of Crime. *The Sunday Times*, no. 5860, 4 August 1935, p. 7.

Review of *A Girl Died Laughing* by Viola Paradise, *Fate Laughs* by Herbert Adams, *Blue Water Murder* by Philip Atkey.

D113 Murder at the Opera: Spirited Stories. *The Sunday Times*, no. 5861, 11 August 1935, p. 7.

Review of *Murder in Time* by Lillian Day and Norman Lederer, *The House of Wraith* by Edward J. Millward, *Blood on the Heather* by Stephen Chalmers.

D114 Confusion and Crime: Trials of a Woman Detective. *The Sunday Times*, no. 5862, 18 August 1935, p. 7.

Review of *The Communist's Corpse* by Richard Wormser, *A Killer and His Star* by H. M. Stephenson.

1937

D115 Famous Scottish Trials. *The Sunday Times*, no. 5955, 30 May 1937, p. 12.

Review of *Mainly Murder* by William Roughead.

1940

D116 The Technique of the Sermon. *The Spectator*, no. 5823, 2 February 1940, p. 150.

Review of *The Art of Preaching* by Charles Smyth.

D117 A Drama of the Christian Church. *The International Review of Missions*, vol. XXXIV, no. 136, October 1945, pp. 430–432.

A review of *The House of the Octopus* by Charles Williams.

1947

D118 *The Road Goes On*: A Nation's Veins and Arteries. *The British Weekly*, vol. CXXI, no. 3140, 2 January 1947, p. 203.

Review of C. W. Scott-Giles' history of British roads from Roman times to the present.

1949

D119 Conan Doyle: Crusader. *The Sunday Times*, no. 6564, 6 February 1949, p. 3.

Review of *The Life of Sir Arthur Conan Doyle* by John Dickson Carr.

D120 Between Two Worlds. *The New York Times Book Review*, 21 August 1949, p. 7.

Review of *Many Dimensions* by Charles Williams.

1950

D121 The Theologian and the Scientist. *The Listener*, vol. XLIV, no. 1132, 9 November 1950, pp. 496–497, 500.

Review of Fred Hoyle's *New Cosomology*. Letter to the Editor in reply to a letter regarding "The Theologian And The Scientist." *The Listener* vol. XLIV, no. 1134, 23 November 1950, p. 594.

D122 Men and Books: Charles Williams. *Time and Tide*, vol. 31, no. 48, 2 December 1950, p. 1220.

1955

D123 Christianity Regained. *Time and Tide*, 1 October 1955, pp. 1263–1264.

Review of *Surprised By Joy* by C. S. Lewis.

E

BROADCASTS, PLAY PRODUCTIONS, FILMS, AND RECORDS

BROADCASTS

The Written Archives Center of The British Broadcasting Corporation has furnished most of the following list of broadcasts. Some entries were found by consulting *The Listener* and *The Radio Times*. German, Italian, and other overseas programmes are not listed. Only the earliest productions are listed; several of the programmes were broadcast many times. *Starred items were published as well as broadcast; consult the Index.

E1   28 June 1930 – *Behind the Screen, Part III.

A contribution to a detective story written in five parts by five authors.

E2   23 July 1930 – Plotting a Detective Story.

Talk with Anthony Berkeley.

E3   10 January 1931 – *The Scoop, Part I.

A contribution to a detective story in twelve parts by six authors.

E4   4 April 1931 – *The Scoop, Part XII.

E5   29 December 1931 – *Trials and Sorrows of a Mystery Writer.

Talk.

E6   16 January 1932 – On The 9.20: Conversations in the Train III.

Participation in a discussion.

E7   5 March 1932 – On The 9.20: Conversations in the Train IX.

E8   3 March 1934 – Seven Days Hard.

Talk in a series by famous people on how they spent a typical week.

E9 6 April 1934 – *Dilemma.

Short story.

E10 19 January 1937 – London Theatre 10: *BUSMAN'S HONEYMOON.

Excerpts read from the play, featuring the cast at The Comedy Theatre.

E11 31 January 1937 – *Would You Like To Be 21, Again? I Wouldn't.

Appeal on behalf of the Over 30 Association.

E12 6 March 1937 – Radio Gazette 22.

An account of her initiation into The Detection Club and a short sequence on BUSMAN'S HONEYMOON.

E13 24 November 1937 – Bells over London.

Extract from THE NINE TAILORS read.

E14 10 June 1938 – Detectives in Fiction. : *The Learned Adventure of the Dragon's Head.

Short story.

E15 25 December 1938 – *HE THAT SHOULD COME.

Nativity play.

E16 5 March 1940 – *Absolutely Elsewhere.

Short story.

E17 11 August 1940 – *Creed or Chaos: Christ of the Creeds.

E18 13 August 1940 – Calling All Women.

Talk.

E19 18 August 1940 – *Creed or Chaos: Sacrament of the Matter.

E20 5 March 1941 – *Religions Behind the Nation.

Talk.

E21 June-July 1941 – God the Son.

Six talks for the Forces Programme:
8 June 1941   Lord and God.
15 June 1941   Lord of All worlds.
22 June 1941   The Man of Men.

29 June 1941   The Death of God.
6 July 1941   The World's Desire.
13 July 1941   The Touchstone of History.

E22 14 December 1941 – Answering You. Replies to questions from Canada and the USA.

E23 21 December 1941–18 October 1942 – The Childrens' Hour: ★THE MAN BORN TO BE KING.

In twelve plays:
21 December 1941	I. Kings in Judea.
25 January 1942	II. The King's Herald.
8 February 1942	III. A Certain Nobleman.
8 March 1942	IV. The Heirs to the Kingdom.
12 April 1942	V. The Bread of Heaven.
3 May 1942	VI. The Feast of Tabernacles.
31 May 1942	VII. The Light and the Life.
28 June 1942	VIII. Royal Progress.
26 July 1942	IX. The King's Supper.
23 August 1942	X. The Princes of this World.
20 September 1942	XI. King of Sorrows.
18 October 1942	XII. The King Comes to His Own.

E24 3 April 1943 – ★The Man with No Face.

Short story on Saturday Night Theatre.

E25 16 April 1943 – ★The Man Who Knew How.

Short story.

E26 30 December 1943 – Your Questions Answered.

Reply to a question about the last nurder trial held in The House of Lords.

E27 10 August 1944 – ★The Inspiration of Mr. Budd.

Short story.

E28 2 August 1945 – Detective Quiz No. 1: Corner in Crime.

Participation in a panel discussion with six other writers of detective fiction; edited by John Dickson Carr and chaired by Val Gielgud.

E29 30 August 1945 – Detective Quiz No. 2: Corner in Crime.

Same format as Quiz no. 1.

E30 27 September 1945 – Detective Quiz No. 3: Corner in Crime.

Same format as Quizzes no. 1 and no. 2.

E31 30 March 1947 – ★THE JUST VENGEANCE.
Drama.

E32 2 October 1947 – ★BUSMAN'S HONEYMOON.
Television drama.

E34 2 December 1947–6 January 1948 – ★WHOSE BODY?
Dramatised in six weekly episodes.

E35 24 February 1948 – Mystery Playhouse: Where Do We Go from Here?
Drama by Sayers and other members of The Detection Club.

E36 28 August 1949 – Mosaic: ★The War Cat.
Poem.

E37 21 November 1949–9 December 1949 – A Book at Bedtime: ★MURDER MUST ADVERTISE.
Read by Alan Wheatley.

E38 9 July 1950 – Mediaeval Cosmology and the Imagination: Dante.
Talk.

E39 26 September 1950 – ★The New Cosmology.
Review of talks by Fred Hoyle.

E40 28 July 1951 – Canterbury and Religious Drama.
Talk.

E41 2 February 1952 – In Town Tonight.
Interview.

E42 12 May 1952 – Religion and Philosophy: Some Christian Books and Their Authors.
A discussion of Sayers' translation of Dante.

E43 30 July 1953 – ★THE MYSTERIOUS ENGLISH.

E44 29 November 1953 – Talking of Books.
Two extracts read from the Introduction to GREAT SHORT STORIES OF DETECTION, MYSTERY AND HORROR.

E45 1 January 1954 – Sherlock Holmes Centenary Birthday Tribute.

Lord Peter Wimsey, played by Dennis Arundell, paid tribute to Sherlock Holmes and remembered when as a boy he consulted Holmes about a lost kitten.

E46 24 August 1954 – 14 September 1954 – *THE NINE TAILORS.

Dramatised in four episodes.

E47 18 September 1956 – Religion and Philosophy.

Extracts from THE DIVINE COMEDY: PURGATORY read.

E48 22 April 1957 – *MURDER MUST ADVERTISE.

Dramatised.

E49 3 October 1957 – *BUSMAN'S HONEYMOON.

Television drama.

E50 19 December 1957 – Today.

Obituary read by Val Gielgud.

E51 20 December 1957 – Woman's Hour.

Personal reminiscences of Sayers by Dr. E. V. Rieu.

E52 8 December 1960 – *THE ZEAL OF THY HOUSE.

Drama.

E53 3 March 1963 – The Detection of a Snob.

Quotations from Sayers' books.

E54 25 May 1963 – *STRONG POISON.

Dramatised.

E55 17 June 1964 – An Act of Worship: *The Journeyman.

Poem read.

E56 22 December 1964 – Christmastide Readings and Carols.

Extract from HE THAT SHOULD COME read at Salisbury Cathedral.

E57 28 April 1965 – Viewpoint: Dorothy L. Sayers 1893–1957 Impressions of a Writer.

BBC television discussion.

E58 13 May 1968 – Renaissance Literature.

Included excerpts from THE DIVINE COMEDY: HELL.

E59 12 November 1968 – Story of Crime and Detection: ★The Man with Copper Fingers.

E60 6 March 1969 – Viewpoint: ★The Homeless Bishop – Richard of Chichester.

Television reading of Sayers' Introduction to C. M. Duncan-Jones' *S. Richard of Chichester*.

E61 6 April 1970–1 June 1970 – Lord Peter Wimsey Stories.

Seven stories from LORD PETER VIEWS THE BODY and the story, "In the Teeth of the Evidence", broadcast in a weekly series.

E62 10 June 1970 – Now Read On: ★THE DOCUMENTS IN THE CASE.

Discussion with exerpts read.

E63 18 April 1971 – Sunday Reading.

Excerpts from UNPOPULAR OPINIONS.

E64 18 March 1972 – Saturday Night Theatre.

UNNATURAL DEATH dramatised.

E65 29 April 1972 – Lord Peter Wimsey.

A talk by Janet Hitchman with extracts from books and stories in which Wimsey appears.

E66 15 February 1973 – Jack de Manio Precisely: An Interview with Muriel St. Clare Byrne.

Poem, ★For Timothy, read.

E67 1972–1975 – Masterpiece Theatre.

Television productions of: 5 April 1972 CLOUDS OF WITNESS: June 1973 MURDER MUST ADVERTISE; April 1974 THE NINE TAILORS; 2 June 1974 THE UNPLEASANTNESS AT THE BELLONA CLUB; and 23 July 1975 THE FIVE RED HERRINGS with Ian Carmichael as Wimsey.

PLAY PRODUCTIONS

The following list does not include plays which were written for radio broadcast; for those and for plays which were published, consult the Index. (Only first productions are listed.)

E68   1915 – *Pied Pipings or the Innocents Abroad.*

Going-down play at Oxford 1915. Sayers was the musical director and played the leading role, in addition to writing parts of the play.

E69   16 December 1936 – BUSMAN'S HONEYMOON.

Written in Collaboration with Muriel St. Clare Byrne, the play opened in London at the Comedy Theatre and ran about 400 performances. The play had a brief trial run in Birmingham. Reviewed in *The Times,* 17 December 1936, 14b; *New Statesman* 12:26 December 1936, p. 1065; *Spectator* 157; 25 December 1936, p. 1122; *Theatre World* 27: January 1937, p. 11.

E70   12–18 June 1937 – THE ZEAL OF THY HOUSE.

Written for the Friends of Canterbury Cathedral; first performed at the Chapter House during the Canterbury Festival. Reviewed in *The Times,* 14 June 1937, 12c; 29 March 1938 London production at the Westminster Theatre. Reviewed in *The Times,* 30 March 1938, 12b.

E71   10–17 June 1939 – THE DEVIL TO PAY.

Written for the Friends of Canterbury Cathedral first performed in the Chapter House during the Canterbury Festival. Reviewed in *The Times,* 12 June 1939, 10d.; 20 July 1939 London production at His Majesty's Theatre; reviewed in *The Times,* 21 July 1939, 12b.

E72   8 April 1940 – *Love All.*

A light comedy produced at the Torch Theatre, London. Reviewed in *The Times,* 10 April 1940, 6e; *The New Statesman,* 19: 13 April 1940, p. 493; *Time and Tide,* 21: 13 April 1940, p. 392.

E73   15–26 June 1946 – THE JUST VENGEANCE.

Performed in Lichfield Cathedral during its 750th Anniversary Festival. Reviewed in *The Times,* 17 June 1946, 6a.

E74   2 July 1951 – THE EMPEROR CONSTANTINE.

Performed during the Colchester Festival, at the Playhouse Theatre, 1951. Reviewed in *The Times,* 4 July 1951, 8d.; 5–26 February 1952–*Christ's Emperor.* A shortened version of THE EMPEROR CONSTANTINE, performed at St. Thomas's Regent Street, London. Reported in *The Times*, 11 January 1952 6e.

FILMS

E75 1935 – THE SILENT PASSENGER.

Screen play by Basil Mason based on Sayers' original, unpublished story commissioned by Phoenix Films. Reviewed in *The New Statesman*, 20 July 1935, p. 95. Wimsey, in a minor role.

E76 1940 – BUSMAN'S HONEYMOON (American title: HAUNTED HONEYMOON).

Screenplay by Moncton Hoffe, Angus Mac Phail and Harold Goldman based on the play (A24) by Sayers and M. St. Clare Byrne. Reviewed in *Illustrated London News*, 31 August 1940, p. 292; *The New Statesman*, 14 September 1940, p. 259; *Theatre Arts*, November 1940, p. 787; *Time*, 18 November 1940, p. 85.

RECORDS

E77 THE SONG OF ROLAND (A57) Caedmon Records #TC2059 LP 33–1/3 rpm 2 vol.

Read by Anthony Quayle.

E78 Records for The National Institute for the Blind: LORD PETER VIEWS THE BODY; STRONG POISON; THE NINE TAILORS; HAVE HIS CARCASE; BUSMAN'S HONEYMOON.

F

LECTURES

The following is as complete a list of lectures given by Sayers as could be discovered and substantiated by consulting the usual reference works, her letters, books, and articles, and her agent's records. She surely gave a good many more than these recorded, which illustrate her popularity as a writer and lecturer and the range of her interests. ★Starred items were also published; consult the Index.

F1   On Detective Novelists. Given at a dinner of the University Section and Authors' and Journalists' Section of the Forum Club reported in *The Times*, 27 November 1930, 5d.

F2   On Detective Novels. Given at *The Sunday Times* Book Exhibition, 23 November 1934.

F3   ★A Toast to Oxford. Given on the occasion of M. K. Pope's retirement at the Somerville College Gaudy dinner 1934; printed as "What Is Right with Oxford?"

F4   ★Aristotle on Detective Fiction. Given at Oxford, 5 March 1935, according to Sayers in UNPOPULAR OPINIONS. Addressed to the English Association 21 June 1935 at Conway Hall, reported in *The Times*, 24 June 1935, 12c.

F5   On Detective Fiction. Given at the Oxford Union, November 1935.

F6   The Future of the Mystery Novel. A "New Paths in Literature Lecture" given at The City Literary Institute and announced in *The Cresset*, January 1936, p. 13.

F7   ★Doing a Man's Job. Given to the Junior Branch of the National Council for Women's Service, 14 October 1936.

F8 The Modern Detective Story. Given to the Sesame Imperial Club, 27 October 1936.

F9 The Importance of Being Vulgar. Given 12 February 1936, to judge by internal evidence, to a club.

F10 *An Account of Lord Mortimer Wimsey. Given to Confraternitas Historica at Sidney Sussex College, Cambridge, 7 March 1937. Other lectures on the Wimseys were given the same day by C. W. Scott-Giles, Helen Simpson, and Muriel St. Clare Byrne.

F11 The Comedy of Horror. Given to the English Association, March 1937, on detective fiction.

F12 Crime Detection in Fact and Fiction. Given to the Trinity Literary Society, Glasgow, 6 December 1937, according to *The Glasgow Herald*, 7 December 1937, 7d. Sayers advises would-be murderers that methods used in detective fiction are too elaborate to succeed in real life.

F13 The Playwright. Given at Chelsea School circa 25 August 1938.

F14 *Are Women Human? Given to a Women's Society, 1938, according to Sayers in UNPOPULAR OPINIONS.

F15 The Dictatorship of Words. Presidential address to the Modern Language Association Conference of Educational Associations at University College London, 5 January 1939, reported in *The Times*, 6 January 1939, 7a.

F16 Detective Stories as a Token of Virtue. Given to the Stationer's and Newspaper Makers' Company at a Livery Luncheon, 15 February 1939, reported in *The Times*, 16 February 1939, 11f.

F17 Our National Attitude Toward the Theatre. Given at the Chapter House Canterbury in conjunction with the Canterbury Cathedral Festival (10–17 June 1939) production of THE DEVIL TO PAY, reported in *The Times*, 16 June 1939, 12b.

F18 Religious Drama and Production. Given to a meeting of the Coventry Diocesan Youth Council and Friends of Coventry Cathedral, 30 September 1939; announced in *The Times*, 1 August 1939, 15e.

F19 ★Creed or Chaos? Given to the Church Tutorial Classes Association Bienniel Festival at Derby, 4 May 1940.

F20 ★The Mysterious English. Given in London, 1940, according to Sayers in the printed pamphlet.

F21 ★The Church's Responsibility. Given to the Archbishop of York's Conference at Malvern, 8 January 1941, reported in *The Times*, 19 January 1941, 7c.

F22 ★Work and Vocation. Given at the Dome, Brighton, 8 March 1941. Printed as "Vocation in Work" and "A Plea for Vocation in Work".

F23 ★The Other Six Deadly Sins. Given at Westminster, 23 October 1941.

F24 On Detective Fiction. Given to the Czechoslovak Institute, reported in the *Times Literary Supplement*, 31 January 1942, p. 49.

F25 ★Creative Mind. Given to the Humanities Club at Reading in February 1942, according to Sayers in UNPOPULAR OPINIONS.

F26 ★Why Work? Given at Eastbourne, 23 April 1942.

F27 ★Church and Theatre. Given at St. Anne's House, Soho, June 1943 as one of a series of lectures, "Christian Faith and Contemporary Culture". This lecture is incorporated in the articles "Types of Christian Drama" and "Sacred Plays". See also The Social Significance of the Theatre (F51).

F28 England, the Empire, Its Laws and Govenment. Given to the Witham and District Girls' Training Corps, Company No. 534 at Witham, 11 October 1943.

F29 ★Towards a Christian Aesthetic. Given as one of the Edward Alleyn Lectures 1944.

F30 ★The Faust Legend and the Idea of the Devil. Given to the

English Goethe Society, 22 February 1945, at University College London.

F31 ★Making Sense of the Universe. Given at Kingsway Hall on Ash Wednesday, 6 March 1946. One of the "Religion and Philosophy" lectures which Sayers, Charles Williams, T. S. Eliot, Ronald Knox and others gave for the "Christian Mission" in London.

F32 ★The Divine Poet and the Angelic Doctor. Given to the Aquinas Society 1946.

F33 ★The Eighth Bolgia. Given to the Society for Italian Studies at Cambridge, August 1946.

F34 Idylls of the King. Given first at Wellington College, Berkshire, 19 February 1947; also given at Girton College, Cambridge, 11 August 1949; St. Anne's Soho 13 October 1952; and Bedford College, London, 11 March 1953.

F35 ★The Lost Tools of Learning. Given to a Vacation Course in Education at Oxford, 13 August 1947.

F36 ★Dante's Imagery: I Symbolic. Given in 1947 to the Society for Italian Studies Summer School at Cambridge.

F37 Dante's Imagery: II Pictorial. Given in 1947 to the Society for Italian Studies Summer School at Cambridge.

F38 ★Dante's Virgil. Given to the Virgil Society 1948.

F39 On the English Language. Given to the English Association, 3 July 1948, reported in *The Times*, 5 July 1948, 6d.

F40 ★The Meaning of Purgatory. Given in August 1948, to the Society for Italian Studies Summer School at Cambridge.

F41 ★The Meaning of Heaven and Hell. Given in August 1948, to the Society for Italian Studies Summer School at Cambridge.

F42 ★The City of Dis. Given to the Confraternitas Historica, Sidney Sussex College, Cambridge circa 1948.

F43 ★The Paradoxes of *The Comedy*. Given to the Society for Italian Studies, Oxford, 17 August 1949.

F44 ★The Comedy of *The Comedy*. Given 16 August 1949 to the Society for Italian Studies Summer School at Cambridge.

F45 On King John and the Magna Charta. Given to a meeting at the Public Hall, Witham, in support for Aubrey Moody, the Conservative candidate, 22 February 1950.

F46 The Revival of Rhetoric. Given at the English Festival of Spoken Poetry, Bedford College, 17 July 1950.

F47 ★The Cornice of Sloth. Given to the Society for Italian Studies Summer School at Exeter, August 1950.

F48 On the Emperor Constantine. Given to the Inner Wheel Club, Witham, 6 March 1951.

F49 On Change-Ringing. Given at the Canterbury Festival of Britain in July 1951.

F50 ★Dante's Cosmos. Given to the Royal Institution, 23 February 1951.

F51 ★The Social Significance of the Theatre. Inaugural lecture at St. Anne's House, Soho, Autumn 1951. On the Church and the Theatre, possibly incorporated in "Types of Christian Drama" and "Sacred Plays".

F52 ★Dante and Milton. Given to the Summer School of Italian Studies Summer School at Cambridge, July 1952.

F53 ★The Poetry of the Image in Dante and Charles Williams. Given to the Chelmsford Arts Association, July 1952.

F54 ★The Teaching of Latin: A New Approach. Given to the Association for the Reform of Latin Teaching, 26 August 1952.

F55 ★The Fourfold Interpretation of *The Comedy*. Given circa August 1954, to The Society for Italian Studies Summer School at Cambridge.

F56 ★On Translating the *Divina Commedia*. Given to a British Council course for Italian teachers of English at Girton College Cambridge, 23 August 1954.

F57 ⋆Poetry, Language and Ambiguity. Given to the Oxford University Socratic Society, 3 June 1954.

F58 ⋆The Writing and Reading of Allegory. Given as a Sarah Walker Memorial Lecture at the Training College, Darlington, 10 November 1954.

F59 ⋆Charles Williams: Poets' Critic. Given to a conference at Milland Place, Lipbook, Hampshire, 23 August 1955.

F60 ⋆*Oedipus Simplex*: Freedom and Fate in Folk-lore and Fiction. Given to the Royal Institution of Great Britain, 11 November 1955.

F61 ⋆The Beatrician Vision in Dante and Other Poets. Given as the Herford Memorial Lecture to the Manchester Dante Society, 14 March 1956.

F62 ⋆Dante Faber: Structure in the Poetry of Statement. Given to the Cambridge University Italian Society, 8 May 1956.

F63 ⋆The Poetry of Search and the Poetry of Statement. Given to the Oxford University Spectator Club, 30 October 1956.

F64 ⋆The Translation of Verse. Given to the Oxford University English Club, 6 March 1957.

G

MANUSCRIPT COLLECTIONS

Privately owned manuscripts are not listed. Italicized titles have been given to untitled pieces. ★Starred items were published; consult the Index. AMS = autograph manuscript; TMS = typed manuscript; TCC = typed carbon copy; ALS = autograph letter signed; TLS = typed letter signed; pp. = pages; *ll.* = leaves; pagination and number of leaves include title-pages.

G1 DEPARTMENT OF WESTERN MANUSCRIPTS BODLEIAN LIBRARY
Oxford OX13BG ENGLAND

The following list has been prepared from information provided by the Department of Western Manuscripts, Bodleian Library; the manuscripts were displayed during the Winter 1977–78; at the time of the preparation of this bibliography, information was not available as to which items will become part of the permanent collection.

G1.1 Socks. (Poem) AMS.

G1.2 An Oxford Kalendar for Somervillians. (Poem) AMS.

G1.3 Experiments in Metre. (10 Poems) 16 pp. AMS. Rondeaux: ★To M. J. – To Sleep – Memory – When Eve went out ... – Any Girl to any Man – Whence are you ... ?; Leander; Ballades: Fortune is Fickle – ★I leaned my head upon my hand; ★Matter of Brittany.

G1.4 ★The Last Castle. (Poem) AMS.

G1.5 ★Hymn in Contemplation of Sudden Death. (Poem) AMS.

G1.6 ★To Members of the Bach Choir on Active Service. (Poem) AMS.

G1.7 To H.P.A. (Poem) AMS.

G1.8   The Lyttel Geste of Saint Hugh of Oxford. (Short verses) AMS, some signed "D.R."

G1.9   Pied Pipings or, Innocents Abroad: A modern fairy play. (Play) 19 pp. TMS, plus a cartoon of Dr. H. P. Allen and a photograph of Sayers as "H. P. Rallentando".

G1.10   ALS to "Tiddler" (Miss Dorothy H. Rowe) signed "H. P. Rallentando".

G2   GUYMON COLLECTION OF DETECTIVE AND MYSTERY FICTION
Occidental College
Los Angeles, California 90041

G2.1   *In the Teeth of the Evidence. (Story) 23 pp. AMS on ruled looseleaf note paper, includes revisions and corrections.

G3   HOUGHTON LIBRARY
Harvard University
Cambridge, Massachusetts 02138

G3.1   A collection of letters to John Cournos 1922–1923.

G4   MUGAR MEMORIAL LIBRARY SPECIAL COLLEC-TIONS
Boston University
Boston, Massachusetts 02215

G4.1   Three letters to Robert Speight 1943–1944 on THE MAN BORN TO BE KING.

G5   HUMANITIES RESEARCH CENTER
University of Texas
Austin, Texas 78712

G5.1   *Bibliography of William Wilkie Collins. (Bibliography for Cambridge Bibliography of English Literature) 25 pp. AMS; 21 pp. TMS with AMS revisions plus 2 TCC's with autograph corrections; 3 pp. galley proofs (2 sets).

G5.2   *WILKIE COLLINS: A CRITICAL AND BIOGRAPH-
ICAL STUDY. (Biography) 28 pp. AMS Chapter I with
note "Portrait of William Collins"; 23 pp AMS Chapter
II; 22 pp. AMS with TMS additions Chapter III; 28 pp.
AMS Chapter IV; 31 pp. AMS Chapter V; 34 pp. AMS
fair copy Chapter I on lined paper with red ink footnotes;
23 pp. TMS Chapter I plus two TCC's.

G5.3   *The Dates in "The Red Headed League". (Article) 16 pp.
TMS.

G5.4   *Dorothy L. Sayers Reveals the Origin of Lord Peter
Wimsey. (Article) 1 p. TCC published as "How I Came to
Invent the Character of Lord Peter".

G5.5   *Gaudy Night. (Essay) 7 pp. TMS.

G5.6   *PAPERS RELATING TO THE FAMILY OF WIMSEY.
(Pamphlet) 14 pp. TMS (does not appear to be the *original*
TMS).

G5.7   Memoranda of agreement with Albatross Verlag: 2 pp.
printed document, signed dated 13 March 1934, regarding
continental distribution of THE NINE TAILORS; 2 pp.
printed document, signed on 1 *l.* dated 17 July 1946, regarding a Portuguese translation of THE NINE TAILORS;
2 pp. TCC of a printed document, signed regarding continental distribution of GAUDY NIGHT.

G5.8   Last Will and Testament. 4 pp. TCC of the handwritten
document dated 1939, plus a legal statement regarding pro-
bation of the Will and payment of tax dated 3 March 1958.

G5.9   Materials relating to a critical and biographical study of
Wilkie Collins: (a) Sayers' collection of printed Collins
materials including 37 of his works in several issues and
editions, many with Sayers' autograph notes; 14 titles about
Collins; photographs of Collins' diary and 8 playbills for
Collins' plays; (b) Sayers' collection of 24 of Collins' manuscripts and proof copies; (c) Sayers' collection of 152 autograph letters written by Collins 1860–1889, including a

letter from Collins to William D. Booth, 20 September 1870 with an autograph note by Sayers about the play *Man and Wife*; plus 14 autograph letters to Collins 1888–1890; (d) two booksellers' catalogues and four pages from catalogues listing books by or about Collins with Sayers' autograph notes; (e) a file of 3 × 5 cards of AMS notes on Collins arranged under headings including each work by Collins and a variety of biographical and critical topics; another file prepared by M. L. Parrish; (f) notebook 11 × 7 cm. 8 pp. AMS notes on Collins' treatment of women in his novels and on detective fiction; (g) notebook 16 × 10 cm. 55 *ll*. AMS notes on Collins' work arranged alphabetically with some miscellaneous notes, doodles and drawings; (h) notebook 20·3 × 15 cm. entitled "Wilkie Collins 1824–1854" including a list of Collins' residences, Collins' family tree, followed by brief notes arranged by month within the thirty years; (i) notebook 15 × 7 cm. 32 *ll*. AMS notes on book reviews of Collins' works, collectors of Collins' works, Collins' understanding of women, a drawing of a woman in 19th century costume, notes on bells for THE NINE TAILORS; (j) notebook 15 × 7 cm. 48 *ll*. AMS notes comparing Collins to Dickens, on Victorian themes and literary techniques as related to Collins' work, etc.; (k) notebook 20 × 16 cm. 35 pp. AMS notes on Collins' bibliography; (l) list of Collins' contributions to *All the Year Round* 5 pp. AMS 4 *ll*.; (m) Love Affairs of Wilkie Collins. 8 pp. TMS with autograph revisions; (n) folder 24·5 × 20 cm. enclosing 14 pp. AMS 10 *ll*. list of Collins' library; (o) Envelope with AMS notes on illustrations for the study of Collins enclosing a 2 pp. AMS outline for nineteen chapters and a 3 pp. AMS outline for twenty-two chapters; (p) chronological list of Collins' novels and plays 3 pp. AMS; (q) 14 pp. AMS notes on Collins' books and variant editions, stained and torn; (r) notes on Collins' letters 26 pp. AMS on half-sheets; (s) 4 pp. AMS notes on Collins and opium plus 12 pp. AMS notes comparing Collins' work to that of Hardy, Dickens, etc.; (t) miscellaneous AMS extracts: from *Pall Mall Gazette*; a letter from George Augustus Sala to Collins with a newspaper extract; from Christie's sale catalogue 22 February 1890; from Anderson Galleries sale catalogue January 1929; plus extracts copied by Sayers' research assistants; (u) miscellaneous AMS: notes about Collins' tour of Switzerland and Italy with Dickens; notes about Collins' mother and portraits; notes on the dramatic version of "The Evil Genius"; notes on *Blind Love*; notes on original manuscripts of Collins; notes on Elizabeth Harriet Bartley; notes on Ferrucio Busoni's interest in Collins; genealogical tables of Collins' family; notes on the Geddes family (on a brown envelope); brief outline of eight chapters for a study of Collins; (v) drawing with AMS notes of Collins' grave at Kensal Green; (w) type-scripts, notes and letters, prepared or transcribed by May Osler or other research assistants with scattered Sayers' autograph notes including a British Museum ticket of application for books (with Sayers' autograph notes).

G5.10 Letters relating to Sayers' work on Collins: (a) postcard from Edmund Sidney P. Haynes with Sayers' autograph notes; (b) TCC to Howard Seavoy Leach 16 July 1928; (c) TCC to the Editor of *The Hornsey Journal* 12 March 1929 (published 29 March 1929); (d) collection of letters from Graham Pollard 1929–1934 with a list of Collins' English and American first editions and letters from William Seymour, some autograph notes by Sayers on the letters plus 1 p. and a small card of Sayers' autograph notes; (e) letter from J. L. Fenn, September 1930, plus 3 pp. typed list of Collins' books with some marks by Sayers; (f) letter from Michael Sadleir, 6 December 1932, with Sayers' autograph notes; (g) collection of letters from A. May Osler February-September 1933 with scattered Sayers' autograph notes; (h) two letters from Morris Parrish with Sayers' AMS extract of a letter from Parrish; (i) TCC letter to Raphael King 20 February 1936; (j) TLS with autograph correction to James Sandoe 6 January 1944; another TLS to Sandoe 20 March 1944; (k) four letters from James Sandoe 1944–1945; (l) typed note to Terence Ian Armstrong-Fytton,

July 1957; (m) a collection of letters to Sayers from many correspondents, largely about Collins.

G5.11 Letters not relating to Sayers' work on Collins: (a) ALS to Leonard Green, 29 August 1919, about her poems in *Oxford Poetry* and on friendship; (b) TLS to Edgar Jepson 15 February 1928 about "The Tea Leaf"; (c) TLS to P. M. Stone 3 March 1928 about S. S. Van Dine's novels and a new Lord Peter novel; (d) 8 TLS to The Richards Press 1928–1931 requesting permission to include various stories in the first and second series of GREAT SHORT STORIES OF DETECTION, MYSTERY AND HORROR and on American copyright problems; (e) Christmas card with autograph note signed to T. Fytton-Armstrong 23 December 1930 (postmark); (f) ALS to Terence Ian Fytton-Armstrong 27 January 1931; (g) TLS with autograph note to Ernest Bramah 30 January 1931; (h) ALS to Ernest Bramah 13 February 1931; (i) ALS to Ernest Bramah 14 April 1931; (j) ALS to J. H. S. Rowland 31 March 1931; (k) ALS to Hugh Walpole 24 April 1933; (l) Autograph card to Hugh Walpole 30 April 1933; (m) ALS to Mrs. Belloc Lowndes 20 February 1934; (n) TLS to R. A. Scott-James 22 November 1938; (o) TLS to Hugh Walpole 3 January 1940; (p) TCC to James Sandoe 8 August 1944 about a bibliography of her works; (q) typed form letter, signed, to Trustees, Civil List Pension Fund, Summer 1951, about John Metcalfe; (r) TLS to John Chamson 14 May 1952 about THE MAN BORN TO BE KING; (s) four TLS to T. H. White 29 October 1954, 15 November 1954, 7 December 1954, 13 December 1954 (which have been misfiled, according to the Humantics Research Center).

G5.12 Three ALS to David Higham and 63 TLS to Pearn, Pollinger and Higham Ltd. (literary agents). Most of the letters are addressed to David Higham or Jean LeRoy; they deal mainly with contracts, legal affairs, difficulties with publishers, refusals to write articles, negotiations for adaptations, new books, articles, etc. These letters are part of the collection of records from Pearn, Pollinger and Higham 1950–1963. Other Sayers related items include typed letters from her secretary, Joyce Wallage, to Pearn, Pollinger and Higham; agents' memoranda, accounting records and miscellaneous correspondence between the agents and publishers, translators, etc. regarding Sayers' work; there is also a play bill for the production of *Christ's Emperor* at St. Thomas's Church produced by Sayers and Graham Suter.

G6 DOROTHY L. SAYERS SOCIETY
Roslyn House
Witham, Essex

G6.1 Letters: TLS to Col. Appleby 3 May 1950 regarding THE EMPEROR CONSTANTINE; ALS to Mrs. Bowen Davies 22 November 1942; ALS to Miss Richards 18 June 1946; copy of a letter to Mr. C. W. Scott-Giles, in French, copied in Scott-Giles' hand; TLS to G. L. A. Spafford 28 March 1947 about H. G. Wells.

G7 MARION E. WADE COLLECTION
Wheaton College
Wheaton, Illinois 60187

G7.1 *Absolutely Elsewhere. (Story) 26 pp. AMS complete.

G7.2 *An Arrow o'er the House. (Story) 20 pp. AMS complete.

G7.3 Arsenic Probably. (Topical article) 4 pp. AMS plus 1 p. TL of rejection from *The Daily News* (London) dated 21 September 1926.

G7.4 *ASK A POLICEMAN: The Conclusions of Mr. Roger Sheringham. (Part of a serial novel) 59 pp. AMS and 4 pp. AMS notes.

G7.5 *Behind the Screen. (BBC serial detective story) 52 pp. AMS including synopsis and notes.

G7.6 *Blood Sacrifice. (Story) 45 pp. AMS complete; see G7.43.

G7.7 *BUSMAN'S HONEYMOON. (Play) 45 pp. AMS 43 *ll.* incomplete; written in collaboration with Muriel St. Clare Byrne, some in Byrne's hand.

G7.8 ★BUSMAN'S HONEYMOON. (Novel) 548 pp. AMS complete.

G7.9 Cat's Cradle. (Play, "A Comedy in Three Acts") 130 pp. AMS complete; performed as "Love All" (E72).

G7.10 Christ's Emperor: Being the Second Part of the Colchester Festival Play, THE EMPEROR CONSTANTINE. (Play) 15 pp. AMS, 11 *ll.* in a notebook (25×20 cm.); 11 pp. AMS stage directions and Biblical quotations. Part of this was printed as the preface to THE EMPEROR CON-STANTINE. "Christ's Emperor" was performed in 1952 (E74). See G7.22.

G7.11 The Comedy of Horror. (Speech) 12 pp. AMS incomplete.

G7.12 The Craft of Detective Fiction I. (Speech) 13 pp. AMS outline, incomplete.

G7.13 The Craft of Detective Fiction II. (Speech) 6 pp. AMS 3 *ll.*, rough draught; 15 pp. AMS complete; 12 pp. TMS with autograph corrections.

G7.14 ★Creative Mind. (Speech) 21 pp. AMS 20 *ll.* complete; see G7.90.

G7.15 ★The Cyprian Cat. (Story) 20 pp. AMS complete; see G7.43.

G7.16 ★THE DAYS OF CHRIST'S COMING (Card text) 6 pp. AMS.

G7.17 Detection Club Speech. (Speech) 6 pp. AMS on detective story writing as a cottage industry.

G7.18 Detectives in Fiction. (Speech) 6 pp. AMS complete.

G7.19 ★Dilemma. (Story) 13 pp. AMS version "A"; 12 pp. AMS version "B" (published). See G7.43.

G7.20 ★Dr. Watson, Widower. (Essay) 26 pp. AMS. See G7.90.

G7.21 ★THE DOCUMENTS IN THE CASE (Novel) 383 pp. AMS complete; written in collaboration with Robert Eustace (Dr. Eustace Barton), some of whose correspondence is also in the Wade Collection.

G7.22   *THE EMPEROR CONSTANTINE. (Play) 239 pp. AMS, some scenes from Act III missing; 9 pp. AMS preface; 2 pp. AMS programme note; plus prompt book and other materials not in Sayers' hand. See G7.10.

G7.23   The Enchanted Garden. (Card text) 14 pp. AMS; 12 pp. TMS; adapted from "Orlando Inamorato" by Boiardo, planned as a card to be illustrated by Fritz Wegner.

G7.24   *EVEN THE PARROT. (Satire) 42 pp. AMS 24 *ll.*; plus 17 illustrations and first proof copy with autograph corrections.

G7.25   *Fantastic Horror of the Cat in the Bag. (Story) 35 pp. AMS complete; in a notebook, see G7.49; see also G7.48.

G7.26   *Fascinating Problem of Uncle Meleager's Will. (Story) 35 pp. AMS complete; in a note book, see G7.50; see also G7.48.

G7.27   *FIVE RED HERRINGS. (Novel) 512 pp. AMS; Chapter 24 incomplete.

G7.28   *THE FLOATING ADMIRAL. (Serial novel) 128 pp. AMS Chapter VII, notes for the chapter, and solution; plus 14 pp. TCC.

G7.29   *The Fountain Plays. (Story) 22 pp. AMS; p. 7 incomplete. See G7.34.

G7.30   The Future of the Jews in England Now: Rambling Meditations on the Subject of Christian Duty. (Article) 22 pp. AMS; 17 pp. first proof with autograph corrections; 14 pp. AMS additional material. Apparently written for, but not included in, the book *The Future of the Jews*, a collection of essays published in London by Lindsay, Drunmond, 1945, and printed by Sherratt and Hughes.

G7.31   *GAUDY NIGHT. (Novel) 640 pp. AMS complete.

G7.32   *Griselda and the Little Cat.* (Story) 7 pp. AMS incomplete.

G7.33   *The Gulf Stream and the Channel. (Essay) 11 pp. AMS complete. See G7.90.

G7.34 ★HANGMAN'S HOLIDAY. (Collected stories) See The Image in the Mirror (G7.41); The Queen's Square (G7.65); The Man Who Knew How (G7.52); The Fountain Plays (G7.29).

G7.35 ★The Haunted Policeman. (Story) 33 pp. AMS; 32 pp. TCC.

G7.36 ★HAVE HIS CARCASE. (Novel) 230 pp. AMS plus 9 *ll.* notes, and letters regarding the novel.

G7.37 ★HE THAT SHOULD COME. (Play) 25 pp. AMS complete with a copy of the sheet music.

G7.38 Herod the Great. (Play) Unfinished plans for a trilogy, The Cruel Life and Death of Herod the Great, King of Jewry: Part I The Son of Esau; Part II The Seed of Cain; Part III The King of the Jews; 35 pp. AMS notes and rough draught; 24 pp. AMS Act I "A" version; 26 pp. AMS Act I "B" version, plus 8 pp. TMS; 23 pp. TMS Act I with autograph corrections.

G7.39 The Horrible Story of the Missing Molar. (Story) 6 pp. AMS incomplete; in a notebook, G7.50.

G7.40 If You Want War. (Article) 4 pp. AMS.

G7.41 ★The Image in the Mirror. (Story) 45 pp. AMS, see G7.34.

G7.42 The Importance of Being Vulgar. (Speech) 23 pp. AMS.

G7.43 ★IN THE TEETH OF THE EVIDENCE. (Collected stories) See Absolutely Elsewhere (G7.1); Dilemma (G7.19); An Arrow o'er the House (G7.2); Scrawns (G7.68); Nebuchadnezzar (G7.59); Blood Sacrifice (G7.6); Suspicion (G7.76); The Leopard Lady, Part II of Smith and Smith Removals (G7.70); The Cyprian Cat (G7.15).

G7.44 Introducing Lord Peter. (Story) 48 pp. AMS unfinished.

G7.45 ★THE JUST VENGEANCE. (Play) 87 pp. AMS 68 *ll.*; most of the last song by the choir missing, otherwise complete with notes, cast, miscellaneous materials.

G7.46 ★The Learned Adventure of the Dragon's Head. Pasteboard original of the Sayers' illustration which accompanies the published story.

G7.47 *The Leopard Lady. 32 pp. AMS complete. Originally titled "Smith & Smith Removals II: The Leopard Lady". See G7.43 and G7.70.

G7.48 *LORD PETER VIEWS THE BODY. (Collected stories). See The Undignified Melodrama of the Bone of Contention (G7.87); The Unsolved Puzzle of the Man with No Face (G7.91); The Piscatorial Farce of the Stolen Stomach (G7.63); Adventure of the Cat in the Bag (G7.25); The Fascinating Problem of Uncle Meleager's Will (G7.26).

G7.49 Lord Peter Wimsey-Amateur Sleuth. (Notebook 20 × 15·5 cm.) *Adventure of the Cat in the Bag ("Fantastic Horror of the Cat in the Bag" G7.25); The Tooth of Time (Essay) 4 pp. AMS; Nor M? (Essay) 4 pp. AMS; Wilkie Collins (G7.94).

G7.50 Lord Peter Wimsey-Unprofessional Sleuth. (Notebook 20·5 × 16·5 cm.) *The Fascinating Problem of Uncle Meleager's Will (G7.26); The Horrible Story of the Missing Molar (G7.39); fragment about the publication of TRISTAN IN BRITTANY 2 pp. AMS; quotation from *History of Fortunatus* and notes on Lord Peter 18 pp. AMS; *The Romance of Tristan 38 pp. AMS translation for TRISTAN IN BRITTANY (G7.86); notes on knitting stockings 2 pp. AMS.

G7.51 *THE MAN BORN TO BE KING. (Play) 633 pp. AMS; 18 pp. TMS; 1 p. music score; several scenes missing; some miscellaneous notes on Sherlock Holmes, etc., are included.

G7.52 *The Man Who Knew How. (Story) 25 pp. AMS.

G7.53 The Master Key: A Lord Peter Wimsey Story. 15 pp. AMS incomplete, written after BUSMAN'S HONEYMOON.

G7.54 *THE MIND OF THE MAKER. (Theological treatise) 206 pp. AMS; 36 pp. TMS; postscript and 1 p. from Chapter XI missing; includes incomplete revised Chapter XI.

G7.55 The Modern Detective Story. (Speech) 8 pp. AMS incomplete. See F8.

G7.56 The Mousehole: A Detective Phantasia in Three Flats. (Story) 12 pp. AMS unfinished, early Lord Peter Wimsey story in a notebook, 20×16·5 cm., with part of THE UNPLEASANTNESS AT THE BELLONA CLUB (G7.89).

G7.57 MURDER MUST ADVERTISE. (Novel) 507 pp. AMS including floor plans and advertising solgans.

G7.58 N or M? (Essay) 4 pp. AMS in a notebook (G7.49).

G7.59 *Nebuchadnezzar. (Story) 16 pp. AMS complete; see G7.43.

G7.60 *THE NINE TAILORS. (Novel) 43 pp. AMS with 63 pp. AMS notes in a notebook 20·5 × 16 cm., plus 2 sketches, a pasteboard map, 23 *ll.* miscellaneous AMS notes.

G7.61 *NOAH'S ARK. (Card text) 3 pp. AMS; 3 pp. TMS.

G7.62 Les Origines du Roman Policier. (Speech in French) 12 pp. AMS.

G7.63 *The Piscatorial Farce of the Stolen Stomach. (Story) 33 pp. AMS complete; see G7.48.

G7.64 On the Profession of Murder. (Speech) 15 pp. AMS complete.

G7.65 *The Queen's Square (Story) 24 pp. AMS complete, see G7.34.

G7.66 Quem Queritis? (Poem) 1 p. AMS complete.

G7.67 *The Scoop. (BBC serial) 32 pp. TMS with autograph corrections and note, broadcast version of Chapters I and XII; 10 pp. TCC Chapter I revised version; 20 pp. TCC Chapter I with autograph corrections; 16 pp. AMS Chapter XII; 14 pp. AMS outline, notes, synopsis.

G7.68 *Scrawns. (Story) 21 pp. AMS complete; see G7.43.

G7.69 The Situations of Judkin: 1 The Travelling Rug. (Story) 35 pp. AMS complete.

G7.70 Smith and Smith Removals. (Stories) 28 pp. AMS; Part I The House of Poplars, complete; Part II *The Leopard Lady, see G7.43 and G7.47.

G7.71 ★THE SONG OF ROLAND. (Verse translation) 394 pp. AMS in thirteen notebooks; 11 pp. notes plus 1 p. notes on a detective story and 1 p. notes regarding Charles Williams. 28 pp. AMS, part of the introduction, torn out of one notebook and placed in a folder with 3 pp. TMS of introduction.

G7.72 Spic and Span. (Story) 9 pp. AMS incomplete.

G7.73 ★THE STORY OF EASTER. (Card text) 9 pp. AMS.

G7.74 ★Striding Folly. (Story) 20 pp. AMS; 22 pp. TMS, written in 1935 or earlier, published 1939.

G7.75 ★STRONG POISON. (Novel) 370 pp. AMS complete.

G7.76 ★Suspicion. (Story) 29 pp. AMS complete; see G7.43.

G7.77 ★Talboys. (Story) 32 pp. AMS; 36 pp. TMS dated 1942 in Sayers' hand.

G7.78 ★The Tale of Adam and Adam. (Card text) 21 pp. AMS published as THE STORY OF ADAM AND CHRIST.

G7.79 ★They Tried To Be Good. (Eassay) 11 pp. AMS 6 *ll.*; see G7.90.

G7.80 Thrones, Dominations. (Novel) 177 pp. AMS 176 *ll.*; unfinished sequel to BUSMAN'S HONEYMOON.

G7.81 ★A TIME IS BORN. (Preface) 6 pp. AMS 4 *ll.* complete.

G7.82 ★A Toast to Oxford. (Speech) 11 pp. AMS; complete, published as "What is Right with Oxford"

G7.83 The Tooth of Time. (Essay) 4 pp. AMS in a notebook, see G7.49.

G7.84 ★Towards a Christian Aesthetic. (Essay) 14 pp. AMS complete, see G7.90.

G7.85 *Trent's Last Case:* A Critique (Speech for broadcast) 5 pp. AMS complete.

G7.86 ★TRISTAN IN BRITTANY. (Translation) 38 pp. AMS incomplete in a notebook, see G7.50.

G7.87 *The Undignified Melodrama of the Bone of Contention. (Story) 83 pp. AMS plus pasteboard sketch; incomplete; see G7.48.

G7.88 *UNNATURAL DEATH. (Novel) 333 pp. AMS incomplete.

G7.89 *UNPLEASANTNESS AT THE BELLONA CLUB. (Novel) 257 pp. AMS incomplete, part in a notebook with The Mousehole, see G7.56.

G7.90 *UNPOPULAR OPINIONS. (Essays) See Towards a Christian Aesthetic (G7.84); Creative Mind (G7.14); The Gulf Stream and the Channel (G7.33); They Tried To Be Good (G7.79); Dr. Watson, Widower (G7.20); Galley proofs with autograph corrections.

G7.91 *The Unsolved Puzzle of the Man with No Face. (Story) 34 pp. AMS incomplete; see G7.48.

G7.92 Untitled story. (Fragment) 14 pp. AMS 7 *ll.*; about a soldier near Ravenna in 1944 who encounters Dante.

G7.93 *Who Calls the Tune? (Story) 10 pp. AMS complete.

G7.94 Wilkie Collins. (Notebook G7.49) 4 pp. AMS list of letters; 12 *ll.* AMS notes in the back of the notebook on articles, obituaries, secondary sources.

G7.95 The Wrecker. (Film scenario) 22 pp. AMS complete. Written for Gainsborough Pictures Ltd. but not used for the 1928 film.

G7.96 *THE ZEAL OF THY HOUSE. (Play) 158 pp. AMS; 33 pp. TMS with some autograph corrections; 16 pp. TCC, plus a photograph and a stage diagram.

G7.97 Letters: TLS to S. C. Roberts 23 December 1937; autograph postcard signed to Frederick Mason (n.d.); TLS to Canon A. L. Wright 21 March 1946; TLS to Hilda M. Wilson 27 July 1951; ALS to Michael Williams 24 May 1948; four ALS to Michal Williams 28 June 1948–4 January 1956; ALS to Michal and Michael Williams 5 May 1950.

ADDENDA

B41-A DRESSING THE PLAY 1953

THE HOW TO DO IT SERIES. NUMBER 48 | DRESSING THE PLAY | by NORAH LAMBOURNE | [design: two figures in period costume] | THE STUDIO PUBLICATIONS London & New York

Collation: [A]⁸ B–F⁸ 48 leaves.
p. [I] DRESSING THE PLAY; p. [II] blank; p. [III] title-page; p. [IV] *First published* 1953 | [publisher's device] | printer's notice; p. [v] CONTENTS; pp. 6–8 PREFACE; pp. 9–94 text; pp. 95–96 BIBLIOGRAPHY.

24·6 × 18·5 cm. Bulk: ·75/1·25 cm. Cream wove paper; cream wove endpapers; trimmed. Bound in red cloth; back and front blank; spine [top to bottom, in black:] DRESSING THE PLAY Norah Lambourne | [upright, in black:] [publisher's device] | STUDIO

Price: 15s; number of copies not known. Published 1953. Dust jacket: red in white and aqua.

Notes: Sayers' contribution is The Preface (pp. 6–8); there are photographs of scenes from *The Zeal of Thy House* (p. 45) and *The Emperor Constantine* (p. 46) and of two necklaces made by Sayers (p. 70).

C27-A Veronica. *The Quorum*, vol. I, no. 1, n.d. [1919–1920], p. 22.

Poem.

C27-B Prayer to the Holy Ghost Against Triviality. *The Quorum*, vol. I, no. 1, n.d. [1919–1920], p. 23.

Poem.

INDEX

Books by Sayers, edited or translated by Sayers are in SMALL CAPITALS; books by other authors, journals and newspapers are in *italic*. Short pieces by authors other than Sayers are introduced by #.

Dent, J. M. & Sons, A22, B30
Desdichado, A2
The Detection Club, A14, A29, B18, C41, C42, C44, C77, E12, E35
Detection Club Speech, G7.17
Detection Medley, B21
Detection of a Snob, E53
Detective and Physician: Re-Enter Mr. Fortune, D100
Detective Authors' Troubles: A New Wills Crofts Experiment, D36
Detective Cavalcade, C67
Detective Novel Problems: Are "Serious" Stories Wanted?, D81
Detective Quiz Nos. 1–3: Corner in Crime, E28, E29, E30
Detective Stories and a Thriller: Crime, Colour and Humor, D32
Detective Stories: Another First-Class "Thorndyke", D18
Detective Stories as a Token of Virtue, F16
Detective Stories for the Screen, C87
Detective Stories of the Week: An American Nut Worth Cracking, D2
Detective Stories of the Week: The Whole Scale of Toughness, D1
Detectives in Fiction (Speech), G7.18
Detectives in Fiction: The Learned Adventure of the Dragon's Head, E14
The Development in the Crime Novel: "Obelists En Route", D33
THE DEVIL TO PAY, A31, A46, E71
Devil, Who Made Thee?, C128
#Diamond Cut Diamond, A7b., c., A13a., C67
#The Diary of Mr. Poynter, A20
Dickens, Charles, A7, A13a.
Dickson, Carter, B21, (*The Bowstring Murders*) D62, (*The Plague Court Murders*) D95, (*The White Priory Murders*) D111
The Dictatorship of Words, F15
Dilemma, A32, B13, E9, G7.19
Dilnot, George, (*The Real Detective*) D24
Dingwall, Peter, (*The Poison Duel*) D35
Dirt Cheap, A32, C69
The Divine Comedy, see The Comedy of Dante Alighieri
Divine Comedy, A43, C118
The Divine Poet and the Angelic Doctor, A56, F32
Dix, Maurice B., (*The Fleetwood Mansions Mystery*) D54
Dr. Thorndyke Comes Again: Fine

Entertainment, D73
Dr. Watson, Widower, A43, G7.20, G7.90
Dr. Watson's Christian Name, A43, B28
THE DOCUMENTS IN THE CASE, A10, A4e.I., E62, G7.21
The Dogma Is the Drama, A30, A45, A60, C84
Dogma or Doctrine, C125
Doing a Man's Job, C71, F7
Doodles, C79
DOROTHY L. SAYERS OMNIBUS (Gollancz), A8a.IV., A11a.II., A12a.II.
DOROTHY L. SAYERS OMNIBUS (Harcourt), A3d.I., A6b.II., A12b.II.
Dorothy L. Sayers Reveals the Origin of Lord Peter Wimsey (How I Came to Invent the Character of Lord Peter) G5.4, C65
Dorothy L. Sayers Society, G6
#The Double Admiral, A13
DOUBLE DEATH (*Night of Secrets*) A29, C77, see also "The Riddle of the Poisoned Nurse"
#Double Demon, A20
Doubleday, Doran, A14b., B17b.I.
Dowding, Lord, B42
Downside, The Abbot of, B42
Doyle, Conan, A7, C67, see also "The Dates in 'The Red-Headed League'", "Dr. Watson's Christian Name", "Dr. Watson, Widower", "Holmes' College Career"
A Drama of the Christian Church, D117
Drama in an Air Liner: Criminals and Cranks, D90
Dramatists Play Service, A24b.
Drewett, John, B25
#A Drop Too Much, C67
The Drunkard, A2
#Duello, A13
Duke Hilary, C7
Duke, Winifred, (*Skin for Skin*) D91
#The Dumb Wife, A20
Duncan-Jones, Caroline Mary, B39
Dunsany, Lord, A20, B10
Dutton, Charles J., (*The Circle of Death*) D21
Dutton, E. P., A22, B30
Dwyer, James Francis, A20

E. F. A. G., see "Geach, E. F. A."
Earp, T. W., B1, B2, B3, B5
East, Roger, (*Murder Rehearsal*) D2, (*Candidate for Lillies*) D32, (*Twenty-*

Impossible Alibi (Absolutely Elsewhere) C52, A32, A61, B14, E16, G7.1
In a Telephone Cabinet, A13a.
IN THE TEETH OF THE EVIDENCE, A32, A11d.ii., G7.43
In the Teeth of the Evidence, A32, A61, E61, G2.1
In Town Tonight, E41
The Incredible Elopement of Lord Peter Wimsey, A18, A61
The Inexperienced Ghost, A13
Ingram, Kenneth, B26
Ink of Poppies, C76
Inner Wheel Club, F48
The Inoffensive Captain, A13a.
Inquest, A20
Inside Story of a Murder: An Imaginary Diary, D80
The Inspiration of Mr. Budd, A32, B7, C36, E27
The Insured Life, C140
The International Review of Missions, D117
The Interruption, A20
Introducing Children to The Bible, C141
Introducing Lord Peter, G7.44
INTRODUCTORY PAPERS ON DANTE, A51
The Invisible Man, C67
The Iron Pineapple, A13
Irregular but Likeable: Perry Mason Again, D86
Irwin, Margaret, A20, B19
Is there a Definite Evil Power . . . ?, B40
Is This He That Should Come?, C110
The Island, A20

Jack de Manio Precisely, E66
Jackson, Joseph Henry, B18
Jacobs, T. C. H., (Sinister Quest) D57
Jacobs, W. W., A7, A13, A20, B10
James I., B37
James, M. R., A7a., A20
Jameson, Storm, B27
Jarrett, Cora, (Pattern in Black and Red) D77
Jellema, Roderick, A60
Jepson, Edgar, A7, A13a., A14, A22, B21, (The Grinning Avenger) D35
Jerome, Jerome K., A7
Jerrold, Ianthe, B21
Jesse, F. Tennyson, A29, B11, B15
Jesus, if against my will, A2
John O'London's Weekly, C151, C152, C153, C168
Jones, E. B. C., A1

The Journeyman (The Priest's Tale: The Journeyman) E55, B4
The Judge Corroborates, A20
A Jungle Graduate, A20
THE JUST VENGEANCE, A42, A46, E31, E73, G7.45
Justus Judex, A2

Kahn, Joan, B18
The Kalendar of Unholy and Dead Letters Days (Pantheon Papers), A60, C178
Kantor, MacKinlay, A20b.
Keeler, Harry Stephen, (The Travelling Skull) D61
Kendral, Carleton, (The Clue of the Forgotten Murder), D105
Kennedy, Margaret, B19
Kennedy, Milward, A13, A14, A17, A22, B10, B15, B21, (Corpse in Cold Storage) D42, (Poison in the Parish) D98
Keverne, Richard, (Artifex Intervenes) D48, (He Laughed at Murder) D82
Key, Robert E., B42
Keyes, Michael, (Murder Cruise) D64
Khan, Aga, B42
Kiddy, Maurice G., (The Jade Hat Pin) D10
The Kindergarten Plays, C1
Kindon, Thomas, (Murder in the Moor) D7
King, C. Daly, A22, C67, (Obelists En Route) D33, (Obelists Fly High) D90
King, Rufus, (Murder by Latitude) D7
King, Sherry, (Between Murders) D104
The King Waits, A13
The King's English (The English Language) B16, A43, C56
Kingston, Charles, (Poison in Kensington) D60
Kirk, Laurence, A20, (Whispering Tongues) D50
Kitchin, C. H. B., (Crime at Christmas) D70
Knight, G. H., A26, A31
Knox, Ronald A., A13a., A14, A22, B7, B12, B17, (The Body in the Silo) D1, (Still Dead) D47
Komroff, Manuel, A13b., A20b.
Krumgold, Joseph, (Thanks to Murder) D111
Kyle, Sefton, (The Life He Stole) D64

Labiche et Molière au "Picturedome",

The Playwright, F13
Playwrights Are Not Evangelists, C189
A Plea for Vocation in Work (Vocation in Work) C143, B26, see also "Work and Vocation"
Pleasant People in a Crime Novel, D101
Plotting a Detective Story, E2
Plum, Mary (The Broken Vase Mystery), D20
Plummer, T. Arthur, (*Creaking Gallows*) D37
PocketBooks, A4*f.*, A6*b.*III., A15*b.*, A16*c.*
Poe, Edgar Allan, A7, A13, A22
The Poem, B8, C32
Poetry, Language and Ambiguity, A59, F57
THE POETRY OF SEARCH AND THE POETRY OF STATEMENT, A59
The Poetry of Search and the Poetry of Statement, A59, F63
The Poetry of the Image in Dante and Charles Williams, A56, F53
The Poet's Cat, B32
Pointers, C82
The Poisoned Dow '08, A18
#Poker-Face, A20
Polar Calendar (Pantheon Papers), C176
The Polar Synthesis: A Sermon for Cacophony-Tide (Pantheon Papers), A60, C180
#Policeman's Cape, C67
Pollard, Graham, A27, (*An Enquiry into the Nature of Certain Nineteenth Century Pamphlets*) D55
Pollefexen, Claire D., A20*a.*
Pond, E. J., (*The Ince Murder Case*) D61
The Portable Murder Book, B18
Post, Melville Davisson, A20, C67
Pot Versus Kettle, C127
#The Prayer, A13
The Present Status of the Mystery Story, C43
Pretty Sinister—If You Have Ears Prepare to Shed Them Now, D57
Prevention Is Better Than Cure, C106
Price, Evadne (*The Haunted Light*), D8
Priestly, J. B., B10, B11
The Priest's Second Tale: The Master-Thief, B6
The Priest's Tale: The Journeyman, B4, E55
#The Primate of the Rose, A13*a.*
#Prince Charlie's Dirk, A7
The Problem of Uncle Meleager's Will (The Fascinating Problem of Uncle

Meleager's Will) C33, A8, A61, G7.26, G7.48, G7.50
Problem Picture, A37, A60
Problems of Religious Broadcasting, C162, C163
The Professional Sleuth: Scotland Yard in Fiction, D74
The Professor's Manuscript (The Secret of the Mystery Professor), A32, C105
Profile by Gaslight, B28
Projects At School, C173
#Proof, A7
The Prophets, A53
Propper, Milton, (*The Divorce Court Murder*) D69
Prothero, John, B15
The Psychology of Advertising, C80
Publications of the English Goethe Society, C160
Publisher's Weekly, C95
Punch, C176, C178, C179, C180
Punshon, E. R., B18, B21, C67, (*Proof Counter-Proof, The Cottage Mystery*) D7, (*Information Received*) D9, (*Death Among the Sun Bathers*) D40, (*The Cross-Word Mystery*) D49, (*Mystery Villa*) D74, (*Death of a Beauty Queen*) D106
Puppets or People in Stories of Crime?, D106
#The Purloined Letter, A22
Pussydise Lost, C171
Pygmalion, B3

Quayle, Anthony, E77
Queen, Ellery, C67, (*The American Gun Mystery*) D2, (*The Siamese Twin Mystery*) D25, (*The Ellery Queen Omnibus*) D29, (*The Chinese Orange Mystery*) D54, (*The Adventures of Ellery Queen*) D92, (*The Spanish Cape Mystery*) D99
Queen Mary's Book for India, B28
The Queen's Square, A18, A61, G7.65
#The Queer Door, A13*a.*
#The Queer Feet, A13*a.*
Quem Queritis?, G7.66
#A Question of Coincidence, C67
Quiller-Couch, A. C., A7, A13, A20
Quince, James, (*Casual Slaughters*) D109

#The Race of Orven, A13*a.*
Radcliffe, Garnett, A20
Radio Gazette 22, E12
Radio Times, C91, C94, C157
"Rallentando, H. P." (pseudonym for

This book is set in Monophoto Bembo by Asco Trade Typesetting Limited of Hong Kong. It is probable that the typeface was originally named for Cardinal Pietro Bembo, a humanist of the early sixteenth century; Stanley Morison revived the face in 1929 for the Monotype Corporation, and it was recently adapted again for the Monophoto process. Cushing-Malloy Inc of Ann Arbor, Michigan, has printed the book on acid-free paper. The Short Run Bindery Inc of Medford, New Jersey, has bound the book in pyroxylin impregnated cloth.